COMPOSING MUSIC FOR GAMES

The world's most authoritative and comprehensive guide for launching and maintaining a successful career as a video game composer.

Composing Music for Games is a guidebook for all those who aspire to have a successful career as a video game composer. It offers a pragmatic approach to learning, intensified through challenging project assignments and simulations. The principles and practices presented here have been tested and proven both in the classroom and in the professional world of game development. Through research, interviews and personal experience, author Chance Thomas begins with the foundation of scoring principles applicable to all media, and then progresses serially through core methodologies specific to video game music.

- In-depth exploration of music scoring for video games
- Powerful blend of aesthetic, technique, technology and business—all necessary components for a successful career as a video game composer
- Colorful case studies, tutorials and challenging tasks to keep you engaged from start to finish
- A companion website: www.focalpress.com/cw/Thomas that contains audio samples and video tutorials to demonstrate principles and techniques from the book, plus resources for classroom assignments, PowerPoint slides, and more!

CHANCE THOMAS is a composer, educator and entrepreneur. His music has underscored blockbuster commercial success and critical acclaim, including an Oscar, an Emmy and billions of dollars in video game and film sales worldwide. Game credits include *DOTA 2*, *Lord of the Rings Online*, James Cameron's *Avatar*, *Heroes of Might and Magic*, Peter Jackson's *King Kong* and many more. As an educator, Chance works with universities, colleges and conferences to help students and professionals navigate the intersection of music scoring, technology and business. He has served on advisory boards for Full Sail University, Brigham Young University, the Game Developers Conference and the Game Audio N̶̶̶̶̶̶̶̶̶̶ iness interests range across studios, publishing ̶̶̶̶̶̶̶̶̶̶ rting a music career spanning more than thir

COMPOSING MUSIC FOR GAMES

THE ART, TECHNOLOGY AND BUSINESS OF VIDEO GAME SCORING

CHANCE THOMAS

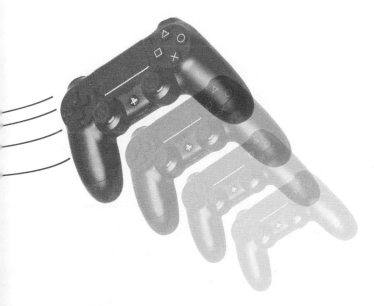

 CRC Press
Taylor & Francis Group

CONTENTS

BUSINESS

EVOLUTION

APPENDAGES

CRC Press
Taylor & Francis Group
6000 Broken Sound Parkway NW, Suite 300
Boca Raton, FL 33487-2742

Library of Congress Cataloging in Publication Data
CIP data has been applied for

ISBN: 978-1-138-02141-9 (pbk)
ISBN: 978-1-315-77774-0 (ebk)

Typeset by Alex Lazarou

Visit the Taylor & Francis Web site at http://www.taylorandfrancis.com
and the CRC Press Web site at http://www.crcpress.com

Printed and bound in the United States of America by Sheridan

This book is dedicated to my dearest and
most treasured mentors in music:

PATRICIA ANN THOMAS

The first and finest musical influence in my life

DORIS VAUGHN

My devoted, tough and exacting piano teacher

MANTA AND CANYON

Rowdy, high school-era rock band mates

JIM ANGLESEY

The most inspiring college professor I've known

This book is further dedicated to all those engaged
in mentoring today's aspiring score composers.
Your influence will resonate for generations untold …

INTRODUCTION

It's all about the ones and zeroes.[1]

M ost video game programs start at address zero and increment up.[2] So it is with this textbook on music scoring for video games. While most books begin with Chapter 1, this book begins with Chapter 0. Why Chapter 0? Because Chapter 0 designates a point of origin rather than a first step on a subsequent ladder of learning. Chapter 0 is, in effect, ground zero for this topic. It offers no first principles of scoring. It enumerates no specific techniques or strategies. Rather, the purpose of Chapter 0 is to establish a perspective, a vantage point. It offers the reader a subjectively focused lens through which the remainder of the book may be best understood.

This is indicative of the didactic strategy employed throughout the text. Early chapters will establish a foundation of universal principles. Later chapters will teach specific methodologies and techniques based on those principles.

Aspiring video game composers who digest the underlying principles and philosophical framework in the early part of the text will find greater success in learning the applied techniques given later in the text. Such a grounded approach is calculated to give diligent readers a much needed competitive edge. Music scoring for games is a crowded profession. Thousands of hopefuls wash out. Thus, understanding the *why* of music scoring will more fully empower the educated composer to make superior selections of *what* and *how* when opportunity knocks. Getting those decisions right will make all the difference.

Given the importance of getting those decisions right, how can a student, professional or professor feel confident that this book will steer aspirants in the right direction? A word about the author's qualifications will be reassuring. Many textbook authors are brilliant academics but have limited experience applying their methods in the professional world. By contrast, this textbook is authored by a composer/educator who has personally researched, invented, tested, observed, absorbed, refined and applied these concepts in a dizzying array of commercial video game scores since 1996, from shoestring-budget indies to high-stakes blockbusters. Readers may be familiar with some of these scores: *DOTA 2, Lord of the Rings Online, James Cameron's Avatar, Monopoly Streets, Heroes of Might and Magic, Dungeons & Dragons Online, Champions Online, Littlest Pet Shop, Peter Jackson's King Kong, Disney's Ghosts of Mistwood, Dinosaurs 3D, Earth and Beyond, Marvel: Ultimate Alliance, War of the Ring, Left Behind, Unreal II, X-Men: The Official Game, Quest for Glory V* and many more.

Thus, the principles and practices offered here have been tested and proven, not only in the classroom, but in the furnace of crunch-time game development and the marketplace of competitive commerce. The depth, diversity and useful application of theory and practice brought to bear in this book is second to none in the world.

The bulk of this educational material is presented generally and objectively throughout the text. However, most chapters also contain focused excerpts from the author's own music scoring experiences. These first-person accounts appear in sidebar segments under the caption **Peek Behind the Curtain**. Such personal windows into the trenches of game scoring are among the book's most unique and valuable features.

Having said that, no single individual possesses all the answers. That is why dozens of outside specialists have also offered their insights exclusively for this textbook. These distinguished experts, many of them the author's personal friends, are featured in special chapter subdivisions labeled **Guest Lecture**. These guest lecture segments add rich layers of clarifying detail, specific application and color commentary to the principles and practices discussed.

Applied learning assignments and exercises follow handy summaries at the end of each chapter, offering students and teachers opportunities to test and put into practice each principle and technique taught in the body of the text. To assist with analysis and scoring assignments, copyright-free and cleared external resources are available at the book's online resource center. Links are included in the text of the book.

Any reader who makes a vigorous study and application of these materials will put themselves in an aggressive position to succeed as a professional video game composer. To all those who so embark, the author and publisher wish a prosperous journey and the very best of success!

REFERENCES

1.   Richard Gregory. Digital Marketing Agency website: http://richardgregory.co.uk/tag/gaming/.

2.   Craig Alexander. Email exchange with author. January 30, 2014.

PERSPECTIVE

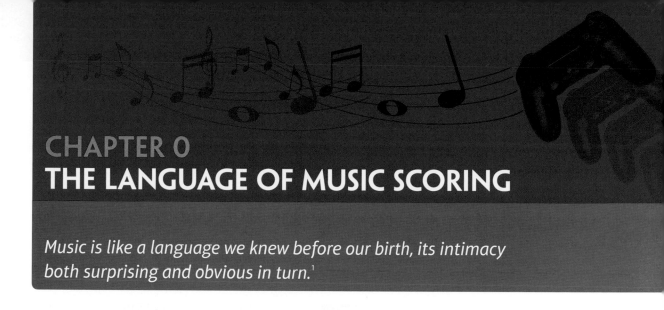

CHAPTER 0
THE LANGUAGE OF MUSIC SCORING

Music is like a language we knew before our birth, its intimacy both surprising and obvious in turn.[1]

Imagine this scenario. An auditorium is filled with music students. A large projection screen displays an image from an obscure video game level. None of the students have seen the image before. The lecturer asks, "How would you score this level? What would your music sound like?" The students begin calling out ideas—specific instruments, harmonies, rhythmic patterns, mixing processes, etc. The group's ideas are written down as they come, raw, unscreened and unedited.

When the list is complete the lecturer continues, "So according to the ideas you have just generated, the music should sound like … this?" The lecturer pushes a button and an audio file begins to play. The students' faces light up with surprise and delight, as the pre-recorded music sample inevitably resembles their own spontaneous list in remarkable detail.

This experience is as predictable as it is notable. The same result has occurred time and time again over many years of lecturing to music students all across America. How is this possible? How do the real-time, stream-of-consciousness musings of random student groups inevitably reflect specific compositional choices made offline and in advance by an individual composer?

The answer is critically important for those who hope for proficiency in music scoring. After all, if predictable expectations exist for how music conveys specified meaning and context, composers who are unaware of such expectations (or choose to ignore them) risk impotence or irrelevance in their work. An intuitive framework for finding answers can be established when we consider music scoring as a language.

MUSIC SCORING AS LANGUAGE

Languages are mutually understood constructs for conveying human thought or feeling. They consist of components, patterns and variants which organize abstract ideas into communication packets intended to elicit understanding in other humans. Because the range of human thought and feeling is enormous, successful languages are rich, varied and serviceable at many levels.

In the opening scenario, students demonstrated a mutual understanding of the components, patterns and variants they expected to hear in music which would appropriately underscore a represented game level. These expectations evidence the students' intrinsic awareness of an underlying musical communication system, or language, used to connect human understanding within a given setting and/or dramatic condition.

This is good news for music students and professionals alike. In viewing music scoring as a language, we arrive at the happy conclusion that music scoring consists of known components, patterns and variables which can be identified, learned and mastered.

IMMERSION

Individuals immersed in a given language naturally acquire a familiarity with that language over time. They develop expectations about its conveyance and assign meaning to certain modes of expression, patterns and dynamics. Children cultivate speaking patterns and acquire vocabulary in much the same way. In a media-saturated culture, familiarity with scoring language distills naturally from years of exposure to music scores across many formats.

EXPLORING THE SCORING LANGUAGE

Scoring language has been in development for many centuries, tracing its roots back to liturgical chanting, theater, dance and opera. Sacred music, as it came to be called in the ancient Catholic Church, communicated a feeling of the divine to its listeners.[2] In the Grecian theater, music communicated the commencement of the dramatic extravaganza and provided important contextual breaks in the action.[3] In seventeenth-century France, ballet music first began to express dramatic content with instrumental songs, telling their stories without words.[4] Program music, opera, radio drama, silent movies, musical theater and many other forms of dramatic communication have contributed to the components and structure of music scoring language. This progression continues to the contemporary visual media of the present day.

Throughout all of this rich musical history, conventions have developed which are recognizable and repeatable. Thus they become useful templates for communication. Meanings have come to be assigned to modes of expression, patterns and dynamics. Such expectations, templates and patterns in music scoring

PEEK BEHIND THE CURTAIN

The Scoring Language of *Avatar*

In March of 2009, I received an unexpected phone call from music agent Noemie Dupuy. She said Ubisoft wanted me to submit a music demo for a new game they were developing called *Avatar*. It was based on an upcoming film of the same name by James Cameron. I hadn't the foggiest idea what *Avatar* was, but I sure knew about James Cameron. I immediately expressed my interest. She arranged to have Ubisoft send me the scoring brief.

When the document arrived, I was stunned by its brevity. There were no screen shots, no descriptive sections of game design, only a single paragraph describing the project in the most generic terms. As I recall, it read something like this: *Explorers from Earth mine alien jungle planet. Conflict ensues.*

Today, millions have watched *Avatar*. They have a strong sense of the aesthetic of the music, if not the actual film score. But back in March of 2009 I had none of that. *Avatar* was a complete mystery to me. And yet, somehow those few words in the scoring brief gave me everything I needed to know. Somehow I could hear what that sounded like. My exposure to the language of music scoring had been so immersive, I was able to create a winning music demo from just the few words in the scoring brief.

form a complex etymological system capable of communicating a broad range of human emotions and dramatic conditions. In simpler terms, they form a deeply expressive language.

Every language possesses both components and structure. Every language has vocabulary, syntax, grammar and idioms. These constituents and constructs help to organize and convey thoughts and feelings through recognizable patterns. Likewise, music scoring has its own *vocabulary*, *syntax*, *grammar* and *idioms*.

Vocabulary of Music Scoring

What is vocabulary? **Vocabulary** comprises the universe of words available to communicate ideas in a given language. Each word has meaning—some independently, some only in combination with other words. Some words even have multiple meanings dependent on context. The same is also true for the language of music scoring. Music scoring's vocabulary consists of *notes*, *beats*, *articulations* and *tonal colors*. Each of these musical elements has the ability to convey meaning to a listener, sometimes in isolation but most frequently in combinations.

If a bassoonist were to play a single note—for example, a staccato, fortissimo Eb—it would be broadly interpreted as communicating a comic sense of surprise. On the other hand, if a staccato Eb is played fortissimo on a trumpet, it will be widely perceived as alarm. But the same pitch played on the bassoon as a whole note, mezzo piano dynamic with a slow vibrato, communicates instead a feeling of melancholy or mystery. And if that same Eb on the bassoon were followed by a C (minor third down) played in the same way, it would convey sadness.

Music scoring vocabulary is anything but random. Notes, timbres, rhythms, articulations—these are all carriers of meaning. Some communicate in a universal and predictable way because of how their vibrations connect with human biology. This is a fascinating phenomenon which will be explored in later chapters. Other parts of the scoring vocabulary provide understanding because of their ubiquitous idiomatic usage. But make no mistake, each kind of note a composer selects has informative inferences in the scoring language. It is imperative for composers to recognize the built-in implications of each element, so as to avoid delivering the musical equivalent of gibberish.

Syntax of Music Scoring

The arrangement of vocabulary into meaningful structure constitutes *syntax*. The minor third combination cited above was a simple example of syntax. Only two notes, but meaningful structure nonetheless. That particular structuring of notes known as a minor third constitutes meaningful structure because it *consistently* communicates the emotion of sadness. This works not only when the minor third is played by a bassoon (or any number of other instruments) but even in spoken dialog.

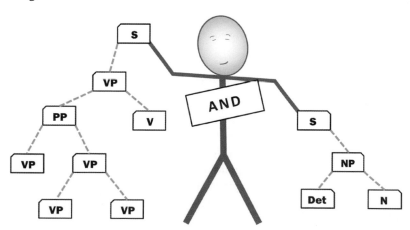

GUEST LECTURE
THE SYNTAX OF
PITCH INTERVALS

Megan Curtis, Tufts University

A 2010 study published on the website for the National Center for Biotechnology Information found that the interval of a minor third conveys sadness not only in music, but also in speech.[5] Using software to analyze speech intervals, Megan Curtis was able to clearly identify when study participants intoned a minor third in their speaking. They "consistently used a minor third to express sadness." Curtis was able to conclude that, "For sad speech there is a consistent pitch pattern. The aspects of music that allow us to identify whether that music is sad are also present in speech ... the minor third consistently was judged to convey sadness."

More complex combinations of vocabulary can bring tremendous depth and duplicity of meaning to musical expression. A powerful example from the cinematic literature is "Anakin's Theme" by John Williams in *The Phantom Menace*. Williams opens by communicating innocence and potential with a rising melody on the flute in the key of E major, lifting to F# major. As the theme develops, large downward intervals in the melody with sophisticated harmonic changes communicate unseen complexity within the boy. Alternating dissonances in the strings continually resolve, then dissolve again in a constantly evolving harmonic tussle. This communicates the internal struggle between good and evil swinging back and forth inside Anakin's conscience. As the piece winds toward its conclusion, the melody tries to rise but cascades downward each time, struggling now against the inevitable. There is a growing sense of deepening struggle, finally yielding to the emergence of the *Imperial March* (Darth Vader) theme in A minor on the low strings. As a harp plucks the final A near the bottom of its register with a menacing rumble, the boy's fate is sealed. The transformation from innocence through deepening turmoil and finally into darkness is communicated with such skill and clarity in part because of William's expert command of music scoring syntax.

On the other end of the spectrum, syntax can also be used skillfully to reinforce and amplify a singular focused connotation. Consider Koji Kondo's beloved video game theme from *Mario Brothers*. The sense of safe, bouncy, adventurous fun is reinforced with every choice the composer made. The tune is lilting and infectious, alternating between cliché and refreshing originality. This communicates both familiarity and adventure. The tonality is

rooted in C major, the most innocuous of keys. Though it takes an occasional foray into minor harmony, these are only brief forays. The tune always returns home, reinforcing the sense of safety. Lots of staccato notes emphasize the bouncy action. Chromatic chordal movements alternate with traditional dominant-to-tonic cadences, reinforcing the theme of safe harbor adventure, simplicity mingled with the unexpected. Everything about the music is phrased in the scoring syntax of safe, bouncy, adventurous fun.

Grammar of Music Scoring

Grammar consists of rules which bring convention to communicative expression. Grammar helps establish predictability and clarity, so communication is efficient, elegant and effective. Consider the clarity of this sentence in the English language, "*John wants to eat the entire pizza.*" This can be expressed formulaically as follows: *Subject + main verb + infinite verb + adjective + object*. It then becomes a simple process to plug and play an enormous array of variables without any loss of clarity in expression. "*Megan needs to comb her long hair.*" "*Phillip prefers to walk short distances.*" "*Brittany plans to steal my composing gig.*" And so on.

Most composers resist thinking about music in formulaic terms. But the grammar of music scoring really is just that. It is a set of formulas through which a composer's creativity can be easily and consistently understood. Music scoring grammar does not limit the composer any more than English grammar limits creative writing. In fact, it frees it. By providing a commonly understood framework, scoring grammar provides a path to more effective communication.

Consider the following examples of music scoring grammar:

Sonata Form:
Exposition + Development + Recapitulation

Movie Trailer Score:
Introduction + Development + Build + Climax

Video Game Victory Stinger:
Major Tonality + Full Orchestration + Flourish + Resolve

None of these structures force the composer into a corner. They can free the composer to focus their imagination on those distinguishing traits of the score that will add to its unique flavor. All this while still effectively communicating the dramatic narrative of the media to a broad audience.

Idioms of Music Scoring

Certain modes of expression take on such character, perhaps even beyond their literal meaning, that they become known as idioms. "Watch your mouth!" is an archetypal example. Taken a step further, idioms can become collections of interrelated parts from the source vocabulary, syntax, grammar and even intonation of a given language. Idioms then become useful shortcuts for colorfully conveying style and flavor. For example, in the animated film *Cars*, a tow truck named Mater uses idiomatic speech to emphasize the down-home, unsophisticated but sincere nature of his character. Even a single line tells the audience most of what they need to know. "Dad gum! I'd give my left two lug nuts for somethin' like that!"[6]

Musical idioms, or genres, abound. Jazz. Rock. Country. Folk. Hip Hop. Trance. Reggae. Speed Metal. Barbershop. The list could unfold for pages. Each one is recognizable because of its peculiar combination of musical elements. Each is a shortcut useful in communicating a given set of characteristics to an audience. Yet there can also be great creativity and diversity within each one. Again, to emphasize the point: structure by itself does not shackle the creative mind!

Within music scoring language there are many specialized idioms as well. The Lydian scale conveys a sense of wonder. A string section playing behind the bridge communicates fear. French horns and choir are idiomatic for epic. Electric guitars are idiomatic for contemporary edge. Hundreds of such instances could be cited. In each case, the scoring idiom gives the composer a reliable framework with which to convey a clearly comprehensible flavor, again aiding the audience in understanding the emotional narrative or abstract subtext.

SUMMARY

The illuminating and encouraging message of this opening chapter is that music scoring is a language. It is comprised of known components, predictable structure and creative variation. While a comprehensive treatise on music scoring language is not intended, enough broad principles and specific examples have been presented to establish the foundational idea for the purposes of the remaining text. Music scoring is a language. It is a codified means of communicating ideas to the human mind. It is knowable, learnable and repeatable.

Modern music students and young professionals have already acquired strong scoring sensibilities through immersion in the scoring language. Immersion is an inevitable condition in today's media-saturated culture, imprinting aspects of music scoring *vocabulary, syntax, grammar* and *idioms* deeply into the subconscious mind, if not also to the conscious mind.

However, accrued sensibility about a language does not equate with mastery of that language. Consider the differences in expression between a third grader's summer vacation essay and a Shakespearean soliloquy. Both make use of the vocabulary, structure and cadence of the English language. The ample difference between the two comes largely in the degree of sophistication with which the language is exercised for purposes of clarity, depth and aesthetic delight.

So it is with the language of music scoring. It can be learned, mastered and nuanced toward a staggering array of purposes. Fundamentals are acquired with exposure and practice so that even beginners may learn to convey simple ideas with competence. Deeper nuances must be plumbed and mastered, leading to enhanced artistry, originality and elegance of expression. Education, experimentation and practice are the price of mastery. Beginning with Chapter 1, this book will take the dedicated student on a journey of exploration and education, offering opportunities for application and practice along the way, in a marvelous examination of the powerful language of music scoring.

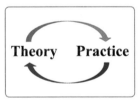

APPLIED LEARNING

1. Write a verbal description of music score for a military base in a high state of alert.

2. Consider the visual image on the facing page. Describe the music you would write for this game level. Outline its musical components in as much detail as possible. Then listen online (www.FocalPress.com/cw/Thomas) to an excerpt from the author's original score. Note any similarities and differences between the author's choices and yours. Defend your choices in light of this chapter's perspective.

3. Create a thirty- to sixty-second music demo based on the following scoring brief: *Telepathic aliens inhabit surface of windswept ice world. Furry trolls invade from underground.* Before composing, identify the elements of music scoring vocabulary in writing—syntax, grammar and idiom—which you will use to make your demo accessible and compelling to a broad audience.

REFERENCES

1. *Quest for Glory V: Dragon Fire* soundtrack liner notes by Chance Thomas. Published by Sierra Online Entertainment. © 1998 Sierra Online Entertainment.

2. http://www.newadvent.org/cathen/09304a.htm.

3. http://ablemedia.com/ctcweb/netshots/tragedy.htm.

4. *Hila Shachar, Behind Ballet*: http://www.behindballet.com/ballets-grandfather-jean-baptiste-lully/ and Wikipedia http://en.wikipedia.org/wiki/Ballet_(music).

5. From website: http://www.ncbi.nlm.nih.gov/m/pubmed/20515223/.

6. *Cars*. Pixar Animation; 00:33:41 into the movie.

PRINCIPLES

CHAPTER 1
TIMELESS PRINCIPLES OF MUSIC SCORING

Ride the horse in the direction it's going.[1]

There is ample room for originality in music scoring. But there is also much of convention. Convention is valuable in achieving the primary purpose of music scoring (or any other language), which is to communicate understanding. Convention does not prohibit creativity. Rather, it offers a comprehensible framework within which creativity can be concentrated, and through which it can have the most impact. Think of convention as a bang-for-the-buck proposition. As many music theory teachers have undoubtedly told their squirming and impatient music students, "You must learn the rules before you can break them intelligently."

This chapter will examine several core conventions of music scoring. To lay the broadest possible foundation, many examples in this chapter will be drawn from movies, television, commercials and other forms of visual media, including games. Subsequent chapters will narrow the focus considerably, highlighting video games exclusively.

CATEGORICAL FUNCTIONS OF MUSIC IN VISUAL MEDIA

Diegetic Music

Prevalent among articles and texts on music scoring is the term *diegetic*. This is a highly specialized term which, as of the date of this publication, still finds no entry in *Webster's Unabridged Dictionary*. Yet the word is widely used by dramatic theorists and educators in the visual arts. It traces its origin back to the fourth century BC, to the writings of Plato. In his book, *The Republic*, Plato introduces the term diegetic to mean any type of entertainment (drama, epic poem, etc.) which is narrated, or described by the narrator.[2]

In modern music scoring, **diegetic music** has come to mean music whose source is visible in the narrative, or music whose source is implied to be present by

DIEGETIC MUSIC IN BIOSHOCK

BioShock's licensed soundtrack helped contribute to the immersive atmosphere of the game with real world licensed music reminiscent of Rapture's time period. Most of [the songs] came from the mid-Twentieth century and cast a feeling of the past in the ruins of a fallen utopia … The licensed songs were designed to be source music as if heard by the characters emanating from radios, phonographs and jukeboxes rather than as incidental music heard from the game's score.

Audio director Emily Ridgway explains the choice to use diegetic music. "The songs themselves, there's a really interesting juxtaposition of … a happy quirky musical … razzle dazzle number and then … how the world is ending … It was supposed to mirror the optimism and the decay at the same time … those two things sort of coexisting with each other."[4]

the depicted action.[3] Framed another way, if characters represented in the narrative can hear the music, then the music is performing a diegetic function.

For example, a documentary depicts a down-on-his-luck, middle-aged man in a public square playing guitar. The guitar is emanating from the scene. The music source is part of the visual narrative. Other people appearing in the scene can hear the man playing his guitar. Therefore, the guitar we hear has a diegetic function in the documentary. Similarly, envision a young woman in exercise clothing selecting a tune from her docked iPod. The song emanates from a physical object visible in the scene. The music source is part of the visual narrative. The girl doing aerobics can hear it. The exercise music is performing a diegetic function.

In addition, sources of music which are implied but unseen in a narrative also perform a diegetic function. The ragtime piano music heard in the background of a honky-tonk bar scene is diegetic for the scene. Even if the audience never sees the musician tickling the ivories, the music is implied to originate from within the bar. The source of the music is assumed to emanate from within the scene itself.

As mentioned, the word diegetic is common in scholarly texts and educational materials. However, it would be uncommon for a creative director to ask a working composer to provide diegetic music. Instead, they would typically use the term *source music*. Even newcomers can grasp this term easily. The expression is reflective of its definition—music for which the source is visible or implied in the scene. These two terms, diegetic music and source music, may be used interchangeably.

Non-Diegetic Music

In most forms of visual media, the great preponderance of music is non-diegetic. While diegetic music requires a source which is visible or implied in the narrative, non-diegetic music does not. Thus, **non-diegetic music** is music whose source is neither visible to the audience nor implied to be present in the action.[5] Non-diegetic music is never heard by the characters in a scene.

This is another term with frequent mention in textbooks and scholarly articles, but not much usage in the professional world. Among directors and score composers, non-diegetic music is simply referred to as underscore or soundtrack. Underscore typically implies instrumental music which supports the visual presentation. Soundtracks may include instrumental underscore but frequently also includes vocal songs. As a side note, when a voice (or voices) behaves like an instrumental color in the orchestration rather than a focal point for lyrics, then the vocals are considered part of the underscore.

When professionals use the term *music score* they are almost always referring to non-diegetic music in support of a visual presentation. In this book, non-diegetic music will be referred to as music score or underscore. Likewise, the process of creating such music will hereinafter be referred to as music scoring.

Since the preponderance of a composer's work for visual media is focused on music scoring, the balance of this chapter will be dedicated to its exploration.

CONVENTIONAL FUNCTIONS OF MUSIC SCORING

Everyone loves a great music score. But what is music actually doing within the context of a visual presentation? What are its various roles and functions? Conventional purposes of music scoring can be distributed among six broad categories—*setting the mood, heightening emotion, propelling the action, providing contextual clues, enhancing the aesthetic* and *contributing to structural unity*. Each of these functions will now be examined in some detail.

Setting the Mood

Many film and game directors will use an establishing shot to quickly orient their audience to a particular sense of place and time. In a similar way, composers use underscore to orient their audience to the proper emotional tone for the scene. This is called *setting the mood*.

An establishing shot for a medieval tale might open showing a grassy field with a hilltop castle looming in the background. The sky is cloudy with a light rain falling. Scattered trees show the faint tint of gold and red on their leaves, telegraphing the onset of autumn. A column of mounted soldiers comes snaking its way out of the castle, down the hill and toward the foreground. This opening image offers the audience many facts about the narrative.

But how should the audience feel about it? Are the soldiers friendly or adversarial? Is the situation mundane, triumphant or grim? Perhaps everything is altogether ambivalent. An establishing shot can communicate many facts about the scene, but may tell the audience very little about how to interpret the scene at an emotional level. Without a device for introducing emotional narrative into the scene, an audience may be left in the dark.

Cue the strings. Underscore is a wonderful device for priming the emotions. The right music can instantly tell an audience how to feel at the opening of a scene or game level. It can draw out the human emotion and lead people along toward the director's intent. This power of underscore to narrow, focus and delineate the intended mood or feeling (among many possibilities) is one of the most rudimentary and indispensable functions music performs in visual media.

Consider this example. In the Disney film *Frozen*, an early scene opens with a wide establishing shot showing a twisted mountain peak in the foreground. Blizzard conditions are evidenced by darkened skies, swirling winds and heavy snowfall. A fierce and rugged mountain range is visible in the background.

Yet, when the music score enters, rather than broadcasting ominous threat or epic adventure, it draws the audience toward a feeling of tender loneliness. A piano sounds gently on a series of soft, minor riffs turning major at the end of the phrase. A bit sad, a bit lost, with a glimmer of hope for the future. With this musical introduction, the audience is perfectly primed to hear the scene's main character express her feelings of isolation, confusion, determination and freedom. The music score has narrowed, focused and delineated the intended emotion among the many possibilities. It has properly set the mood for the scene.

Heightening Emotion

Entertainment often presents an amped-up version of reality. Sometimes this is taken to the very extreme. Consider the Terran soldiers in *Starcraft*. They aren't just big, tough and muscular. They are enormous, virtually indestructible and almighty. Their hand-held guns aren't just large. They are the size of a living room entertainment center. Everything about the Terran soldier is completely over the top.

Exaggerating reality isn't limited to video games. Projecting a close-up of an actor's face on a 50-foot-wide movie screen (even more for IMAX) is exponentially larger than life. And dressing a Wagnerian diva in a shield-bra is nothing if not hyperbole.

Thus, not surprisingly, music scores in such amplified versions of reality serve to intensify the experience *even more*. And while CGI and cinematography work at the visual level, music scoring goes straight to the heart. Whatever an audience may feel when playing a game level or watching a scene in silence, the right music score will multiply. This function of music scoring is referred to as ***heightening emotion***.

To illustrate, a gamer who explores the shadowy depths of Sschindylryn in *Dungeons and Dragons Online* with the sound muted may experience some feelings of anxiety and anticipation. But by adding the growling dissonance of a dark orchestra and distant chanting, the composer can raise the emotional stakes significantly. Now, instead of anxiety, the player experiences fear. Instead of anticipation, she feels excitement mingled with dread.

Nowhere is raising the emotional stakes more important than in an action score. In this role, underscore elevates human biological response, drawing an audience into the visual media akin to actually being there. The pulse quickens. Respiration increases. Mental focus narrows. According to a growing body of evidence from peer-reviewed scientific research, "Stimulating music increased plasma cortisol, ACTH, growth hormone, and norepinephrine level . . . The brainstem interprets

[such] music as signals related to survival, and then initiates corresponding physiological responses."[6] For reference, ACTH stimulates the secretion of adrenal cortex hormones. As many a game designer knows intuitively, action music really does get the adrenaline pumping.

Thus we see that action music tricks the body into releasing a cocktail of hormones comparable to what it would secrete in an actual fight-or-flight situation. This intensifies the impact of a visual representation, super-charging the emotions. This functionality makes action music a key factor in creating the sense of immersion, or suspension of disbelief, which directors pursue and audiences crave.

Propelling the Action

When music is added to a visual presentation, it has the ability to bring a new sense of movement and pacing to the program. This is called *propelling the action*, and is another conventional function of music scoring. There are many ways in which a music score can move action forward in a visual presentation. One way is by adding a pulse to the scene or level. Human physiology and movement are both rhythmic in nature, as is music. Connecting these to a story or gameplay activity taps into an innate sense of drive, giving a sense of propulsion to a dramatic sequence.

Another way music propels action is by providing through-narrative or, in other words, by attaching an emotional meaning to the visual action. Music can take a horrific scene of battle and make it feel noble, heroic or tragic.

The action-propelling function of underscore can also help to carry an audience through mundane

PEEK BEHIND THE CURTAIN

Music Score as Adrenaline

Many times developers will hire me to add an adrenaline rush to the game. I like to go back to the early twentieth-century Russian masters for my inspiration—Stravinsky, Prokofiev, Shostakovich. The non-traditional orchestral techniques they pioneered are incredibly effective at provoking fear, fire and unease in a listener. I call on them generously in my work!

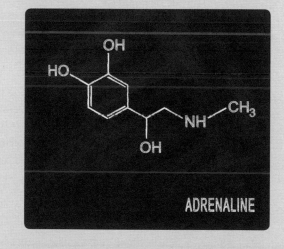

ADRENALINE

stretches of visual slog. In the movie *Ben Hur*, several minutes of film are devoted to watching a group of men row back and forth while confined to the galley of a Roman ship. Although the editor worked in many cuts to show different angles, close-ups and otherwise inject variety into the scene, without music it remains several minutes of seeing men push wooden sticks back and forth. An old adage comes to mind about watching paint dry . . .

Enter the music score. Miklos Rozsa propels the action forward with a relentless piece built on trombones and low strings. The music matches the rowing speed as the hortator hammers out the tempo. The pace of rowing quickens as the scene unfolds. The music synchronizes with the action beat for beat. Counter motifs in the cello rise and fall against the driving repetition of the score, like so many waves crashing against the hull. The score and scene are mesmerizing together, almost hypnotic in their combined effect upon the mind. This action-propelling function of underscore completely transforms the experience. A scene which would otherwise be tedious becomes riveting instead.

Providing Contextual Clues

Contextual clues connect something an audience is currently
experiencing with something else they need to understand
outside the boundaries of the current scene. Underscore
often offers this function through the use of leitmotif, a
musical phrase tied to a character, location or other important
element of the drama. In Peter Jackson's film *The Fellowship of
the Ring*, the score by Howard Shore performs this function
throughout. When the One Ring is picked up, the underscore
offers a hint of Sauron's sinister theme. When Frodo stops to
gather strength or perspective by reflecting on his homeland,
the Shire melody returns. When the Uruk Hai are coming,
Saruman's industrial war-complex leitmotif plays to alert
the audience and trigger their bodies' ACTH response (see
Heightening Emotion above).

Contextual clues can also be provided through instrumental
palette choices. Just as the use of an establishing shot was
discussed as a visual tool, so the composer's instrumental
palette can clue the audience to time and place through
music. As a case in point, consider that any pure nature scene
(no manmade elements) is historically neutral. Similarly,
many fantasy game levels could be interpreted through any
number of cultural filters. The selection of instruments used
in the underscore can provide useful contextual clues about
dramatic framing, time period, culture, etc.

Enhancing the Aesthetic

Aesthetic is a human judgment of input from the surrounding
world, with a resulting appreciation for that which is
esteemed to fit a pleasurable ideal. The natural senses and
developed sensibilities can respond with deep satisfaction to
that which charms a person's aesthetic. Food, art, clothing,
architecture, furnishings, automobiles and entertainment
are all evaluated in part based on their aesthetic appeal.
Even a person's initial response to another human being is
influenced by aesthetic.

AESTHETIC APPEAL

The smell of cinnamon rolls baking in the
oven. Ocean surf pounding against a rocky
shoreline. A gentle touch on soft skin.
A fiery sunset. Miles of tall, green trees.
Each of these reach the human sense
of aesthetic. Entertainment, like nature,
offers a staggering array of flavors for the
consumer. There is something essential
to our humanity about an appreciation of
shape, color, form, cadence and so forth.
Entertainment may be judged as boring,
thrilling, offensive, touching, engaging or
otherwise based largely on its aesthetic
appeal.

Given its pervasive reach, little wonder directors and producers of visual media devote such significant resources to developing what they believe will be an appealing aesthetic for their products. Actors and actresses are chosen in part based on their good looks. Art direction is meticulously contrived to convey a discernible style which audiences can detect, connect with and respond to. Camera placement and movement, color correction, pixel density and many other factors are scrutinized for their contribution to the overall aesthetic of the final product.

With the notable exception of opera and musical theater, the music score typically arrives at the end of this process. At that point, the essential aesthetic of a production is generally well established. The function of the music score now is to enhance the existing aesthetic. For example, long shadows and Dutch angles in a horror game are enhanced by using dissonant harmonies and abrasive textures in the underscore. The bright colors and clean surfaces of a commercial for bathroom cleanser are enhanced with major chords and bouncy rhythms. In this function, music enhances the existing aesthetic, rather than trying to supplant it. The music score is always in the service of the visual content.

Contributing to Structural Unity

Structural unity has to do with the harmoniousness of individual components to an overarching main idea. The greater the cohesiveness of all contributing factors to a central point, the greater the structural unity. This includes the interplay of both micro and macro elements, as well as considerations of within and between. Macro elements may include geographic locations, set pieces or world designs. Micro elements run the gamut from rivet patterns on machinery to minding the axis of action. Within and between are best understood as within the same production (for example, acts one through three of the same play) and between different but related productions (sequels, expansions, etc.).

Music can help connect the dots between all of these disparate elements in at least three important ways. First, by matching the visual aesthetic. Second, by keeping an appropriate continuity with the emotional narrative. Third, by maintaining cohesiveness within the score itself. A brief look at each follows.

First, music contributes to structural unity by matching the visual aesthetic. Cultural connections offer an obvious way in which music can match a visual aesthetic. Consider a jungle setting. Structural unity between the visual and the music would typically call for tribal rhythms, ethnic woodwinds and chanting of some kind. Does this mean all jungle narratives will end up having the same score? Of course not. As a case in point, the alien jungle of *James Cameron's Avatar* and the prehistoric jungle of *Peter Jackson's King Kong* drew out very different scores from their respective video game and film composers. Though all four scores include tribal rhythms, ethnic woodwinds and chanting, each has its own distinct aesthetic which matches its respective visual content. Consider that the uplifting chant for *Avatar* is lyrical, fully orchestrated, tightly performed by a female chorus and lightly South American in its flavor. By contrast, the chanting provided for *King Kong* is vicious, primitive and accompanied only by furious drumming. Even though both approaches match their respective jungle-themed visual aesthetics perfectly, they could hardly be more different from each other.

Matching the visual aesthetic can also be accomplished through stylistic mirroring. The bright and playful sound of *Super Mario 3D World* is a perfect match for the game's primary colors, bouncy action and innocent gameplay. On the other hand, a futuristic cityscape may find its stylistic mirror in a purely electronic score. Thus the intuitive pairing of Giorgio Moroder and Skrillex for Disney's 2015 *Tron* video game.

Second, music can contribute to structural unity by keeping an appropriate continuity with the emotional narrative. Emotional narrative is the subtext, the path along which the director or designer intend to take the audience's feelings. To cite an archetype, consider the romantic comedy. Two people meet and begin dating. Some kind of conflict/misunderstanding/event-out-of-their control breaks them apart. Overcoming some weakness/challenge and gaining understanding brings them back together. The emotional narrative follows a simple path, similar to an uppercase letter "N". Things look up, then they go down, then they go up again. In the end everything works out, a modern equivalent to happily-ever-after. Effective music in romantic comedies supports this structure, tending toward pleasant and hopeful without ever taking itself too seriously. This kind of score matches the emotional narrative and contributes to the overall structural unity of the film.

Third, music can contribute to structural unity by maintaining cohesiveness within the score itself. Recognizable form, such as theme and variation, is an effective application of this principle. The sustained use of Marty O'Donnell's iconic theme throughout the Halo franchise comes to mind. Each time this theme plays, the player is instantly connected to their memories of the game and their experiences in that universe. Themes are powerful tools for building continuity between a production and the audience.

Another manifestation of cohesiveness in the score and its contribution to structural unity is through stylistic continuity. A score should sit within its defined stylistic

hulu

STRUCTURAL UNITY

Hulu's 2009 Super Bowl commercial featuring Alec Baldwin (www.youtube.com/watch?v=W5j961bMrfI) playfully mocked every cliché about the bad effects of television and turned them into selling points. The music score also hit a grand slam in terms of structural unity.

1. *Matching the visual aesthetic.* The commercial's visual setting is a direct knock-off of the *Men in Black* HQ. The music score takes on the same cryptic playfulness of the MIB movie scores, offering an effective connection to the visual setting.

2. *Keeping continuity with the emotional narrative.* There is a duality in this emotional narrative. At one level is the MIB parody, with the idea that television is a secret alien plot to create mushy, edible brains. But at another level, it portrays a smug friskiness through the alien spokesman's matter-of-fact mocking commentary. The music dances at both levels, offering enough wonder and suspense to support the alien plot, but also bouncing around with enough mickey-mousing motion to suggest the cartoon-like premise.

3. *Maintaining internal cohesiveness within the score.* The score retains its palette and personality from top to bottom. Celeste backed by orchestra runs throughout. A harmonic motif of minor triads moving by half steps opens and closes the spot. Start-and-stop scoring is continuous. With consistent palette, harmony and scoring approach, the music remains internally consistent. The structural unity of the spot is supported by the score every step of the way.

parameters, whatever they may be, in order to retain its cohesiveness. It is almost easier to make this point by considering its opposite. Imagine the sense of disconnect an audience could feel if a film score were divided into thirds—Alexandre Desplat takes the opening act, Trent Reznor scores the middle and Alan Menkin brings it home!

There is an additional form of continuity in media that is more logistical than philosophical. Games sometimes pause to load the next level. Films may have flashbacks, montages and edit points. Plays have scene changes and intermissions. There are any number of operational limitations that can cause an interruption or shuffling of the narrative flow. In quality entertainment, every effort is made to minimize such disruptions of continuity and their impact.

Music score is an element that can ameliorate such moments of interruption or discontinuity. "Music can tie together a visual medium that is by its very nature, continually in danger of falling apart."[7] By playing through load screens and across scene changes, music can mask disruptions and help keep the consumer engaged. Music can also provide a through-thread that links disruptions in the dramatic flow to overarching themes or previous connections.

Score gravitates to moments when narrative continuity is the most tenuous, to points of linkage on which the narrative chain depends: the transition between sequences, the flashforward and flashback, parallel editing, the dream sequence, and the montage . . . Music [score] responds to potentially disruptive shifts in space and time with its own continuity, often in the form of continuous playing and frequently through reliance on extended melody.[8]

CONVENTIONAL TOOLSETS USED IN MUSIC SCORING

Each of the music scoring functions examined above inform a composer's purposes. They define the end. But what of the means? What resources are available to the score composer to facilitate his success in generating music to fulfill those functions? Attention now turns to an initial exploration of several conventional toolsets at the composer's disposal.

Palette

The *palette* for a particular score is defined as the collection of tonal colors and sonic textures utilized in that score. Palette includes a broad range of variables, including whether to use acoustic or electronic instruments (or both), ensemble and/or solo instruments, performance ranges, recording approach and mixing style. Anything which impacts the tonal color or sonic texture of a score becomes part of the palette of that score.

Palette is the first toolset many professional composers will grab when beginning a new score. Ramin Djawadi, composer for the television series *Game of Thrones*, is one. "At the beginning of each project I like to create a palette of sound for that particular project."[9] Beginning with the palette selection helps to set up another type of framework

PEEK BEHIND THE CURTAIN

Structural Unity in LOTR Music

In 2001, Vivendi-Universal Games announced their license from Middle-earth Enterprises (formerly Tolkien Enterprises) to develop video games based on the writings of the late J. R. R. Tolkien. Preserving the integrity of the IP was a contractual priority in the license, manifested in the hiring of a franchise Music Director, a franchise Design Director and a franchise Art Director. These directors were tasked with creative vision and guidance for five different development studios in four different states working on six different games. I was hired to be the Music Director. My mandates were to preserve quality, authenticity and continuity.

I needed a strategy to ensure the structural unity of music scores to the original source material and across all the different games. I had spent several years studying the Tolkien works, and had a good handle on the story, setting and characters. But to ensure structural unity in the music, I needed much more than that. I needed source data about music in Tolkien's world. I resolved to go meticulously through each book, making note of every reference to music, instruments, song, voices, sounds—even registering the impact of music and sound on the surrounding world. I found hundreds of such references and inferences in the literature. After culling them from the books, I correlated each reference by race, so that we would know authoritatively what kinds of instruments Hobbits played, what constitutes the vocal range of a Dwarf, and how Elven singing can effect people and surrounding environments. These findings were codified in a detailed document called the Tolkien Music Style Guide. Everyone working on music for these games received a copy.

Lord of the Rings is such an iconic fantasy creation. All of the music had to be just right. I began to wonder if even a thoroughly researched Style Guide would be enough. To prevent a proliferation of incompatible scoring approaches, I felt I should take the strategy one step further. We needed thematic continuity as well.

With this determination, I created a cycle of themes for the key races highlighting important locations in the lore for each race. The themes incorporated and embodied all of the authoritative references and resulting creative direction outlined in the Style Guide. These theme cycles became audible musical examples of the Style Guide's textual directives. Every development studio received finished mixes of the theme cycle for each race, plus extensive stems and underlying MIDI files.

The music was well received. VUG registered over a million downloads of the themes from its website. That was back in 2004 when a million downloads still meant something. But more than popularity, the continuity we crafted helped to keep all of the games orbiting around an authoritatively based musical center. I'm happy to report that the themes have held up remarkably well. In 2012, I composed a new score for the *Riders of Rohan* expansion to *Lord of the Rings Online*. Parts of this expansion put players in the roles

within which creativity can find expression. It also boosts productivity.

Convention often informs the composer's choice of palette. Audience expectations are well developed from years of media immersion. Recalling the auditorium exercise of chapter zero, music students tended to call out ideas for a score's palette first. Perhaps palette choices are the most easily recognizable and quickly envisioned components of a score. For example, in looking at an image of an ice planet, it may be much easier to recommend bowed cymbals than it would be to select specific notes for a fitting melody. Likewise, a rainforest scene calls to mind ethnic woodwinds and tribal drums more readily than a specific tempo or metric. Cultural expectations regarding palette come quickly to mind and are deeply ingrained. The wise composer will take advantage of these expectations.

Orchestration

Closely aligned to a composer's choice of palette is how the selected palette is utilized to bring color and character to the composition. Students will find that orchestration is meagerly defined by mainstream dictionaries. Most say only that it is arranging music for an orchestra or band. Certainly at the most elementary level, orchestration is that. But it is so much more than just that. As described by Samuel Adler in his book, *A Study of Orchestration*, "Orchestration and instrumentation . . . illuminate many important areas of music. After all, texture and timbre clarify the form as well as the content of a host of compositions. Furthermore, specific orchestral colors and even spacing of chords in the orchestral fabric give special personality to the music."[10]

For the score composer, *orchestration* involves the clothing, coloring and articulation of the score's components across all the available timbres of a selected palette. It may be instructive to compare a piece of music to a bare store manikin. Think of the head as the melody, the body as harmony, arms as counter melodies and ornamentation, and the legs as rhythm. In its bare state, the form and shape of the manikin are clearly discernible. But think how dramatically the impression is changed by clothing the manikin with a bright Hawaiian shirt, colorful shorts and a straw hat. For a contrasting look, change the color of the clothing to black, add dark sunglasses and remove the hat. The effect is markedly different. Many such transformations may be imagined. In each case, though the manikin itself is exactly the same, the impression is significantly altered by how it is clothed, colored and articulated.

of Frodo, Sam and Boromir, so I went back and quoted from the original theme cycle. The players loved it. My personal email inbox and the game's online forums lit up with bubbly comments from players who recognized the themes and felt the connection to their previous LOTR gaming experiences. Oh, how the human mind craves effective continuity and responds to it!

So it is with orchestrating a music score. Choices of instrumentation, range, voicing, dynamics and articulations all have a significant impact on how the body of music is perceived. Consider that Alexander Courage chose to introduce his ten-note fanfare for the television series *Star Trek* with a French horn section, repeated in modulation by the trumpets. It could have been introduced by tuba and repeated by a bassoon ensemble instead. Although the notes, rhythm and harmony would have been unchanged, oh what a different impact that particular orchestration choice would have had!

Orchestration is a big job. There may be thousands of large and small orchestration decisions involved in a major music score. Even if the palette is small and specialized, such as a zydeco band, there are still many decisions to make. Which part of the rhythm goes to the washboard and which to the drummer? Will the accordion harmonize against a guitar melody, or vice versa? Will they switch roles? How, when and in what manner will the fiddle play? Probably the only question that doesn't need much consideration is whether the bass part will be played by the bass player.

Spreading the score across a full orchestra multiplies the composer's options exponentially. For a simple exercise, consider the following twenty-plus questions that need to be considered and answered to make even the most rudimentary decision for a single orchestral scoring cue: "How shall I introduce the melody?"

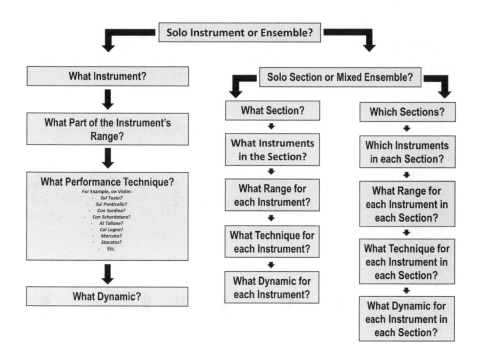

Harmony

Harmony is created by sounding two or more simultaneous but differing pitches. Pitches may be combined according to long-established or evolving conventions. Early classical harmony developed combinations of three pitches, or triads. Such triads include the tonic, third and fifth notes of a scale. Later classical harmony added the seventh. Jazz harmony expanded by allowing increasing numbers of simultaneous pitches and altering combinations of chord tones by half steps one way or the other (flat 5, sharp 9, etc.). Twentieth-century harmony went even further by creating large and unconventional note combinations referred to as polychords and clusters. All of these combinations and their resulting effects are available to the score composer.

As palette conventions are shaped by cultural expectations, so harmonic conventions are shaped by biological expectations. Simply put, humans are wired to respond in predictable ways to given harmonies. Researchers at Cornell, Tufts and McGill Universities have demonstrated specific and measureable physiological

ORCHESTRATING REVIEWS

Critics had a lot to say about the original video game score for *Peter Jackson's King Kong*. There was so much in the press about the game's music that it became possible to correlate multiple reviewer remarks with the specific score tracks they were commenting on. During this correlation it was discovered that adjectives selected by the critics could be reliably connected to specific orchestration techniques. The same pairings popped up again and again. Here are ten examples:

What They Said	What It Means Musically
Exciting	Rapid contrapuntal lines
Sumptuous	Added sevenths and ninths in the string choir
Atmospheric	*Sul tasto*, polychords, clusters
Menacing	Sharp dynamics in the low brass
Eerie	*Sul ponticello*, tremolo
Foreboding	Suspensions, low brass, low strings
Sweeping	Arpeggiated strings, unison lines, glissandi
Expressive	Effective dynamics and typecasting
Relentless	Repetitive lines against changes
Epic	French horns and classical choir

changes occurring in response to musical harmony which match the body's reaction to fundamental emotional states. For example, people experiencing sadness will evidence a lower body temperature, decreased skin conductivity, elevated blood pressure and a slowing pulse. When exposed to minor harmonies, test subjects evidenced the same physiological readings as those who experienced real sadness. Major harmonies produced respiratory changes and limbic system responses identical to happiness. Dissonant harmonies increased pulse rates and lit up areas of the brain associated with fear.[11]

Future studies may find comparable correlations between more complex chords and additional emotional states. Mirrored physiological responses may even be discovered for progressions of harmonies. Composers and academics will no doubt benefit from additional scientific inquiry in the years ahead, yielding new evidence and findings to better explain the interplay between harmony and human physiology.

Meanwhile, one thing is clear. Harmony provides the composer with a direct path to the human nervous system. Such powerful, biologically ingrained connections are a composer's gold mine. They are also risky to ignore. Composers making selections against the grain of these conventions should only do so with careful consideration and deliberate purpose.

Rhythm

Rhythm is reflected in the speed, pacing and pattern of beats in a musical composition. Rhythm also exists in the speed, pacing and pattern of visual content. Of all aspects of a score for visual media, most careful attention must be given to rhythm to ensure that it acts in the service of the scene. Film composer John Williams has said, regarding rhythm, "My own belief is that the first and most important issue in scoring films is tempo. If the music is quicker than the editorial rhythm it may seem to slow the film down, and the reverse is also true. You need to get into the rhythmic 'pocket.' We know we've got it right when it's riding with the action in an effortless way."[12]

Rhythm also connects with human biology in ways the composer can take advantage of. People experiencing sadness are slow and sedate, listless even. Music scoring which imitates this slow rhythm can match the feeling. Happiness and excitement rev up the emotions with energy. Music scoring imitates this with energetic rhythms. The connections are scientifically proven.

Melody

There is a charming saying ascribed to Oklahoma songwriter Woody Guthrie. It goes something like this, "Don't sing me a sad tale about your momma. Sing me a happy tune." When one thinks of singing a happy tune, they think of melody. When one thinks of whistling a tune, they think of melody. When someone complains about a song stuck in their head (*"It's a small world after all, It's a small world after all . . ."*), melody is always the culprit.

Melody is a succession of individual notes that form a phrase, a pattern or a musical sentence. Melody is

GUEST LECTURE
CONJURING FEAR

Jason Graves
(*Tomb Raider, Dead Space*)

Music is all about emotion, and fear is a very powerful emotion. So what scares us? More often than not it's simply the unknown—the masked figure, the shadow in the hallway, the shark fin on the water. As a composer, there are very specific things that evoke fear. Anything that the human ear relies on for stability and a "home base"—specific key centers, constant rhythms, familiar sounds, even the very structure of written music—can be twisted and harnessed to throw the listener off guard. Randomness, otherwise known as "chance music" or aleatoric music, is often engaged. I try especially hard to create sounds that are unrecognizable and unfamiliar, very much along the lines of classical composers such as Krzysztof Penderecki and György Ligeti, who are the true pioneers in aleatoric music.

PEEK BEHIND THE CURTAIN

Manipulating Emotion

While the player is playing the game, a great music score is playing the player. Being a video game composer is like having access to a vast array of switches, knobs and sliders to seduce and manipulate the player's emotions, drawing them deeply into the experience. Harmony is probably the biggest knob on the panel. I use it relentlessly to manage the player's feelings. For any composer who wants to give each player the richest, most immersive and impactful experience possible, harmony is the perfect partner.

always monophonic. It may certainly be harmonized by one or even hundreds of supporting parts. But the melody is a musical sequence of specific pitches which could be sung (in some octave) by the human voice, the original monophonic instrument.

Tying a discussion of melody to the human voice is not only metaphorically instructive but may also be existentially revealing. The brain appears to latch onto melody similarly to how it latches onto a person's voice in conversation. This is not surprising. In thinking of music as a language, melody is that component which most closely resembles the rise and fall of human speech. It could be that because of this resemblance, the brain processes melody as it does speech, as if the melody were conveying the important rational information of a piece of music, or the facts. Thus, those parts of the brain which have evolved to interpret and capture important facts become most engaged when exposed to melody, improving recognizance and recall. It is only a hypothesis, but it is interesting to note how fiercely the mind locks onto melody. Perhaps future research will uncover more that can clarify the correlations between melody, language and physiology.

Theme

One specialized use of melody in music scoring is the theme. A melody becomes a *theme* when that melody is tied to a particular character, setting, dramatic situation or overarching idea. Themes provide contextual clues and reinforce struggles, conflict, payoffs. They are memorable, or become memorable through meaningfully targeted repetition.

In EA's *Monopoly Streets*, an energetic and infectious theme introduces the game and underscores the menu while players set up options and choose their characters. It is an exciting and catchy tune, portending good times to come. Versions of the theme repeat at strategic moments in gameplay to reinforce this feeling, such as when a player passes "Go" and whenever they earn a monopoly. When a player finally wins the game, their character is lauded on a victory stand accompanied by a full-blown celebratory version of the theme. The theme sets up expectations from the very beginning of the game, then delivers on those expectations throughout the experience to give the player a series of recurring and connected emotional payoffs, culminating in the climactic payoff of winning the game.

A character theme, also known as a leitmotif, can be equally effective. By evolving a character's theme across their story arc, the music heightens the emotional experience for an audience following along and identifying with a character's journey, struggles and ultimate endpoint. In the Broadway musical *Wicked*, composer Steven Schwartz introduces an ambitious, aspiring leitmotif for Elphaba which he refers to as the "Unlimited" theme.[13] "Come with me, think of what we could do together," Elphaba says to Glinda, as her voice takes flight on the theme, "Unlimited, Together we're unlimited, Together we'll be the greatest team there's ever been." This melody returns during the song, "The Wizard and I" as the story unfolds and the witches' paths diverge. Elphaba's story is noble and tragic, as her ambitions fade and her trajectory veers wildly from early dreams. The theme makes its final tentative appearance as she sings in the end, "I'm limited. Just look at me, I'm limited." This recurring melody, this theme for Elphaba, adds a unifying thread to the musical and brings the character's story arc straight to the heart.

A great theme is a nifty memory hook for human emotions. When the players experience a great moment in the game and that moment is simultaneously underscored by a riveting and memorable theme—the moment becomes magical, a

RHYTHM AND HARMONY

For today's score composers, rhythm and harmony are the music scoring equivalent of "the old one–two punch". Rhythms reinforce the body's biological responses to harmony. Some of the scientific research cited earlier about harmony also mentioned rhythmic stimuli. Not surprisingly, similar results were discovered. Slow rhythms reinforced the body's reaction to sadness. Upbeat rhythms have a predictable correlation to happiness. And so on. Because of their immersion in the scoring language for many years, most music students and young professionals already know this intuitively.

MELODY TELLS THE STORY

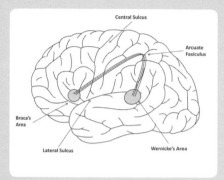

Melody may be considered as the storytelling device in music. For a given musical composition, melody takes the role of narrator. It has been postulated that melody engages those parts of the brain that filter, process and retain language (shown above). Thus the phenomenon can be widely noted that melodies remain in the minds of even the musically untrained. Further research is needed to confirm and codify the correlation.

seminal memory that the player never forgets. Places like Azeroth and Middle-earth don't really exist. But fear, longing, nobility, striving, honor—these do exist. The composer's job is to underscore these feelings at the right places in the game so the player becomes immersed in those emotions. The game is just a fantasy, but the emotions called forth by the theme are very real, thus impressing the experience indelibly upon the player. It could be said that the video game score composer's job is to find and awaken the real within the surreal.

Having a theme alone won't ensure magic. It must resonate with zen clarity, or as John Williams once said, it must sound "inevitable". A great theme should also be deployed just enough throughout the game, but not too much, and in the most impactful context.

Genre

When a particular recipe of ingredients selected from among palette, orchestration, harmony, rhythm and melody yields music of a distinctive and serviceable flavor, that combination of choices can create a musical *genre*. Genre is a French word meaning kind, sort or style.[15] The word genre may be used interchangeably with the word idiom, as presented in the previous chapter on language. When used in music scoring, genre can represent a template of musical components available to the composer again and again to reliably score visual content of a matching style.

Scoring genres come into the professional consciousness when musical and visual elements combine in some distinctive way that resonates with a broad audience. Scoring genres can also come into their own when such a combination finds resonance with a narrow but especially responsive audience. These explain popular genres and niche genres.

Just as there are many different musical idioms, there are many scoring genres. The human appetite for variety is enormous. Diversity of flavor is a hallmark of the natural world, and a deep source of pleasure and satisfaction. Running in parallel to the appetite for variety is the brain's penchant for categorizing and making sense of variety. Scoring genres are effective musical shortcuts to comprehension.

Think of scoring genres as musical recipes or templates. Or to use another analogy, liken scoring genres to the snapshot function of a mixing console. When a mixer finds a given combination of settings that work well together to deliver a mix of a distinctive color, the snapshot function preserves that combination of parameters for quick and effective use in the future.

SUMMARY

Diegetic music originates from within a scene or a level. It functions as part of the visual narrative. It is more commonly called source music. *Non-diegetic music* has neither a visible source nor is implied in the scene or level. It is generally referred to as underscore. Six conventional functions of non-diegetic underscore in visual media are to *set the mood, heighten emotion, propel the action, provide contextual clues, enhance the aesthetic* and *contribute to structural unity*.

Robust and reliable toolsets are available to help the score composer deliver on the conventional functions required for visual media. They include *palette, orchestration, harmony, rhythm, melody, theme* and *genre*. Both human physiology and cultural bias inform the meaning and effectiveness of choices made using these toolsets.

There is no need to reinvent the wheel. Scoring fundamentals may be applied in nearly limitless creative combinations to deliver both

GUEST LECTURE
LEITMOTIF

Gustavo Constantini, Professor of Sound Design, University of Buenos Aires

What is a leitmotif? First things first. Wagner leitmotifs were both a complex form of codification and a way of producing subtle sensations and associations in the listener. It was not mere chance that film music opted so strongly for the Wagnerian approach. According to *Grove's Dictionary of Music*, leitmotif (leading motif) is "a theme, or other coherent idea, clearly defined so as to retain its identity if modified on subsequent appearances, and whose purpose is to represent or symbolise a person, object, place, idea, state of mind, supernatural force or any other ingredient in a dramatic work, usually operatic but also vocal, choral or instrumental." Wagner's flexible way of using musical themes enabled musicians to resolve a lot of problems when films began to include sound. First, to find a structure for organizing musical material. Second, to link characters and situations by means of music. Romantic music entered the film sound field associated with all these technical, psychological and formal aspects, helping narrative film to aim higher. People were aware of the musical code, and the associations with characters and situations allowed directors to delineate and complete plot ideas through sound. [14]

understanding and delight. Convention does not inhibit creativity. Used with skill and imagination, it offers a comprehensible framework within which creativity can be concentrated where it will have the most bearing. Rules must be learned before they can be broken intelligently. Music scoring is a rich and powerful language of expression, a masterful tool in the hands of the well-educated and inventive composer.

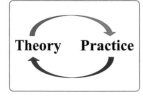

APPLIED LEARNING

1. Find or cite ten examples of diegetic music (source music), two each from video games, films, television shows, theatrical plays or opera and commercials. Describe the contributing role each plays in the visual presentation. Postulate why the director chose to use source music in each instance.

2. Select a video game, film, television show, play or opera of your choosing. Analyze and describe how the composer addressed the six conventional functions of music scoring outlined in this chapter: *setting the mood, heightening emotion, propelling the action, providing contextual clues, enhancing the aesthetic* and *contributing to structural unity*.

3. From the same selection, analyze and describe how the composer used the toolsets of *palette, orchestration, harmony, rhythm, melody, theme* and *genre* to address and fulfill these functions.

4. Watch or download the short film *Masterpiece* from the website associated with this book. (www.FocalPress.com/cw/Thomas). Using the principles learned thus far, describe in writing the principles, functions and toolsets you would apply in scoring this visual work.

5. Create a mock-up of the score you described in #4.

REFERENCES

1. Secondary source, quoting Werner Erhard, in Lynda Obst, *Hello, He Lied: And Other Truths from the Hollywood Trenches* (New York: Broadway Books, 1996), p. 73.

2. Plato, *The Republic*. Book III, 392c.

3. FilmSound website: http://filmsound.org/terminology/diegetic.htm.

4. http://bioshock.wikia.com/wiki/BioShock_Licensed_Soundtrack#cite_note-0.

5. FilmSound website: http://filmsound.org/terminology/diegetic.htm.

6. Mona Lisa Chanda and Daniel J. Levitin, "The Neurochemistry of Music". *Trends in Cognitive Sciences* (April 2013), 17(4): 186.

7. Roy D. Prendergast, *Film Music A Neglected Art: A Critical Study of Music in Films* (New York, W. W. Norton, 1992), p. 221.

8. Kathryn Kalinak. "Music to My Ears: Teaching the Soundtrack". *Indiana Theory Review* (Spring/Fall 1990): 9.

9. Victoria Ellison. "*'Game of Thrones'* Composer Ramin Djawadi: I'm Just Trying to Create Something Magical (Q&A)". *The Hollywood Reporter* (April 15, 2013).

10. Samuel Adler. *A Study of Orchestration* (New York, W. W. Norton, 1989), p. 3.

11. *The Economist.* "The Biology of Music" (February 12, 2000), also available online: http://www.economist.com/node/329414 . See also Tufts University: http://ase.tufts.edu/psychology/music-cognition/emotion2009.html.

12. http://www.dlwaldron.com/JohnWilliamsbio.html.

13. Carol di Giere, *Defying Gravity: The Creative Career of Steven Schwartz from* Godspell *to* Wicked (New York, Hal Leonard), Chapter 20.

14. Gustavo Constantini. FilmSound website: http://filmsound.org/gustavo/leitmotif-revisted.htm.

15. http://www.etymonline.com/index.php?term=genre.

CHAPTER 2
DISTINGUISHING PRINCIPLES OF VIDEO GAME SCORING

And now for something completely different.[1]

A successful video game score will fulfill each of the six conventional music scoring functions outlined in Chapter 1. It will *set the mood, heighten emotion, propel the action, provide contextual clues, enhance the aesthetic* and *contribute to structural unity*. Additionally, a video game score must also effectively address the unique game-centric challenges of *score flexibility, scale* and *game function*. This chapter presents an exploration of these challenges and a foundational discussion of principles for effectively addressing each.

SCORE FLEXIBILITY

A favorite scene from George Lucas's *The Empire Strikes Back* depicts Han Solo and Princess Leia stealing a passionate kiss. A memorable exchange ensues as Leia breathlessly confesses her feelings. "I love you," she says. "I know," he replies in a tender deadpan. Tension mounts as worried glances pass back and forth among the key protagonist characters. Han is being prepped for carbonite freezing as Darth Vader sets a trap for Luke Skywalker. Solo is lowered into a metal pit and frozen in carbonite amid a billowing puff of smoke. The music score heightens the emotion, enhances the aesthetic and propels the action forward moment by moment, using tools of harmony, orchestration and rhythm—even Chewbacca's bellowing voice—all leading up to the climax. The music delivers on its various roles in perfect sync with the action.

However, rewind the scene for a moment and imagine how it might play out differently as a video game. Han and Leia are kissing. The guards pull them apart. The score begins to raise the tension. Leia is just about to say, "I love you," but suddenly receives a pop-up from one of her friends. "We're all heading over to Tatooine to play some mini-games. Wanna come?" Leia quickly replies back, "Totally!" Off she trots, abruptly leaving Han, Darth and everyone in the scene (not to mention the rising music score) far behind. What is a composer to do?

This playfully imagined scenario illustrates a distinguishing fundamental between music scoring for a video game and music scoring for any other type of visual media. A video game score must be **flexible** in real-time, capable of responding instantaneously to unpredictable dramatic changes in musically relevant ways.

Consider the problem from another angle. A player's character (PC) enters the game world and begins to explore a forest. After two minutes of exploration, a troll enters play and battle ensues for ninety seconds. When the troll is vanquished, the PC does a seven-second victory dance, then teleports to another world. This would be a simple scenario for any competent composer to score. Two minutes of mood-setting and aesthetically enhancing exploration music. Ninety seconds of rousing fight music to heighten emotion and propel the action. A victory flourish which transitions into seven seconds of dance music. All concluding with a magical embellishment as the player teleports away. Sounds like a remarkably simple and straightforward scoring assignment. Some might be tempted to ask, "So what's the big deal with scoring games?"

What's the big deal, indeed! The big deal is that the next player may spend *twenty minutes* exploring the forest instead of *two*. They may pick every flower and turn over every rock and click on every tree trunk. They may decide to go back and collect all the magic mushrooms or sit by a brook to soak in the ambience. Still another player may cut straight through the forest in a beeline for the troll. After just fifteen seconds of fighting, the troll may land a particularly effective blow and decimate the player's health points. The player might decide to turn around and run away. The music score which seemed so straightforward in the first scenario is clearly inadequate now.

These kinds of variances can multiply exponentially in a video game, transforming one of the most fundamental building blocks of music scoring into an unknowable variable. That fundamental building block is timing. **Timing** consists of entry points, duration and exit points for any given musical composition in a score. Think of timing as an *x*-axis running along underneath the game experience with each integer representing seconds, minutes, hours or even days.

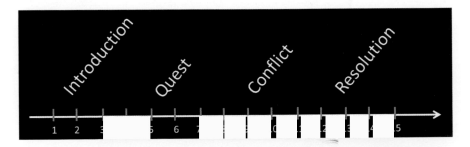

In traditional music scoring, each important action or dramatic development occurs at a specific and consistent point along the x-axis, or at a given moment in time. In the afore-mentioned scene from *The Empire Strikes Back*, Leia says, "I love you," eight seconds after Han is pulled away. At twenty-two seconds, Chewie starts to bellow and Han's descent into the pit begins. Solo's descent lasts exactly fourteen seconds until the carbonite freeze is triggered. Such important actions and dramatic events develop for specific durations along the x-axis, occurring at specific points in time. Traditional score composers target such dramatically relevant timings and move their music score forward along the timeline toward these important points as needed. Logistically, this is not a difficult proposition.

However, this same approach does not work in video games.

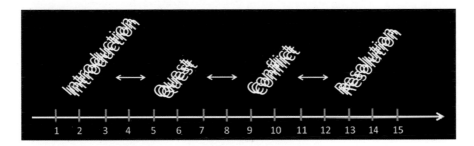

The game timeline is unknowable because it regenerates anew each time the game is played. It unfolds based on moment-to-moment decisions made by gamers of diverse ages, genders, backgrounds, playing styles and even moods. There is always uncertainty as to which actions may be taken next by any given player. Therefore, it is unknowable to the composer as to when key events in the dramatic timeline will occur or how long such events will last.

To solve this problem of elastic timing, composers must learn to think of music structure in flexible terms. Unknown timing necessitates a music score that can stretch, contract and transition as needed. In the wide world of visual media, this is a problem unique only to video games. Fortunately, there are three powerful new tools which can be added to the composer's arsenal, three principles which can assist the video game composer in rethinking music scoring in flexible terms. These principles are *pathing, repetition* and *randomness*.

Pathing

The principle of pathing states that the number and type of dramatic conditions in a game are finite and knowable. Likely transitions between dramatic events can be predicted. Thus, corresponding pathways of music scoring solutions can be mapped out in advance. This principle of pathing allows the composer to plan in advance for options and transitions in the video game score.

If/then statements make good junctures for pathing. If situation A occurs, then implement solution 1 (where A represents a dramatic condition or event in the game, and 1 represents a set of music score instructions). *Pathing* is a plan for what always happens next with the music when a given gameplay event or game transition occurs.

Such dramatic conditions and events within a video game are referred to as game states. A *game state* can be thought of as a node or stage within which a specific type of gameplay experience is offered. For example, the game's menu is a particular game state. Exploring the world is another game state. Various types of events and encounters within the world comprise different and additional game states. There are dozens of game states in a typical modern video game.

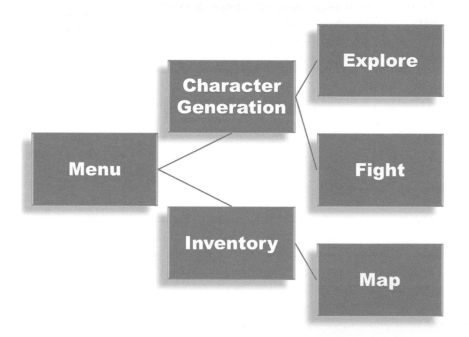

In order to plan appropriate pathing for music between game states, composers need a blueprint which shows all of the relevant game states and the gameplay transitions between them. Such a blueprint is called a *game design document*.

A shorthand version of the game design called a **game flow document** may alternatively be given to the composer.

Game design or game flow documents should outline the number and type of game states planned for the game. These may include menu tasks, tutorials, exploration, chatting, combat, victory, defeat, solving puzzles, crafting and so forth. These game states may unfold slowly, as in an MMO, or they may occur in rapid succession, as they do in a side-scroller. The composer must understand the flow of game states in order to create successful pathing for the music score.

With a solid understanding of game states and their flow, and with a game design document firmly in hand, a composer is ready to begin thinking through the pathing of their score. There are several ways pathing can take shape in a game:

- Pathing can occur sequentially like a row of dominoes.
- Pathing can branch like a tree.
- Pathing can take shape in a matrix.
- Pathing can build like a stack.

Regardless of the structure chosen, the principle of pathing gives composers a powerful tool for building flexibility into their music score. It allows them to plan ahead for options and transitions in the music which will match the anticipated game states and transitions players will encounter during gameplay.

In some cases a specialist in audio who works for the developer, usually the audio director or audio lead, will review the game design document and interpret the musically relevant parts for the composer. In such cases the audio specialist may determine the pathing and give the composer only an asset list showing the itemized music cues to be delivered. In such cases the composer should seek to understand the pathing and ideally participate in pathing plans, as there are many path-related factors which will influence the efficacy of the score.

PLAY GAMES!

Parents and spouses may cringe to hear this, but an understanding of game states and flow is best internalized through experience with playing lots of games. Just as the language of music scoring becomes internalized through exposure to music scoring in media, so acquiring a feel for game progression is best achieved through some amount of immersion in the game experience. Each of the five games pictured above have won the award or been a finalist in the Game Audio Network Guild's category for Best Interactive Score. Seems like a great collection to start with.

GUEST LECTURE
REPETITION, RANDOMIZATION AND PATHING

Chase Combs
(*Forza Motorsport, Guild Wars*)
and **Lance Hayes**
(*Forza Motorsport, Gears of War*)

The core concept behind *Forza Motorsport 5's* soundtrack is that it underscores the player's journey from their garage to the race, and back to the finish line. As you play the game, the music design is actively and adaptively responding to your progress.

If a player is designing a livery or tinkering away in their virtual garage, variety and repetitiveness can be a concern here. So when we were designing the menu music design for *Forza Motorsport 5*, we built a system that utilized multiple stem layers that loaded into memory. Using adaptive mixer changes, we were able to alter the balance between the stems, which allowed us to introduce new elements for a particular UI screen or to remove elements to reduce the score to more of a sonic wallpaper. This all varied depending on the goals of the particular scene, and helped to make the score feel less like a static piece of music and more of an evolving soundscape that followed the player's actions. Adding random music sweeteners timed to bar/beat markers would add additional variety to the score in this area.

Repetition

This is another principle which can assist the video game composer with score flexibility. *Repetition* allows for parts of the score to be repeated as needed while underscoring a persisting game state. This is most effective when the length of music to be repeated most closely matches the expected length of time that a game state will be active for an average player. If a game state will likely persist much longer than is practical for a single music cue, repetition is most effective if the length and structure of music is sufficient to mask the repetition.

A common use of repetition occurs with action music in underscoring a fight scene. Perhaps an average fight in a particular game will last approximately sixty seconds. The composer creates a sixty-second piece of combat music to accompany such battles. However, depending on unknown variables in the player's fighting style, experience and spontaneous decisions, the fight could easily stretch to two or three minutes, maybe longer. Repeating the action music while the fight continues allows for a diversity of gamers while still propelling the action and contributing to the structural unity of the experience.

A warning about repetition is needed, however. As with any other kind of statement, too much repetition of a musical statement will quickly fatigue the listener. Even a brilliant theme will become tiring after multiple repetitions, especially if they occur in close proximity. Very likely by the time the third or fourth repetition begins within a short time frame, it will trigger an unfolding sequence of responses in the listener—recognition, tolerance, mild annoyance, aggravation and finally intolerance. The player will probably turn off the music at this point. Game over.

Even a piece of music that initially thrilled the listener will grow tiresome after too much repetition. Though it can be utilized to assist the composer in achieving flexibility in the score, great wisdom and restraint must be exercised in applying the principle of repetition. The line which divides usefulness from uselessness can be very thin.

Randomness

Randomness is another principle which can increase the flexibility of a video game music score. *Randomness* is evidenced when any one instance of a set has the same probability of occurring as every other member of the set.[2] Randomness in a video game score happens when a single instance or component is selected indiscriminately from a set of related musical components. This allows for increased musical variety in those cases where proliferating a sufficient number and diversity of specific music cues is impractical.

Starting out in this "Homespace", the game states subsequently transition to "Travel", "Pre-Race", "Race" and conclude in a "Rewards" section. The soundtrack was nearly all adaptive with many pathing options along the way.

The various sections included up to twelve stems playing back in a vertical mix that varied dramatically based on player location, as well as offering performance feedback in the race itself. For example, if you are performing well and are in the lead, you get a very full mix of music. However, if you fall back in the pack behind the other racers you get a very different, darker and quieter mix that is there to let you know that things are not going well. All of the music is seamlessly and invisibly mixed in the audio engine as you engage in gameplay.

During a race, changes come quickly and often, so making large musical shifts here can feel jarring and become repetitive quickly. It's also very unlikely that races will present scripted moments for musical embellishment, such as building a swell before a crash. It's much more of a reactive space. Avoiding cue changes here based on game state would make the experience more transparent to the player. For example, if you had a neutral cue that played for most racing conditions and an intense cue that was triggered when you were approaching a car or a car was passing you, you'd probably be alternating between the two cues over and over for the length of the race, as that's a core component of gameplay and something that happens all the time.

With well over 2,000 stems of music we were able to create a very flexible score that was implemented with a focus on variation. Specifically there are 180 minutes of music in eighteen unique tracks that can be randomly assigned to the player experience each time you go back to the Homespace. Additionally, if you spend enough time in the Homespace, the soundtrack will randomly move on to a new Homespace music track to avoid too much repetition, all with the same deep stemming and adaptive options all cued up and ready to play.

Randomization is most effective for game states which persist for several minutes and where the underscore serves primarily in a static function. For example, in a racing game, once the race is underway any number of similar high energy tracks could sustain gameplay with equal fervor. In such cases, randomization is much more effective than repetition. Pulling from a related set of different tunes with similar tempos and similar styles will keep the player seamlessly engaged, while repeating the same song over and over runs a high risk of distracting the player and pulling them out of the continuity of the experience.

Now that was random...

Randomness is least effective when applied across changing or dynamic game states where the emotional context is in flux. For example, a real-time strategy game may progress from exploration to mission mode and then into combat. Each game state addresses different levels of human emotion—curiosity/discovery, duty/adventure and fight/flight. Randomly playing a piece of exploration music while engaging in combat would be ineffective because of its disruption to the structural unity.

This brings up an important filtering point. In applying any of the principles discussed in this section on score flexibility—pathing, repetition or randomness—it should be stated that none of these principles of flexibility trump the six conventional functions of scoring discussed in Chapter 1. Those six functions always have priority. Consider them to be preeminent in scoring hierarchy.

To continue the thought, whenever considering the application of any other scoring principle, be sure to filter that consideration through the conventional functions of music scoring first. If the use of pathing allows for a flexible score but does not propel the action, then it is a fail. If repetition solves the problem of elastic timing but does not enhance the aesthetic, then it is a fail.

SCALE

The problem of scale is another common challenge for video game composers. In this context *scale* refers to the actual or potential length of an entertainment experience. For example, a long movie like *The Hobbit* lasts about three hours. Richard Wagner's entire operatic *Ring Cycle* takes about sixteen hours to perform. But online games like *World of Warcraft* or *Lord of the Rings Online* can take hundreds of hours to play, and may continue offering gameplay for several years.

While it's true that many game experiences are closer in duration to the *Ring Cycle* than they are to *WoW*, the fact remains that video games tend to exist on a scale which is significantly larger than any other form of visual entertainment. A quick sampling of popular games reveals average durations between fifteen and forty hours each.[3]

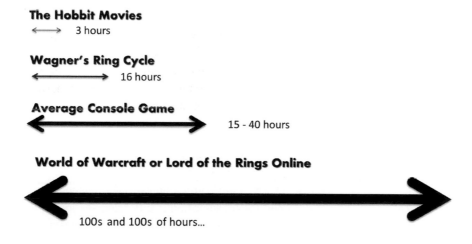

The Hobbit Movies
3 hours

Wagner's Ring Cycle
16 hours

Average Console Game
15 - 40 hours

World of Warcraft or Lord of the Rings Online
100s and 100s of hours...

The scale of such projects creates unique challenges for the score composer. If the game required a matching music score length of between fifteen and forty hours, that would certainly present one kind of challenge. Wagner took over twenty years to write his sixteen-hour opera! But if the music score budget allows for only two or three hours of music to cover the fifteen to forty hours of gameplay, as is typical, then this presents another kind of challenge for the composer. How is it possible to provide fresh and relevant musical coverage for days of gameplay experiences with only two or three hours of music?

This kind of flexibility challenge requires the composer to think about music in terms of increasing its scalability. For example, what kind of composition structure would allow for hours of relevant, non-repetitive musical coverage with only a small number of music assets? One possible solution would be to build and deploy an *ambient music set*, which loosely follows the classical principle of theme and variation. Using a fully arranged introductory theme and a matrix of short variants on selected instruments, the ambient music set brings the player into the aesthetic of the game state and keeps them engaged through periodic refreshing from the instrumental variants. This and other effective methods for addressing this problem of scale will be expounded in later chapters on technique.

It should be noted that casual and social games offer a similar scale challenge, but on a reduced level. Though designed for consumption in bite-sized sessions, the total amount of time people spend playing them, otherwise known as **engagement**, tends to range between two and three hours. For such a game, music budgets of five to ten minutes are common. Once again, the problem of scale must be addressed. How can a ten-minute score effectively serve the musical needs of a three-hour game experience? Chapters 4 and 5 will provide some current answers to this question. With any luck, future innovations from people now reading this book will provide even more effective solutions in years to come.

GAME FUNCTION

The final distinguishing principle of video game music is that of *game function scoring*. This involves underscoring game utilities which may occur outside the direct story arc or dramatic content of the game experience. Providing music for a game's load menu is one example of functional scoring. Here the music function is to mask the delay caused by loading data and assets, though no dramatic action has occurred. Another example is music heard when a player stops the game action to check their inventory for weapons, money or other items of value. These kinds of music cues are tied to game functions rather than game action, hence the term functional scoring.

PEEK BEHIND THE CURTAIN

Functional Music Cues in *DOTA 2*

Composing the video game score for Valve's MOBA game *DOTA 2* was rife with functional scoring cues. We needed music for starting up the game. We needed music for selecting team members. We needed music for finding an opposing team. Choosing which heroes to play required special music. Respawning, purchasing attributes, counting down … all of these operative aspects of the game required bits of functional scoring.

The argument could be made that functional scoring is not unique to video games. In days long past, music was often played in movie theaters while operators switched between reels. Broadway musicals typically begin with an overture or other kind of prelude music. Sports broadcasts utilize music to play in and play out of program segments. But nowhere else in modern visual media is music required for so many functional purposes as in video games.

This then becomes another way to think through the game scoring process. What functions need music? From such a list of functions, an asset list of music and pathing branches can be more fully fleshed out. But which emotions should such functional scoring address, if any? On first glance, many of the game states perform functions that may not clearly seem connected to any emotional condition. But in actuality, they all are. The emotion may be subtle anticipation. It may be a slight emotional drop or lift. For example, a menu score should heighten the emotion of anticipation. An inventory score should set a subtle mood of suspense or pause. Finding loot should offer the player a contextual infusion of "happy", like the sugar rush from popping a few M&Ms.

As with all music scoring conventions discussed in Chapter 1, each of the distinguishing principles of video game scoring in this chapter can be brought back to emotion. Music scoring is and always will be a language of emotion.

SUMMARY

A great video game score is first and foremost a great music score. The conventional scoring principles utilized in creating a memorable and effective music score for film, television or musical theater also apply to music scoring for video games. In addition, there are important distinguishing criteria that apply wholly to video game music, such as *score flexibility*, *scale* and *game function*. The unknowable dramatic timeline in video games makes score flexibility a prime challenge and focus of the composer's efforts. Principles of *pathing*, *repetition* and *randomness* assist the composer in building a flexible and functional score. Problems of massive scale may be addressed with game scoring techniques introduced in Chapters 4 and 5. Game functions offer another window through which to view a video game's music needs. Though these principles distinguish games from other visual media, the score's emotional purpose remains largely the same across all forms of entertainment.

APPLIED LEARNING

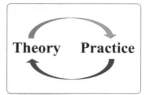

1.   What is a primary difference between the composer's challenge in scoring a video game versus any other type of visual media?

2.   Explain why flexibility is a critical factor in video game scoring. Discuss how pathing, repetition and randomness may be used to create a more flexible score.

3.   How do questions of scale affect a composer's approach to a video game score?

4.   List six game functions that require attention and possible musical solutions in a game's music score.

5.   Describe a scene from a popular movie or television show. Show how that scene could change if it were a video game. Outline possible ways to address the resulting unknowable timeline using principles of pathing, repetition and randomness.

REFERENCES

1.   Announcer, *Monty Python's Flying Circus*. Television show.

2.   Philip Babcock Grove (editor in chief), *Webster's Unabridged Dictionary* (Springfield, MA: Merriam-Webster, 2002), p. 1880.

3.   www.howlongtobeat.com.

CHAPTER 3
APPLIED PRINCIPLES IN MUSIC DESIGN

Ready. Fire. Aim.[1]

Lost in mediocrity are far too many forgettable video game scores that fail to apply the basic scoring principles outlined in Chapters 1 and 2. Some fail to set a compelling mood or enhance the aesthetic of the experience. Some are too repetitive or meander aimlessly without effective pathing. There are many flavors of such mediocrity, but a common cause underpins the majority of them all. The lack of a comprehensive scoring plan dooms many video game scores to oblivion before the first notes are ever written. To quote a catchy couplet attributed to Benjamin Franklin, "If you fail to plan, you are planning to fail."

Yet it is doubtful that any composer sets out with failure as an objective. In fact, most composers are passionate about their work and care deeply about being successful. Regardless, ignorance can leave a composer flailing about in any number of unprofitable directions. Picture a blind sentry assigned to guard a beloved coastline against invasion. No matter the passion felt, no matter the effort expended, no matter the firepower available, such a sentry will underperform an equally motivated watchman who sees clearly and takes careful aim before firing.

In video game development, nothing helps a composer see more clearly than a well-conceived music design. A **music design** is a comprehensive plan which outlines the *purposes*, *tools* and *logistics* for all uses of music within a video game. A music design is like the blueprint for a new studio. It sorts out the shape, dimensions, materials, equipment, wiring, acoustics and décor so that most features and problems can be thought through and resolved well in advance of construction. Likewise, a music design built on solid scoring principles will help the composer envision the particulars of their score ahead of production and plan for success.

Music design encompasses all parts of the composer's work for the game. Music design is based on a developer's **game design** or **game flow** document. These documents are roadmaps which outline all relevant game states and transition points in the game. These are the critical bits of information which a composer must have in order to plan a flexible and functional music score. With the game design or game flow document in hand, the composer analyzes each game state in a three-step process to determine musical *purposes, tools* and *logistics*. This is a comprehensive question-and-answer process which requires brainwork, discipline and creativity.

Steps of Music Design Analysis

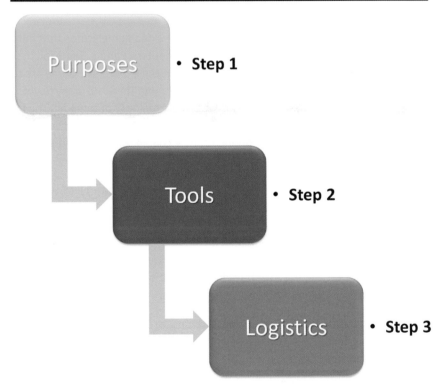

Purposes • Step 1

Tools • Step 2

Logistics • Step 3

STEP 1. PURPOSES

Every game state and transition is first scrutinized for why music may be needed. What **purposes** would music perform for a given game state or transition? Is it setting a mood? Heightening emotion? Propelling action? Providing contextual clues? Enhancing the aesthetic? Contributing to structural unity? Enabling flexibility? Principles taught in previous chapters now find their practical application as each point in the game design is scrutinized for potential scoring purposes.

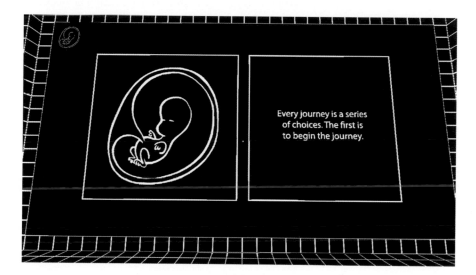

Consider the puzzle game *Antichamber* and its start-up menu. The game design calls for a minimalistic menu. The setting has little or no embellishment, a black box, with white graph lines intersecting across the floor. It resembles the 3D mesh of a basic polygon. Text appears, "Every journey is a series of choices. The first is to begin the journey." Next, a small icon with the instruction "Click here" appears on a wall showing options for the player's journey. The purposes of this menu state are partly utilitarian (game settings and launching gameplay). But there are also more subtle intentions. Is there an emotional or abstract goal here? The abstract goals of this game state include arousing curiosity, perhaps even provoking slight bewilderment. It wants to pique the player's interest and set an amorphous tone for the mind-bending puzzles ahead.

Such scrutiny of each game state will disclose the respective purposes for the composer's music design. Understanding the flow of game states and their purposes is the first step of analysis in the music design process.

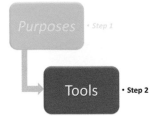

STEP 2. TOOLS

The next level of analysis addresses the necessary scoring **tools**. How will the composer's available toolsets be used to achieve the purposes outlined for each game state and transition? What is the right palette? Orchestration techniques? Harmonic structure? Rhythmic considerations? Melody or theme? Genre? And what of flexibility? What kind of pathing will the music cues, harmonies, rhythms and palette follow? Will repetition be needed? Randomness? Again, foundational scoring principles become the footings a composer relies on for analysis and decision.

Continuing the *Antichamber* example again, the questions now become methodologically focused. For a purpose of arousing an amorphous feeling of curiosity and bewilderment, what palette choices would be appropriate—acoustic ensemble, electronic, orchestral? And what of harmony—would major, minor or poly chords be most effective? Would melody add or detract from this purpose? Is there a genre which offers a shortcut or useful snapshot? Is there a need for specific pathing among a sequence of cues? Will repetition draw the player out of the amorphous feel or reinforce it? And what of randomness, how could it affect the desired end? Thus the first step of analysis, *purposes*, is funneled through a second round of analysis, *tools*, to yield actionable conclusions about the available means.

STEP 3. LOGISTICS

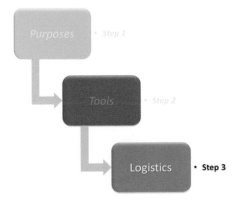

Finally, the **logistics** of each methodology must be contemplated. How will the selected methods be deployed to yield the desired purpose? This layer of analysis covers the range of questions taking in key, tempo, production, implementation strategy, processing and playback technology. Although this level of granularity has not yet been plumbed in the text, later chapters will offer composers powerful tools and templates to use in fulfilling the logistics of their music design.

HYPOTHETICAL CASE STUDY

A hypothetical case study will show how this process works from start to finish in practical terms. In this game, *Winter Frog Crossing*, a frog must safely cross a busy street in the snow.

The game developer provides the composer with the following game flow list and predicted average timing:

1. Load game and start menu; fifteen to sixty seconds.

2. Waiting to cross the road; three to fifteen seconds.

3. Crossing the road; five to thirty seconds.

4. Slipping in the snow; one-second animation.

5. Getting hit by a car; five-second animation and reset.

6. Successfully crossing the road; ten-second animation and reset.

7. Tally points and exit game; fifteen to sixty seconds.

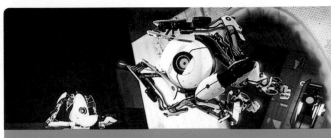

GUEST LECTURE
ADAPTING MUSIC THROUGH LOGISTICAL DEPLOYMENT

Mike Morasky
(Portal, Team Fortress, Left 4 Dead)

There are several cases in *Portal 2* where the music adds channels and complexity as you successfully solve portions of the puzzle, with each additional piece of music actually coming from the device that is participating in the activated gameplay mechanic. Obviously, this can confirm success and heighten the sense of achievement as you complete the puzzle but also turns the mechanics of the puzzle into a sort of interactive music instrument that you can explore by selectively triggering the different channels of music with differing timings and configurations. Most of the interactive music is also positional so that as you move through the space you also change the mix and volume of the music you are hearing, which invites explorations of the space as well.[2]

When beginning work on a game's music design, it is helpful to have a *Music Design Flow Chart* nearby listing relevant music design parameters to assist the composer in working through each step of music design analysis in tandem with the game design or game flow doc. Each game state or transition plugs into the top slot for analysis and decision making through the three key parameters of music design.

Game State or Transition

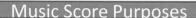

Music Score Purposes

➤ Set The Mood
➤ Heighten Emotion
➤ Propel Action
➤ Provide Contextual Clues
➤ Enhance the Aesthetic
➤ Contribute to Structural Unity

Music Scoring Tools

➤ Palette
➤ Orchestration
➤ Harmony
➤ Rhythm
➤ Melody
➤ Theme
➤ Genre
➤ Pathing
➤ Repetition
➤ Randomness

Music Score Logistics

➤ Key
➤ Tempo
➤ Adaptive Technique
➤ Production Approach
➤ Processing
➤ Implementation

Using the Music Design Flow Chart opposite, the composer plugs in each game state from the developer's game flow and works through each music design parameter, making note of the resulting decisions. Below is one example of how this could turn out, with a completed music design based on the *Winter Frog Crossing* game flow document.

1. Load game and start menu; fifteen to sixty seconds.

    a. Music Purposes—*Set a mood of excited anticipation, introduce the music aesthetic, support the menu state but don't crowd thinking.*

    b. Music Tools—*Upbeat theme song, major/happy harmonies, chiptunes genre, real-time signal processing.*

    c. Music Logistics—*Key of C, 160 bpm, thirty-second cue, play theme on load; duck 3 db and add low-pass filter with menu; loop until gameplay begins.*

2. Waiting to cross the road; three to fifteen seconds.

    a. Music Purposes—*Introduce gameplay mood, heighten the emotion with a tug of anxiety/uncertainty, add to the aesthetic of the scene, maintain structural unity.*

    b. Music Tools—*New music cue, slower tempo, meandering melody, harmonic change, maintain genre, keep fresh and flexible.*

    c. Music Logistics—*Key of F, 110 bpm, fifteen-second cue, stuttered rhythm, alternate large and small melodic intervals with pauses between pairings, three layered stems track, play full mix on first play, thereafter mute any two layers randomly for subsequent loops and replays.*

3. Crossing the road; five to thirty seconds.

    a. Music Purposes—*Raise the emotional stakes, propel the action across the street, add danger element, enhance the aesthetic of the game and maintain structural unity.*

    b. Music Tools—*Evolved version of waiting cue, faster tempo, hints of theme in melody, harmonic surprises, maintain genre, keep fresh and flexible.*

    c. Music Logistics—*Key of G, 120 bpm, twenty-second cue, melody quotes from theme with new instrument, stinger overlay of dissonant harmony punctuated by percussion hits, four layered stem tracks (three layers for base music bed, one layer for melody); add three dissonant harmony/percussion hit stingers; loop layered tracks, randomly choose one, two or three layers for music bed, always play melody, randomly play one stinger for near misses.*

4. Slipping; one-second animation.

    a. Music Purposes—*Clue the player to the slippage, create brief emotional tension and humor.*

    b. Music Tools—*Smear the sound of the music when slipping.*

    c. Music Logistics—*300 ms pitch bend of tracks a half step up and back (or down and back) randomly in real-time on slipping.*

5. Getting hit by a car; five-second animation and reset.

    a. Music Purposes—*Change the mood radically, pack emotional gut punch, stop action immediately, clue the player they lost, add to the impact aesthetic, maintain structural unity.*

    b. Music Tools—*Short music cue, jarring key change, slowing tempo, feeling of quick and abrupt transition.*

    c. Music Logistics—*Rapid chromatic downward chip-glissando transition, key of C# (tritone down), five-second cue, 88 bpm slowing to 60 bpm; play one shot of stinger on getting hit, simultaneous 300 ms fade out of Road Crossing tracks.*

6. Successfully crossing the road; ten-second animation and reset.

    a. Music Purposes—*Bring feeling of climax, highest emotional point of game, propel action to finish line, clue the player they won, add to the celebratory aesthetic, maintain structural unity.*

    b. Music Tools—*Short music cue, identify feeling of victory with game, modulated key, no noticeable tempo change, smooth transition from gameplay music.*

    c. Music Logistics—*Drum roll and whoosh transition, key of A, triumphant version of theme, ten-second cue, 120 bpm with ritard at end; play one shot on reaching safety zone, simultaneous 500 ms fade out of Road Crossing tracks.*

7. Tally points and replay; fifteen to sixty seconds.

    a. Music Purposes—*Mood of happy resolution, celebration, emotions of satisfaction, invite to play again, keep aesthetic, structural unity.*

    b. Music Tools—*Upbeat Theme song, major/happy harmonies, chiptunes genre.*

    c. Music Logistics—*Use same track as first game state, loop as needed.*

A bird's eye view of the entire score is now possible before a single note is written, giving the composer valuable perspective. Does this process take time and mental discipline? Yes. Absolutely. Each game state has been examined. Every musical purpose, tool and logistic has been carefully considered from the beginning of the game to the end. Important preliminary decisions have been made. Each decision has been framed in the context of robust scoring principles. From palette to pathing to technology, every nook and cranny of the music score has been ferreted out, vetted and sorted. This practice pushes the composer to think comprehensively through each step of the score. There are so many benefits. It can raise important questions, point out weaknesses, uncover unexpected bonus ideas and open meaningful dialog opportunities with the developer.

It should be noted here that game design documents may undergo constant revision during the development process. Similarly, the composer's music design is not a static relic, but rather a living document evolving as the design of the game evolves. Regularly checking in with the developer will help keep the composer plugged into relevant game changes so the music design can be adjusted as needed.

Analysis by Principle

One of the underlying ideas in this book is that a grasp of enduring principles will serve a composer better than a collection of techniques alone. A firm grounding in scoring principles will enable the composer to master a staggering array of techniques while always delivering relevance. Techniques may come and go, but scoring principles remain.

GUEST LECTURE
MUSIC DESIGN DOCUMENT

Guy Whitmore, PopCap Games

A music design document begins by imagining how you would like the music to behave in your game. As with any good story, timing is everything, and the only way to get timing right in game audio is to be tightly integrated with the overall design of the game. At the same time, I didn't want *Peggle 2* to become a "music game" or "rhythm game"; to the contrary the score isn't necessary to play the game, but you do miss much of the experience without it. Rule number one for adaptive music design: Often a few well-integrated adaptive audio features will trick folks into thinking the design is more complex than it really is under the hood.[3]

For example, there are seven distinct phrases that play back in progressive sequence as the player makes progress in the level. This progression is tied to the number of orange pegs remaining. The timing of the transitions is purposely oblique, so the player senses the general progression of music but not the specific cause. Often those transitions happen to line up with a visual element that can seem causal while it's not. Also, there's enough change and variation within each of the seven phrases that the player may believe there are more than seven music phrases per set. An illusion of music design complexity under the hood while keeping things manageable for the dev team.

To better reinforce the connection between scoring principles and music design decisions, here is an analysis of the hypothetical music design for *Winter Frog Crossing*.

Set the Mood

Choices of key, harmony and genre are selected based on the mood-setting properties of each musical component.

Load Game/Start Menu	C major connects to human physiology with a happy resonance. Chiptune genre taps into playful nostalgia.
Waiting to Cross	Key modulation to F signals new circumstance (see *Propel Action* and *Contextual Clues* below). F major continues happy resonance.
Crossing Road	Key modulation to G major raises tension slightly and retains happy resonance.
Slipping	Key slide through pitch bending creates moment of disorientation. Sound of chiptune palette adds element of humor.
Getting Hit by Car	Key modulation to C# minor creates jarring and negative mood change to unhappy resonance. Downward chromatic gliss is deflating, but also mildly humorous.
Successfully Crossing Road	Key modulation to A major raises tension slightly and retains happy resonance.
Tally Points and Replay	C major connects to human physiology with a happy resonance. Chiptune genre taps into playful nostalgia.

Heighten Emotion

Players approach a gameplay session with a certain level of built-in positive anticipation. Tempo choices combined with real-time processing and stingers are designed to enhance the player's emotions throughout the experience.

Load Game/Start Menu	160 bpm stirs excitement, raises pulse.
Waiting to Cross	110 bpm settles mood for thinking.
Crossing Road	Tempo increase to 120 bpm raises tension slightly. Dissonant stinger adds startle response effect.
Slipping	
Getting Hit by Car	Jarring and dissonant key change magnifies impact of visual game play. Drastically slowing tempo reinforces deflated feeling.
Successfully Crossing Road	Triumphant idiom escalates pleasure and signals achievement (see Contextual Clues below). 120 bpm tempo keeps up pulse.
Tally Points and Replay	160 bpm stirs excitement, raises pulse.

Propel Action

Changes in key and tempo help to move the action forward from one game state to the next. Some of the same tools used to set a mood and heighten emotion simultaneously propel the gameplay.

Load Game/Start Menu	C major connects to human physiology with a happy resonance. 160 bpm stirs excitement. Chiptune genre taps into nostalgia.
Waiting to Cross	Key modulation to F major moves the action forward from the initial menu state to a state of readiness for gameplay.
Crossing Road	Key modulation to G major with increased tempo and continuous looping supports the player moving their frog across the street. Variety in the arrangement keeps the player engaged without distracting noticeable repetition.
Slipping	Key slide through pitch bending moves with the character's slipping animation. Player feels connected to the screen action.
Getting Hit by Car	Key modulation to C# minor supports the jarring and negative visual of getting hit by a car. Downward chromatic gliss and slowing tempo propel the action to a close.
Successfully Crossing Road	Key modulation to A major raises tension slightly and retains happy resonance. Triumphant idiom escalates pleasure and signals achievement (see Contextual Clues below). 120 bpm tempo keeps up pulse.
Tally Points and Replay	C major connects to human physiology with a happy resonance. 160 bpm stirs excitement. Chiptune genre taps into nostalgia.

Contextual Clues

Structural changes in the music are a strong contextual signal. Stingers, win/lose tracks and real-time processing also connect the player to material changes in the game.

Load Game/Start Menu	3db ducking and frequency spectrum change in music help the player settle into menu navigation.
Waiting to Cross	Key modulation to F major and drop in tempo/rhythmic structure signal new game state.
Crossing Road	Key modulation to G major and tempo increase helps the player feel the game state change to crossing the street. Stingers clue the player to near misses by passing cars.
Slipping	Wavering music alerts player to slippage.
Getting Hit by Car	Every aspect of the music is a contextual clue—tritone modulation, minor key, jarring transition, tempo change and gliss. Components and combination project negative emotion.
Successfully Crossing Road	Every aspect of the music is a contextual clue—whole step modulation, A major key, upbeat tempo, triumphant idiom. Components and combination projects celebratory emotion.
Tally Points and Replay	Opening theme returns player to points of origin, inviting replay.

Enhance Aesthetic

Musical choices have functional, communicative roles. But they can also be artistic, adding to the aesthetic of the experience.

Load Game/Start Menu	Chiptune genre enhances the old-school game style. Catchy theme gives the player a hook to hang their fun on. Major harmonic structure adds to happy feeling.
Waiting to Cross	Evolving arrangement keeps the music fresh. Unobtrusive melody and stuttered rhythm provide a good transition aesthetic.
Crossing Road	Return of theme on new instrument brings familiarity and freshness. Evolving arrangement is pleasing rather than dulling.
Slipping	Pitch bend of entire track is a funny aesthetic.
Getting Hit by Car	Key modulation, chromatic gliss, slowing tempo echoes approach of many 8-bit games of old, reinforcing nostalgic feeling.
Successfully Crossing Road	Key modulation and triumphant composition construction is also a throwback to old games, reinforcing nostalgic feeling.
Tally Points and Replay	Opening theme adds bookend symmetry and keeps the fun feeling going.

Structural Unity

The chiptunes style throughout matches the nostalgic gameplay and art style. Introducing a theme and quoting from it reinforces the internal unity of the music. Matching the game state changes with music changes strengthens the external structural unity of the experience.

Load Game/Start Menu	Opening with an exciting theme fits with the structure of an introduction. Ducking the volume and masking frequencies with the menu conforms to the game state and function change. Chiptune palette remains uniform throughout.
Waiting to Cross	Drop in tempo while modulating up makes a good match for the change in gameplay.
Crossing Road	Upward modulation and increased tempo match raised stakes of new game state. Return of theme reinforces internal cohesiveness of score. Dissonant stinger reinforces gameplay structure of near misses.
Slipping	All elements combine to match slipping—music, visual and gameplay.
Getting Hit by Car	Music solution is a match emotionally, stylistically and mechanically for game state.
Successfully Crossing Road	Music solution is a match emotionally, stylistically and mechanically for game state.
Tally Points and Replay	Return to top bookends the structure. Theme reinforces internal unity.

Pathing

Five levels of pathing are outlined in this design—harmony, tempo, arrangement, processing and tracks. Each allows for cohesive functionality and provides relevant variety to the score.

Load Game/Start Menu	Each point of origin stakes its home territory here. C major harmony. 160 bpm tempo. Thematic melody. Chiptunes genre. Transition path is 500 ms fade-out from existing track, then hard start of new track.
Waiting to Cross	The harmonic path is from C major to F major. This modulation of a perfect fourth creates the feeling of going to something related but new, similar to a bridge. The tempo path is from 160 bpm to 110 bpm. This drops the intensity and gives the game somewhere to go. The arrangement path begins with a full arrangement, then cycles through the different stem versions. Transition path is 500 ms fade-out from existing track, then hard start of new track for "Crossing Road" game state.
Crossing Road	The harmonic path is from F major to G major. This kind of lift provides a feeling of taking it to the next level. The tempo path rises from 110 bpm to 120 bpm, increasing the intensity slightly. The arrangement path begins with a full arrangement, then cycles through the different stem combinations. Stinger triggers when car passes within x (TBD) pixels of character, plays once on top of game track. Transition path is 500 ms fade-out from existing track, then hard start of new track for "Getting Hit" or "Successfully Crossing" game states.
Slipping	Track slide overrides all other music instructions.

Getting Hit by Car	The harmonic path is from G major to C# minor. This dissonant modulation takes the player abruptly down. The tempo path is from 120 bpm to 88 bpm, slowing to 60 bpm. This change also takes the player abruptly out of the road-crossing mode. The transition path is a 300 ms fade of "Road Crossing" track and simultaneous hard start of "Getting Hit" track, which includes a 500 ms roll-in intro. At conclusion of "Getting Hit" track, game returns to "Waiting to Cross" state triggering "Waiting to Cross" music track, hard start.
Successfully Crossing Road	The harmonic path is from G major to A major. This provides a new flavor and degree of lift as it is outside of the circle of harmonies experienced previously in the game. Tempo path is from 120 bpm to 120 bpm, remaining constant. This enables a feeling of continuity for the success of crossing the road. The transition path is a 500 ms fade of "Road Crossing" track and simultaneous hard start of "Successful Cross" track, which includes a 500 ms roll-in intro. At conclusion of "Successfully Crossing" track, game advances to "Tally Points and Replay" state triggering "Load Game/Start Menu" music track, hard start.
Tally Points and Replay	The harmonic path is from A major to C major. This gives a feeling of both lift and return, as the score arrives at the home key. Tempo path is from 120 bpm to 160 bpm, ramping up the excitement for another go-around. Transition path is 500 ms fade-out from existing track, then hard start of new track.

Repetition

Repetition is employed to allow for flexibility in the score. Cue durations are matched to average predicted gameplay as determined by the developer during play testing. Repetition is also managed in such a way as to avoid stagnation.

Load Game/Start Menu	Theme loops while player is getting into game, setting things up and making menu selections. Change in volume and frequency masking at menu add a different look and take the music down to a more subliminal level.
Waiting to Cross	Music track loops while player decides when and where to cross. Changes in arrangement keep the music track fresh.
Crossing Road	Music track loops while player is crossing road. Changes in stem combinations with stinger overlays prevent monotony.
Slipping	No repetition.
Getting Hit by Car	No repetition.
Successfully Crossing Road	No repetition.
Tally Points and Replay	Theme loops while player is reviewing score and making any new menu selections. Real-time processes (ducking and band pass filtering) change color and perception of music.

Randomness

Targeted randomness in three tracks also helps with score flexibility. Random selection of layer combinations and random up or down pitch bending allows for variety without multiplying music assets.

Load Game/Start Menu	No randomness.
Waiting to Cross	Random selection of stems keeps arrangement changing unexpectedly.
Crossing Road	Random combinations of stems keeps arrangement changing unexpectedly.
Slipping	Random up or down pitch bend selection prevents monotony.
Getting Hit by Car	No randomness.
Successfully Crossing Road	No randomness.
Tally Points and Replay	No randomness.

This formal, multilevel analysis is not generally part of a composer's music design process. However, it may be helpful for those working through a music design for the first time. Such post-design analysis verifies the rationale for every musical decision listed in the game's music design. It ensures that each component contributes to meaningful and artistic communication between the game, the score and the player. If any aspect of the composer's music design does not hold up to such scrutiny, it can be called out and adjusted accordingly. Such a thoroughly vetted music design will considerably increase the composer's odds of delivering a music score capable of adding understanding and delight to the player's experience with the game. All within a manageable technical framework and attractive budget.

SUMMARY

The odds of delivering an effective video game score increase significantly when composers take the time to create a comprehensive *music design*. Music design encompasses all parts of the composer's work for the game, addressing the *purposes*, *tools* and *logistics* of music for each game state and transition. Using the *game design* or *game flow* document as a roadmap, the composer addresses each game state and transition, taking them through a step-by-step process of analytic and decision-making parameters based on music scoring principles and toolsets. The Music Design Flow Chart provided on page 62 can bring clarity and focus to the process. The resulting music design becomes the composer's guide for creating a relevant and flexible music score for the game. Changes in game design are reflected with appropriate changes in corresponding parts of the music design, through periodic consultation with the development team as needed.

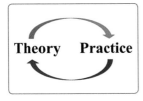

APPLIED LEARNING

1. Choose a game for analysis and play through the completion of one level. Postulate how the music design may have addressed questions of *music purposes*, *tools* and *logistics*.

2. Select a sample game design from the website associated with this book (www.FocalPress.com/cw/Thomas). Create a music design for this game addressing all steps listed in the Music Design Flow Chart on page 62.

3. Complete an analysis of your music design, verifying the function and efficacy of all music design components.

REFERENCES

1. Tom Peters and Robert H. Waterman Jr., *In Search of Excellence* (New York: HarperCollins, Harpers Business Essentials, 2004).

2. www.gamesradar.com/portal-2s-dynamic-music-an-interview-with-composer-mike-morasky-and-five-tracks-to-listen-to-now/.

3. http://www.audiogang.org/peggle2-sonic-joy/.

TECHNIQUES

CHAPTER 4

BASIC MUSIC SCORING TECHNIQUES FOR GAMES

Simplicity is the ultimate sophistication.[1]

Reverse engineering complex systems often reveals simpler component parts under the hood. For instance, at machine level, even the most sophisticated programming code is written with only two digits, 1s and 0s. The binary equivalents in game scoring include such modest but essential techniques as music loops, transitions, tags and stingers. This chapter will introduce students to the mechanics of these and other core music scoring techniques for video games.

MUSICAL BUILDING BLOCKS

Consider for a moment a toy construction set for children. Lego, Tinkertoys, K'Nex—each of these toy building blocks can be an instructive model for understanding how a complex game music score may be constructed from simpler component parts.

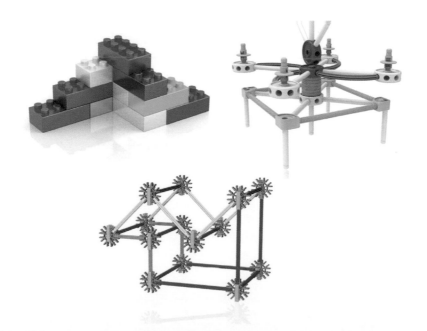

COMPLEX SYSTEMS FROM SIMPLE COMPONENTS

Year after year, thousands of youth ages nine to fourteen gather in teams across North America to build autonomous robots. They also learn to program these robots to perform a staggering array of complex tasks. Surprisingly, as sophisticated as these robots can become, they are built predominantly from the simplest possible components—Lego brand building blocks.

Similarly, many functionally effective and flexible music scores for video games are built from simple components. These musical building blocks include intros, loops, transitions, tags, stingers and cinematics.

Think of each brick, spool or hub as a musical building block delivering certain musical function(s) within the score. Think of each stud, stick and connector as offering a hand-off from one core music function to another. For example, in the simplified figure below, the first block is an intro. Its primary musical functions include setting the mood and establishing an aesthetic. It plays one time only when the player first enters the game world.

Next, the loop block propels action for as long as needed within the boundaries of a defined emotional range. It continues to play while the current game state remains active. Finally, the tag block plays one time when the current game state reaches a point of definitive conclusion, such as a victory or defeat. Its musical functions include providing a contextual clue of finality and adding a bookend opposite the intro, thus contributing to structural unity.

Such a component system of scoring allows for music that can be highly functional. In addition, this building block approach also provides for a score that is both flexible and scalable, two of the distinguishing objectives of game music discussed in Chapter 2. Every block in the illustration fulfills scoring functions learned in prior chapters. To reiterate one of the book's core propositions, these foundational principles of music scoring are pervasive. They will continue to inform scoring techniques throughout this text and across the successful career of composers who understand and apply them.

Now consider a slightly longer chain of components, as illustrated in the figure below:

The chain begins with an intro block and a loop block, as in the previous figure. But in this example the first loop block is followed by a transition block. The transition block functions to propel the action in a new direction and provide a contextual clue that something in the game has changed. The transition block connects to a second loop, which eventually terminates in a tag. Keeping the Lego/Tinkertoy/K'Nex analogy in mind, it is easy to envision how a component-based score of musical building blocks could continue to grow in size and complexity. Such a component-based music score could address any number of game state situations and accompanying scoring requirements.

BASIC SCORE COMPONENTS

With this paradigm of musical building blocks as a backdrop, attention now turns to a focused exploration of six basic game scoring components and techniques: *intros, loops, transitions, tags, stingers* and *cinematics*.

Intro

An *intro* presents a new level, section, gameplay mechanic or other type of beginning within the video game experience. It plays one time as the new game state begins. Its functions typically include setting a mood, establishing an aesthetic, providing contextual clues and contributing to structural unity.

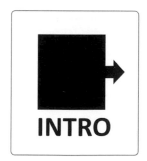

An intro may be short or long. It may be simple or complex. It may fade in gently or begin abruptly. There is tremendous flexibility available to the game composer in determining the type of form an intro will take. The key is to choose the form that best serves its music design function for any given point in the score. Nevertheless, all intros tend to have certain logistical characteristics in common. Intros establish a tonic key for the subsequent section of gameplay. They set up the instrumental palette for the corresponding game state. They will offer a stylistic framework or genre for the subsequent music to follow.

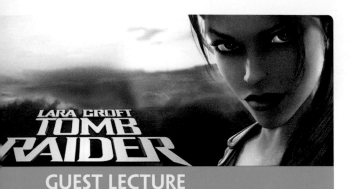

GUEST LECTURE
MODULAR SCORING

Troels Folmann
(Tomb Raider, Transformers)

True adaptive music needs be generated in real-time … It's basically the idea of chopping your score down to very small components and triggering them in a way that compliments the game experience … Essentially, I can place scores for any change in the game, which is naturally a complex and time-consuming process. The trend of games is one of complexity. Everything is getting more detailed, whether it's multiple translucent layers of textures, real-time generated light and shadow maps, massive streaming game worlds and so forth. Audio and music is no exception. The need for dissecting music into smaller fractions is becoming increasingly important in order to support the decisions and experiences of the player.[2]

Most intros trail off with a long fading sustain at the end. This facilitates a smooth hand-off to whatever follows in the music design, whether it is another musical building block or just the ambient sound of the level. In either case, a long and fading sustain makes a nice aural connector.

Loop

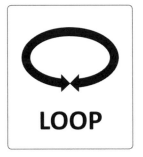

A music *loop* is a piece of music whose end dovetails back into its beginning, resulting in a seamless and potentially never-ending track. Music loops are ubiquitous in games but have acquired something of a shoddy reputation. Since music loops are based on a simple mechanic, nearly anyone with editing software can make one. However, the ability to make a loop does not necessarily equate to making one that works well in a game. Just as owning a knife does not qualify a person to perform surgery, neither does the ability to cut a track qualify as expertise in making great music loops. Creating a music loop that fills game scoring roles elegantly and effectively can be a precise and sophisticated process.

Compositional Considerations

To better understand the process of creating a great music loop for games, first consider the inherent challenges of this peculiar workhorse. As discussed in Chapter 2, a repeating music file can be useful in providing a game score with flexibility and scalability. But recognized repetition soon becomes tiring. Themes in particular, while critically important to the branding and emotional impact of any overall score, are anathema in a music loop. A great theme is memorable. It often possesses some element of musical inevitability married to an element of surprise. Think of that particular combination—memorable, inevitable and surprising. This really does make for great theme writing! To hear such a theme at rare and important points across the dramatic arc of an entertainment experience can be satisfying and exhilarating. However, to hear it repeatedly within the span of just a few minutes would quickly wear thin.

To test this assumption, think about a beloved music theme from the world of science fiction. The *Star Trek* fanfare makes a terrific example. This is a brilliantly executed announcement of heroic arrival coupled with a musical send-off to unknown discoveries yet to come. One need hear it only once or twice in an hour to relish its functionality and style. But imagine hearing it repeatedly as part of a looping music track. Even such a beloved and effective theme as this would soon cross the threshold into antagonism. Therefore, to be on the safe side, composers should generally avoid quoting from their themes inside a music loop. The best place for a theme is inside an intro, transition, tag or cinematic. But not in a music loop!

Orchestration must also be carefully managed in a music loop. A dramatic change of color, an unusual voicing, a stark contrast—in short, any orchestration choice that abruptly draws attention to itself can suffer the same fate as a theme. That is not to say that unusual voicings or dramatic color should be avoided completely. But the composer needs to be careful in how such choices are utilized, so that such choices weave their particular thread into the seamless backdrop, rather than popping out as a striking musical feature.

In fact, it could be generalized that for a music loop, any musical feature that results in arresting the attention of the listener may need to be avoided. There are better places than loops for such musical statements, as we will see later in the chapter. Does this mean that a music loop should be bland and lifeless? Not exactly. The best game scores are filled with thoughtfully conceived and skillfully executed loops that keep the player engaged without periodically or momentarily arresting their attention. But any super noticeable musical feature, no matter how engaging when heard sparingly, can become counterproductive if used in a looping music file. As with all rules, this one can be broken intelligently. Yet emerging composers would be well advised to proceed with caution in these matters and err on the side of restraint.

Knowing what to *avoid* is a good start. But what should the composer *do*? What actually makes for a *good* music loop? A good music loop creates a continual sense of movement within the limited dynamic boundaries of a single emotional state. It should feel like one leg of a journey but never convey a point of arrival. This deserves some additional explanation. Good game design, like good script writing, moves a person's emotions along a path of progression. There are inclines and declines, high points and low points as emotions are manipulated through conflict and resolution, climax and denouement, etc.

In a well-executed game design, this kind of movement feels like a continuous journey for the player. But in truth, it is actually a progression of numerous discrete nodes or game states. Like points on an old-fashioned dot-to-dot drawing or samples of a sound wave, each game state is a snapshot of a particular point on this emotional journey. A music loop which accompanies a given game state must necessarily remain within the boundaries of that emotional node, never rising too high or falling too low. Progression comes in moving from one game state or

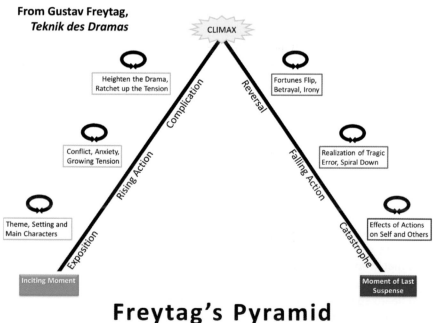

emotional node to the next, and from one musical building block to the next. Great sophistication can be achieved by building a sequence of loops that move the player up and down an emotional hierarchy. Some of these advanced techniques will be explored in the following chapter.

In this chapter, the focus remains on building a single effective music loop. If a successful music loop is intended to convey a sense of movement while remaining within the limits of a single emotional level, how can this be accomplished? What tools are available to the composer to achieve this and how should they be used? Not surprisingly, the available tools are those outlined in Chapter 1: palette, orchestration, harmony, rhythm, etc. Harmony is a particularly effective tool.

To illustrate, consider the well-known harmonic formula of modulating by minor thirds. This works well for an action bed as the progression delivers a continual sense of rise without ever arriving. Readers can hear an example of this by visiting the book's website (www.FocalPress.com/cw/Thomas). The cycle can start in any tonality. In the figure below, the cycle begins in C major.

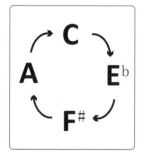

FREYTAG'S PYRAMID

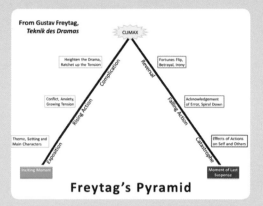

Freytag's Pyramid

An understanding of dramatic form and structure is critically important for the successful score composer. There is a common path of progression among works of drama and entertainment that yields a feeling of satisfaction to the human pysche. Historically, this path is known as Freytag's Pyramid, from Gustav Freytag's *Technik des Dramas*.[3] This, in turn, was based on a study of the book *Poetics* by Aristotle, famously advocating a three-act structure for dramatic works. Roman Horace expanded on this slightly in advocating a five-act structure. The modern writer Joseph Campbell wrote of a seventeen-stage progression called the Hero's Journey. Yet in each model, there is a common sense of progression through conflict, exploration and discovery within a structure that resonates with people. The most satisfying music scores tend to mirror these structures to some degree.

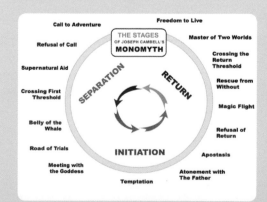

Running the cycle in reverse with minor seventh chords instead of major chords can also work well for a suspense loop.

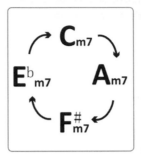

Another workable suspense structure is to build a short progression in a home key, then modulate by tritone to a new key where the same progression is built. It can then modulate back to the original key via tritone without ever sounding like a return home. There are many, many such harmonic structures to discover and explore.

Poly-harmonic textures which morph rather than cadence can also keep a feeling of movement without drawing attention. Ambient granular synths and atmospheric orchestral effects offer the composer a rich palette in which to realize this harmonic approach.

Another great technique is to string together dissimilar but related runs, hits and flourishes on a variety of different instruments in odd rhythms. Ironically, the continual sense of off-balance created by such orchestration and rhythm changes creates its own feeling of background balance, a mantra of sorts that provides consistency because of its continual inconsistency. That last statement is impossible for the author to fully explain (or defend), but most readers will intuitively know that it is true. *Star Wars* games utilizing John Williams' incidental music have done this effectively for years. This is one example of breaking the rules intelligently.

On the other end of the spectrum, a simple groove can also make for an effective loop. Without specific storytelling components in music, such as melody and leading harmonic structures, the repeating pulse simply falls out of player focus and into the subconscious. Such groove loops can raise energy effectively without bludgeoning the sensibilities.

Technical Considerations

All of the foregoing discussion is intended to help in the composition of a successful music loop. But what of its production? What techniques will ensure the transparent conversion of the composer's ideas into a seamlessly looping audio file? Here are a few tips that will help.

When sequencing a new piece of music intended for looping, copy the first two or three bars of the piece and paste them onto the end of the composition. Listen through to make sure the dovetail transition feels seamless. Then record or bounce the tracks out that way. The same is true with a live session. Copy the first two or three measures onto the end of the cue and have the musicians play to the end of the chart, including the repeated measures.

After the loop has been recorded, the optimum edit point must be located. It may not necessarily be the downbeat of the piece. It could easily be somewhere in the first few measures or the corresponding last few measures. Some experimentation will help the composer determine the most natural-sounding place to loop.

Once a spot is chosen, exact edit points must occur where both waveforms of the stereo file cross the 0 db threshold simultaneously. This avoids having clicks or pops in the audio file when it repeats. In this graphic representation of a music loop created for *Marvel Universe*, note that the end of the file has zero crossings for both sides of the stereo wave form.

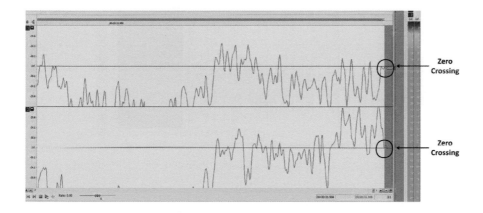

When following all of these points of instruction with precision, the composer should end up with a loop that is musically accurate and clean from pops and clicks. Yet occasionally, something about the transition from the end into the beginning may still be telling. There may be a slightly different color at the beginning than at the end. There may be subtle difference in dynamics, processing and performance. One effective tool that helps to blend and mask these differences is the use of an added reverb tail. Here's how to do it.

First, send the end of the loop into a reverb.

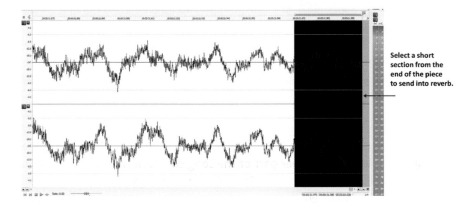

Select a short section from the end of the piece to send into reverb.

Next, capture the tail from the loop point to the end of its ring-out.

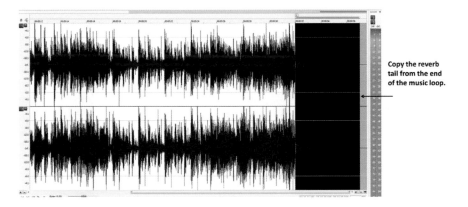

Copy the reverb tail from the end of the music loop.

Finally, cut the tail and overlay it onto the beginning of the loop.

Add the copied reverb tail to the beginning of the piece. It should add to and mix with the existing wave form, rather than replacing it.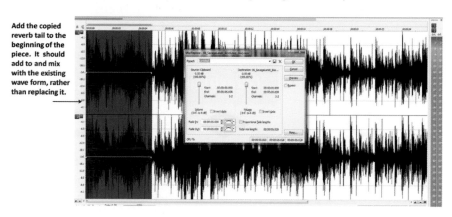

It sounds now as if the end of the piece has played into reverb, and the reverb is bleeding naturally into whatever part of the song comes next. In this case, it is playing back into the beginning of the loop. One final caution is to listen carefully and be aware of unsuspected dissonances or harmonies bleeding over. Other than that, the technique is fairly bullet-proof.

Transition

Transition blocks carry the score from one game state to another. They may transition the score from a loop to a cinematic, from an intro to a loop, or from one loop to another. Almost endless variety exists for what the composer may connect to either end of a transition block. Like the sticks in a Tinkertoy set, transition blocks always have the logistical role of connecting the score from one node to another.

Compositional Considerations

How does one approach the task of composing a transition block for a video game score? A first step is to define the parameters of a given transition. What block is being transitioned from? What are the musical attributes of that block? What block is being transitioned to? What are its musical attributes? These attributes would typically include key, harmonic progression, melody, tempo and palette.

Consider a game design calling for combat with several low-level guards. When the last guard is vanquished, a knight comes out to fight the player in a boss battle scenario. A basic music design might have one combat loop for the guards and a

TRANSITION

second combat loop for the knight. A transition block moves the score from one to another, as shown in the following diagram.

It is time now to define the musical parameters for each "from" and "to" block. For this example, Loop 1 is composed on a pedal point in the key of A minor at 120 bpm. Its palette consists of gran casa, orchestral toms, full string section, trombones, tuba, bassoon and bass clarinet. Loop 2 is composed on a pedal point in the key of E minor at 150 bpm. Its palette adds timpani, cymbals, male and female chorus, horns, trumpets, flute and piccolo.

With this information it is easy now to define parameters for a successful transition block. The transition block for this hand-off must begin in the key of A minor and modulate up to E minor. It must accelerate the tempo from 120 bpm to 150 bpm. It must make a natural evolution in the palette to include or set the stage for the additional colors of the second loop. This can be done in a thousand different creative and interesting ways, but the composer now has the essential information needed to make a musically satisfying transition in the video game score.

For example, a timpani roll on A accompanied by suspended cymbal crescendos across a two-beat pickup measure at 120 bpm. Double bass, cello, tuba and trombones make the same crescendo on A, octaves apart. Piatti crash on the downbeat of the first full measure, with a blat in the low brass on the tonic, followed by G, Bb, C, D and finally Eb on off-beats. The low strings are striking a marcato rhythm following the changes in the brass, with violins accompanied by flute and piccolo taking up an ostinato run which rises and falls high above. The orchestra hits a unison strike across five octaves on the Eb, pauses, strikes again joined by choir and an Ab–Eb rip in the horns, pauses, then hits a rhythmic triple strike followed by a long hairpin (crescendo–diminuendo) on B in the timpani, gran casa, low brass and cymbals.

The stage is now set for the natural-sounding transition to the new key of E minor at the new tempo with the new palette.

Certainly building blocks on either side of a transition can be more complicated than they were in this illustration. Much more complicated! For example, a more sophisticated harmonic structure, erratic tempo changes, radical differences in palette or a prominent melodic change all call for deft handling of a transition block that can effectively hand-off seamlessly between them. In the absence of intricate marker tracking or some other system to keep tabs on changing tonalities, the two extreme ends of a transition block may benefit from techniques that blur the harmonic content, providing a morphing texture rather than a clearly defined modulation. Such techniques include fading in and fading out with poly chords, harmonically amorphous percussion rolls or atmospheric electronic sweeps. These can effectively blend the "from" and "to" connection points with musically nebulous extremities while allowing the composer the ability to make a clear transitioning statement in the middle of the block.

The middle of a transition block may be a good place for the composer to quote from a theme, highlight a unique palette change or show off some other point of musical interest. Since transition blocks typically occur at moments where gameplay is changing anyway, this can be a good time to call attention to the music with something unique and memorable. All of these techniques can be expanded upon and modified to fit the endless variations of adjacent game states which a composer may be called upon to score.

Technical Considerations

In general, a transitional piece of music will start very quietly and end with a fading sustain. Like the icon used to denote the transition block, a niente start and fade-to-black conclusion allows for its seemingly seamless connective properties. These properties of fade-in/fade-out dynamics at each extremity can be easily built into the sequence, live performance or mixed music file using volume curves. The music file below was edited post-mix to ensure smooth fade-in and fade-out properties. Note that each extremity of the transition reaches to zero.

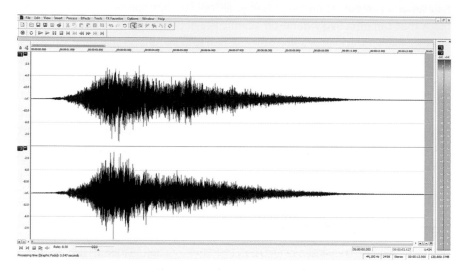

The same thing can be achieved with live performance dynamics, as shown in this excerpt from a string chart.

Beyond this dynamic consideration, there are no other specific technical considerations for the production of an effective transition music file. Of course, typical best practices for any music production apply—clean recordings, jitter-free digital pipeline, no unwanted clipping at any point in the process, consistent file formats, etc.

Think of transition blocks as the connector pieces that link otherwise independent musical nodes to one another, thus creating the illusion of a seamless through-composed music score that matches the player's unpredictable progression through the game.

Tag

The *tag* block brings a sense of finality or resolve to a prior sequence of related blocks in the music design. A tag is a closing gesture, which might play at the successful completion of a puzzle or upon winning a boss battle. A tag may also play when a player fails to provide a correct answer or loses in combat. A tag in a game score can function as both climax and denouement, bringing a game level or other structural construct to its peak and then releasing the tension in preparation for whatever comes next.

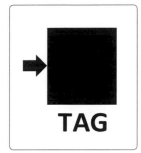

Composition Considerations

The beginning of a tag is subject to the same kinds of compositional considerations as the beginning of a transition block. In order to effect a smooth hand-off, the prior block's harmonic, rhythmic, melodic and palette content must be known and addressed. Matching or blurring musical constructs, as detailed in the transition section above, are utilized as appropriate to begin an effective tag.

The heart of the tag is a clear musical statement defining the player's situation in the game. There can be no ambiguity here. If the tag reflects victory, then the music must provide positive reinforcement to the player, indicating a successful conclusion. If the tag reflects defeat, there can be no mistaking that the moment is lost. This doesn't necessarily mean Dun-Dun-Dun on low strings and timpani for defeat, or a brass fanfare on a dominant-tonic cadence for victory. Clever composers have devised many innovative ways to signal both loss and victory without resorting to cliché.

A composer's approach to creating an effective tag may also benefit from a functional examination in light of the conventional scoring purposes examined in Chapter 1. A tag sets a mood of finality, one way or the other. The tag heightens the player's emotion of succeeding or alternatively failing to accomplish a desired objective. It propels whatever action has preceded and brings it to a close. A tag offers the player a powerful contextual clue regarding their victory or defeat. It should enhance the aesthetic by utilizing those musical colors that best convey the climactic moment of the preceding arc. Finally, the tag should contribute to structural unity, not only

Marty O'Donnell (*Destiny, Halo, Myth*)

The phrase "First do no harm" is famously attributed to the Hippocratic Oath taken by doctors. As video game composers we have our own version of that: "First do no annoying." Don't overstate your theme or any other single musical feature of your game score. It will always, inevitably and inescapably, lead to annoyance. And that just makes people turn off your music. Which means you've failed. Don't fail. Use your themes sparingly and at the right spots in your score.

with its feeling of conclusion in juxtaposition to the intro block (which started the scoring sequence), but also in its choice of cohesive musical elements.

One final compositional note: a tag may be another potentially effective place for a thematic statement in the game. The feeling of victory may be enhanced by quoting from the main theme of the game, or from some other important motif the composer has used to connect the player to the game score. Likewise, a feeling of antagonism or frustrated determination may be enhanced by quoting from a villain's theme. Some tags play often, so care must be taken not to overuse thematic quotes, lest they lose their effectiveness and start to annoy. Please try not to annoy! Saving such thematic statements for major and rare milestones in the game may be best.

Technical Considerations

Unlike a transition block, a tag may begin at any dynamic, depending on its function. A victory fanfare may begin at a full celebratory volume, stopping the prior music node in its tracks to bring the joy. On the other hand, the composer may prefer a more subtle approach, leading into the tag statement with a crescendo. Either approach may be effective, depending on the desired aesthetic. To illustrate, here is a score excerpt from a victory tag in the game, *Might & Magic: Forgotten Wars*. Note that the first measure dynamics are designed to arrest attention (sfzp) and also grow into a lively fanfare (mp < f).

PEEK BEHIND THE CURTAIN

Using Stingers in *Monopoly Streets*

In *Monopoly Streets*, a music loop cycles in the background while the player rolls the dice. For normal rolls, the loop continues uninterrupted. But if the player happens to roll a double, it's stinger time! A short burst of music plays, momentarily overriding the background loop. The same kind of thing happens when the player passes Go, builds a house, achieves a monopoly or lands on Free Parking. I created unique musical stingers that were matched to each of these events in order to inject a shot of recognizable excitement, giving the player a contextual clue that something rare and desirable has just occurred.

I also created stingers to highlight noteworthy moments of misfortune, like landing in jail, paying income taxes and declaring bankruptcy. Those are fun too! Using stingers like these allowed me to score all kinds of important moments in the game as they occurred in real-time. This would have been very difficult to do using any other kind of scoring block.

Stinger

A *stinger* is a short burst of music created to match a specific game event or specific kind of game event. Stingers are unique in that they do not necessarily connect with any other music block in the score. A stinger may stand alone or it may overlay another part of the music. Its usual purpose is to highlight something out of the ordinary or noteworthy occurring in gameplay.

Compositional Considerations

Will there be music playing when the stinger is triggered or will it play out in the open? If the stinger plays over existing music, there are several options to consider. Does the composer want the stinger to seem like a naturally occurring part of the underscore? If so then considerations would include matching the tonality, palette, timing, etc., of the underlying composition. On the other hand, if the composer wants the stinger to dominate the musical landscape, as a momentary replacement to the score, then such considerations are not as critical.

Technical Considerations

For an overlapping stinger, care must be taken to ensure that the summed gain of the two files playing together does not exceed the available headroom. This is easy to test. Simply bring up both files in audio editing software. Copy the stinger and overlay it on the underlying music file at the point of its highest transient, like this:

Step 1. Open both music files.

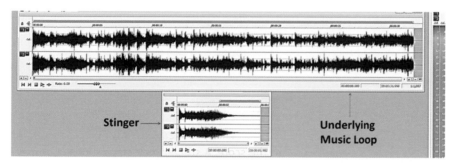

Step 2. Copy stinger and overlay/paste on music loop.

Step 3. Playback and check meters.

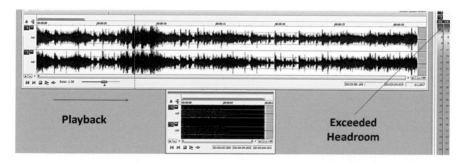

This shows that combining the files results in a signal strength that exceeds the available headroom by 4 db. Now the composer can try a variety of remedies, including reducing file levels (one or both), trying various compression or limiting algorithms, etc., until the desired sound is achieved at combined levels that maintain sonic fidelity. The final screenshot shows the result of a successful test after adjusting the levels.

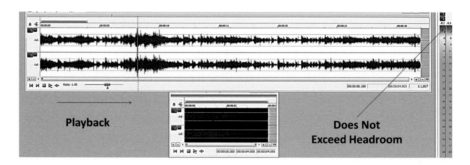

Playback

Does Not Exceed Headroom

Now when the two music files are played together, the sum of their volume does not exceed the available headroom.

Another option to avoid overdriving the audio system is to utilize ducking, which drops the playback level of the underlying music by a specified amount whenever the stinger plays. This can also be tested in editing software (or in-game if the audio system supports it), in order to dial in the exact amount of ducking needed. Referencing the *Monopoly Streets* example above, here is what an excerpt from a Visual Basic script might look like when ducking the underlying music by 6 db while simultaneously playing the music stinger.

x = dice roll

If *x* = double Then

Duck music_loop_…mp3 6db

Play music_stinger_double.mp3

This book will take a more involved look at music implementation in Chapter 8.

Sometimes a stinger will play out in the open, as a standalone musical element. In this case, such tweaking is generally unnecessary. The stinger should then be produced at a desired level in comparison to other elements in the music score.

Cinematic

A *cinematic* is a linear game segment wherein control of the action is temporarily taken away from the player in lieu of programmed content. Think of a cinematic as a short film within the game experience. A cinematic can be pre-rendered through editing and animation or it can render in real-time through scripted code. Pre-rendered cinematics may also be referred to as cut-scenes. Real-time renderings are sometimes called scripted events. This book uses the term cinematic(s) to describe all such pre-programmed linear segments in a game.

CINEMATIC

Cinematics perform a wide variety of purposes for games. A cinematic can set up a new level, conclude a level, give new information, add color, make a transition in the drama, etc. While cinematics are widely relied on for conveying storytelling elements in the game, any function fulfilled by scenes in a play, film or television program may also be fulfilled by a game cinematic.

It's important to note that a cinematic will stop gameplay. This is important for the composer to understand as it has implications for the music design. Transitions into a cinematic may be abrupt. Or they may appear to be completely seamless. Because factors such as technical limitations, implementation skill and aesthetics are all over the map, a composer may be presented with any number of different ways in which cinematics can transition into and out of the gameplaying experience. Take time to ask questions of a developer about how cinematics will interface with gameplay. This understanding will assist the composer in knowing what approach to take in designing music solutions for the most dramatically effective score.

Compositional Considerations

Fortunately, game design documents tend to be very specific about the location and circumstances for playing any cinematic. This means that if the composer has crafted a sufficiently informed music design, all important questions relating to the key, harmonic movement, melody, rhythm and palette for music files playing on either side of the cinematic can be answered with clarity. Thus, the task of scoring the cinematic becomes no more difficult than scoring the next scene in a movie. Modulations, mood changes, palette shifts, etc., may all be affected to produce the desired emotional result.

Musical flow is important. Just as a film composer is careful to craft each new cue in such a way that it makes good musical sense when flowing from the previous scene (and flowing into the following scene), the game composer must do the same with the music underscoring each cinematic. Acknowledging that a picture can be worth more than paragraphs of text, consider these two illustrations to underscore the importance of flow.

Figure A.

Figure B.

GUEST LECTURE
MUSIC FOR CINEMATICS

Benedicte Ouimet, Music Supervisor (*Assassin's Creed, Far Cry, Prince of Persia*)

When I started working for videogames, cinematics were long clips that sounded and looked quite different from the rest of the game. They were fun to work on and nice to watch, but players got restless and skipped them as soon as they could. Nowadays cinematics are a lot more integrated and music has an important role in preserving the immersion. On the technical side, for best results you need to:

Note the smooth flow of colors in Figure A. This represents the gradual unfolding and development of musical color and ideas in a component music score. Notice that the color of the cinematic block blends right in and continues the natural flow of colors as the score moves across the spectrum. Contrast this with Figure B, where the flow is interrupted oddly by the yellow cinematic block. The color of the cinematic block in Figure B has nothing to do with the rest of the color scheme and is oddly out of place. When looking at such a visual representation it appears blatantly obvious that music for the cinematic should be composed in harmony with the flow of the overall game score. Yet surprisingly, many video game scores ignore this important point completely, instead treating each cinematic as an island detached from the balance of the score.

Cinematics can offer the composer an ideal forum to develop the score's thematic material. Since cinematics are generally only seen once per play-through, there is little risk of overexposure for the music which underscores them. Thematic introduction and development across the span of several cinematics in the game can add richness and meaning to the music for players, tying motifs to important characters, locations or dramatic developments. These can be further exploited in other appropriate music blocks later in the score, as mentioned previously.

Finally, the score for a cinematic block must support not only the dramatic ideas conveyed, but also the timing. All of the prior musical building blocks discussed in this chapter can be free-composed, without constraint of any linear timeline. Cinematics are different. They are all about the linear timeline! For a cinematic the music must be composed so that it matches the length and pacing of the visual action. In this way, scoring a cinematic is also a radically different technical endeavor than scoring a game level.

Technical Considerations

Since synchronization to picture is critical, composers must be able to create their music in sync with the moving images. Fortunately, the technology for such synchronized scoring is well established. Each cinematic plays back at a given frame rate, generally ranging between fifteen frames per second (fps) and thirty fps, with some as fast as forty-eight fps. Like an old-time animation flip book, a cinematic plays back each of its "pages" (called frames) at the given number of frames per second to create the illusion of motion.

1. Have the ability to set music entry points at significant moments of the action and/or the dialog, just as you would for a linear medium. This ability comes from the game engine.

2. Have an audio engine that offers many music transition possibilities (on bars, on beats, with different crossfade lengths, with transition blocks, sequences, etc.).

Today we do all that we can to avoid the dreadful, clumsy music cuts that historically marked the start and end of each cinematic, awkwardly setting them apart as separate blocks of score. I usually ask myself these two simple questions. Do we need new music to start with the cinematic? A lot of times you'll find you can let the gameplay music roll, or keep it silent until an appropriate moment comes along. And second, is there a reason why the music has to stop abruptly right at the end of the cinematic? Most of the time there isn't a good reason, but we often do it out of habit.

In the cinematic music briefs I create for the composer, I always mention what music plays before and after the cinematic, so that the composer can match the key, tempo and instrumentation. To be on the safe side, we usually set a center key for the whole score and wander away in friendly keys only. All of these steps help to more seamlessly integrate the music for cinematics into the natural flow of the game score.

Each of these cinematic frames are numbered. The total count of all frames is logged from the beginning to the end of each cinematic. This running time log, including the frame numbers, may be referred to as SMPTE time code, EBU time code or MIDI time code, depending on the system. But each delivers the time information in a standardized format listing the number of hours, minutes, seconds and frames passed. For example, a point occurring precisely two minutes, six seconds and thirteen frames into the cinematic would read like this: 00:02:06:13.

Game developers may deliver cinematics to the composer in any one of a number of currently popular movie file formats. Such may include QuickTime, WMV, AVI or others. The frame rate of each cinematic must be checked and noted so that all composing or recording software synchronized to that cinematic is set correctly and to the same frame rate. Otherwise, drift and mismatching can occur in the timing of the music. Software manuals typically have thorough sections on synchronization which should be read, understood and followed to avoid problems.

SUMMARY

Complex and serviceable video game scores may be built from relatively simple musical building blocks. Music blocks in a game score were compared to bricks, spools and hubs from building sets for children like Lego, Tinkertoys and K'Nex. Six basic music blocks were examined: intros, loops, transitions, tags, stingers and cinematics.

Intros open a new beginning in the game experience. They play one time to set up and establish key musical parameters for the next segment of gameplay. Intros generally fade out at their conlusion. Loops are repeatable music tracks which maintain a specific node within the dramatic arc of the game. They can be most effective if carefully composed so as to avoid either easily recognizable thematic elements or jarring changes that arrest the attention of the player. Transition blocks move the score from one emotional node to another. Gathering the key musical data from the music blocks on either side of the transition allows the composer to build a transition block that will affect a successful hand-off. Transitions often occur at moments when the game is changing noticably and may be a good place to highlight themes or interesting changes in the score texture, voicing, etc. Tags bring a section of score to an effective conclusion. Stingers are short music bursts that highlight some aspect of gameplay. They may play on top of existing music or stand alone. Cinematics provide music to underscore any linear segment of gameplay, including pre-rendered movies or scripted sequences.

CHAPTER 5
ADVANCED MUSIC SCORING TECHNIQUES FOR GAMES

From simple beginnings to staggering complexity.[1]

hapter 4 introduced the idea that composers can build a video game music score using discrete music blocks, analogous to using building set components from Lego, Tinkertoys and K'Nex. Their respective bricks, spools and hubs were compared to intros, loops, transitions, tags, stingers and cinematics in the video game composer's arsenal. Composing a score using these techniques allows for flexibility, expansive sophistication and effective functionality.

Imagine how pathing (introduced in Chapter 2) with such music blocks and connectors could expand outwardly in every appropriate direction, resulting in a virtually unlimited neural network of score options! The complexity, nuance, flexibility and functional impact of such a score would only be constrained by the composer's imagination, time and resources.

Ah yes, resources. Game development teams and publishers tend to guard those carefully, especially when dealing with music. Resource tightfistedness is not just limited to the amount of cash allotted to fund the composer's creativity or production costs. Developers may also keep a short leash on the availability of software engineers to assist in implementation. Also, the amount of memory reserved for music assets has historically ranged from negligible to nominal. It seems that game score development is a continual puzzle of how to make the most effective use of limited resources. Building a music design endlessly outward is a luxury many composers will never experience. Fortunately, innovative thinking can lead to other effective approaches.

For example, what if there were ways to expand the pathing *inwardly*, so that each music block could provide functional variety and nuance even within its own node? What if opening up the metaphorical Tinkertoy music spool revealed additional pathing options on the *inside*?

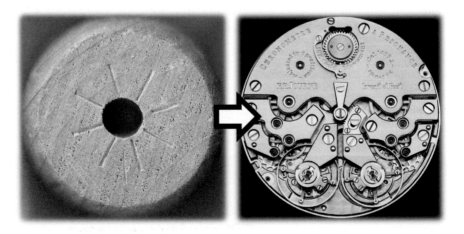

INTERIOR PATHING

When scoring blocks were first explained, it was easy to see how a music score could progress from one type of scoring block to the next. Each block represented a single piece of music underscoring a discrete emotional state or with a singular function to perform in the scoring chain. The music score progressed as it moved along the designated path from one block to the next, as illustrated in the following figure.

However, for the more advanced scoring techniques presented in this chapter, each scoring block will serve as a container for multiple pieces of music, as illustrated by colored subdivisions in the revised block diagram below.

Thus there may be themes and variations in the intro block. There may be several layers of music in the loop blocks. There may be optional choices in the tag and transition blocks. Such additional pieces of music provide the composer with enhanced flexibility to progress and vary the score as needed to meet the complex demands of modern game designs. *Interior pathing* is the combination of design constructs and scripted instructions that tell the game how to handle the order and flow of additional music tracks *within* each individual scoring block.

MUSIC LAYERS

One way to organize additional music tracks within a single scoring block is to utilize layers. When speaking of *music layers*, game composers are describing a group of synchronized music tracks that play back simultaneously, with one or more sounding while all others are muted.

Music layers are much more than sections of an orchestration or stems from a mix session. For the advanced techniques in this chapter, music layers are specifically composed pieces of music that underscore discrete emotional states along the pathway of the game's dramatic arc. They are composed in such a way as to successfully stack on top of each other for synchronized playback—crossfading, muting and unmuting as required by the game's music design.

Some theoretical underpinning may be useful. Recall that in Chapter 2, dramatic timing was described as an *x*-axis running along underneath the game experience. In traditional music scoring, each important action or dramatic development occurs at a given moment in time, or at a specific and consistent point along the *x*-axis.

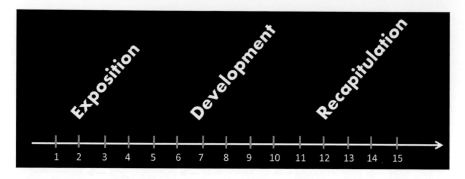

But since games present the problem of an unknowable timeline for important dramatic states, video game scoring requires a different approach. The music layering approach literally turns traditional scoring on its end. Instead of unfolding a procession of successive music states in the dramatic arc along the *x*-axis, music layering provides for the unfolding of music states along the *y*-axis.

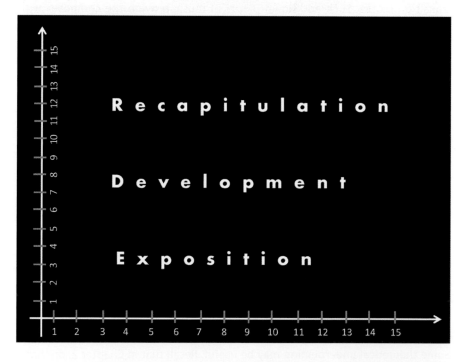

Music layering creates a stack of music cues rather than a series of music cues. Or to put it another way, music layering stacks the succession of emotional states in the dramatic arc on top of one another. This takes advantage of both the *x*-axis and the *y*-axis. The *x*-axis still represents a timeline, just as in traditional music scoring. But the *y*-axis allows for successive parts of the music score to be stacked for instant transitioning.

Layered music blocks generally start with the bottom layer, playing the first piece of music while all others are muted. When the game state changes to questing, a simple crossfade occurs. Or perhaps another track is unmuted, depending on how the layers are set up. Transitions can occur at any time and with minimal coding support. Remember that resources are always limited. Music layers pack tremendous flexibility inside an elegant solution with minimal demands from programming resources on the front end or from computational resources on the back end. This process of transitioning from one scoring state to the next is facilitated by interior pathing up and down as many game states as the scoring block is designed to handle.

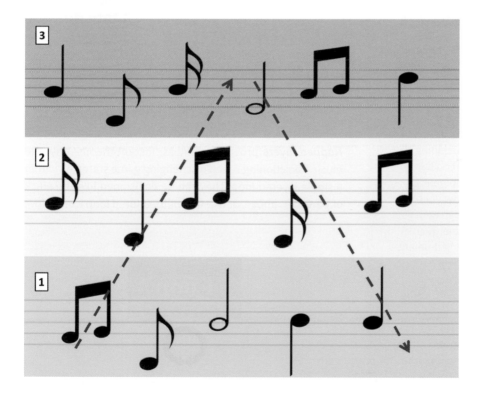

As a reminder, all of these music layers are housed within a single scoring block, and may be thought of as the inward machinations of the figurative Tinkertoy spool introduced at the beginning of the chapter. The remainder of this chapter will focus

WHY USE A MAP?

Imagine if these three pieces of music were used as music layers within the same scoring block. A brief glance at the sheet music will reveal that there is very little in common with the three different charts. What would happen when crossfading from one to the next? Train wreck. It is very likely that at any given moment of transition, different chords would be playing, rhythms would not align and melodies would be incompatible. Such a crossfade would deliver a jarring moment of musical cacophony. That single jarring moment is all it takes to kick a player completely out of the game world, losing the immersion that is so essential to a satisfying gaming experience. No more suspension of disbelief. Composition maps give the composer a tool for aligning the musically relevant components of each piece of music in the stack. This allows for seamless, instantaneous, anytime music transitions.

on four specific music design techniques which approach the scoring puzzle from just such an inward perspective. These advanced techniques are *mapped layers, additive layers, music sets* and *swappable chunks*.

Mapped Layers

Mapped layers provide seamless, instantaneous, anytime music transitioning based on changing game states, all within a single layered loop. They can be envisioned like the stack of pancakes above, or like the multi-colored loop icon below.

With mapped layers, multiple pieces of music are written for progressive game states using a layered composition map. This map ensures that each piece of music written conforms to shared harmonic progressions, dynamics, melodic constructs and sync-able tempi. Locking these key musical variables in place enables instant crossfading between one piece of music and the next in such a way that moving through the various layers of music sounds like a single, through-composed section of score.

Here is a sample section from one of the author's original composition maps. This map provides guidance for composing three distinct pieces of music for exploration, questing and combat, respectively. Notice how each piece of music sits on top of the other, like tracks in a digital audio workstation.

	172 bpm															
					Am +5 E/G#+6	Am	5/6/5	F6 B/F	A6/F	Am/E E7 Am/E	Abm/E F/E		C D Eb F		Eb G C D	
C	Am +11 +13										Am	C/E	Cm/Eb		Cm/Eb	
	fortissimo **Combat**	<	<										*f* *cresc*		*ff* *cresc* *fff*	
	86 bpm															
						Am		F6		Am/E	Abm/E		Cm/Eb			
Q	Am **Quest** E/G#		<	<									*mf* *cresc* *f* *cresc* *ff*			
	forte															
	43 bpm															
										Am/E			Cm/Eb			
E	Am **Exploration** F6		<	<									*mp* *cresc* *m* *cresc* *f*			
	mezzo-forte															

Take a look at the exploration music track first, on the bottom of the stack. The tempo is 43 bpm with dynamics ranging from mezzo-piano to forte. Two points of accent are noted. The harmonic progression is simple and broad, supporting an unobtrusive, contemplative track to underscore the player's survey of the game world.

Now examine the tempo markings for the quest and combat tracks. Notice that they are both perfect multiples of the exploration track's tempo. Look at the harmonic pillars defined in the exploration track. See how they carry through vertically to identical spots in each of the other two tracks? Passing tonalities occur in the upper tracks, but only in between shared pillars. Also notice how the dynamic contour of the exploration piece (including the accents) carries upward in parallel into the other two pieces.

With such a map in place, three different pieces of music can be written to underscore corresponding game states. The resulting compositions will be perfectly compatible for synchronized playback and seamless transitioning. Here is a slightly extended look at the same map, showing the next few measures of score mapping.

172 bpm	Am +5 E/G# +6	Am 5/6/5	F6 B/F A6/F	Am/E E7 Am/E	Abm/E F/E Am C/E	C D Eb F Cm/Eb *f* *cresc*	Eb G C D Cm/Eb *ff* *cresc* *fff*
C Am +11 +13 *fortissimo* **Combat**							
86 bpm	Am	F6	Am/E	Abm/E	Cm/Eb *mf* *cresc* *f* *cresc* *ff*		
Q Am **Quest** E/G#							
43 bpm			Am/E		Cm/Eb *mp* *cresc* *m* *cresc* *f*		
E Am **Exploration** F6							

172 bpm	Fm/E Am/E G/E Bb/E	Dm Dm +11 +5aug	Dm7(4) Dm7(4-3) Bb/D Dm7(-3)	Cm Fm/C	Gm/C	Cm+5	Cm+5
C Am/E Dm/E Db/E Em *fortissimo* **Combat**				*ff* *cresc*	*fff*		
86 bpm	Dm	Dm7(4)	Cm	Cm+5			
Q Am/E Fm/E *Forte* **Quest**			*f* *cresc*	*ff*			
43 bpm	Dm		Cm	Cm+5			
E Am/E **Exploration**			*mf* *cresc*	*f*			

Readers may recall from Chapter 4 that music loops were restricted to a single emotional node, offering a continual sense of movement within the limited dynamic boundaries of that one emotional state. The same rule applies here to individual layers. Each layer functions as one leg of the emotional journey, never rising too high nor falling too low to support the current dramatic state.

Consider how this works in a game. Assume a game design that introduces the player to the game world, then drops into a real-time strategy sequence of exploration, questing and combat. An illustrative block diagram would look like this.

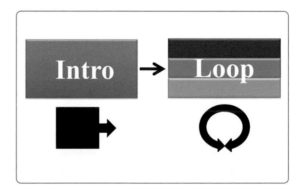

Once the intro block has concluded, the layered loop begins. In this case, the layered loop block is comprised of three layers written to a composition map. The first layer of the loop is an exploration track. It loops for as long as the player remains in exploration mode. At whatever moment in time the player begins a quest, the music will smoothly and seamlessly transition to the questing music track. This then continues to loop for as long as the player remains on the quest. If at any point in time the player is ambushed or chooses to attack, then the music can instantaneously crossfade to the combat music layer. Transitions between each piece of music are always seamless, resulting in a music score experience that sounds like one continuous track created in real-time to support the player's actions during that particular session of gameplay.

This next diagram illustrates the flow of score layers as the game progresses from exploration to questing to combat and back again. Yellow highlights the track that is currently active. Arrows represent crossfades from one track to the next as the player creates or encounters changes in the game state.

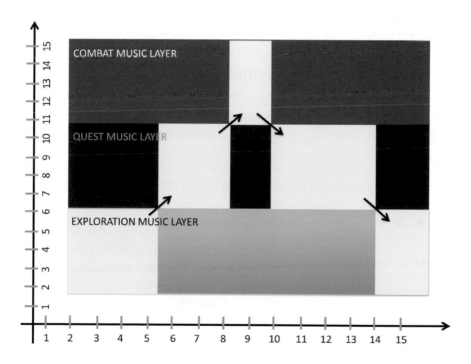

PEEK BEHIND THE CURTAIN

Additive Layers in *Avatar*

The original video game score for *James Cameron's Avatar* was built almost entirely using additive loops of four layers each—exploration, danger, combat and intense action. While the player was exploring, only the bottom layer played while all other layers were muted. I typically composed exploration layers from ambient synth sounds and whole notes with woodwinds, guitars or strings. Harmonies were implied, but often blurred.

Exploration

Once the player crossed a specified threshold within range of a hidden enemy, the second layer faded in on top of the first layer. This is where I brought in *sul ponticello* flavors in the strings, percussion booms and rattles, distant voices, overblown woodwinds, etc. The goal was to set the player on edge just a little bit. I had to always be very careful to use these colors sparingly but adequately in order to give the player enough of a contextual clue that danger was nearby, while still leaving room for the next two layers of score.

The score moves seamlessly up and down in support of the game state changes, no matter how short or long they may be. Note the asymmetrical duration of each game state in the illustration. Such unpredictable changes in timing are handled easily and elegantly with such a scoring system. The music could also change from exploration directly to combat and vice versa, skipping the middle layer entirely if required by certain gameplay circumstances. This is an excellent technique for real-time strategy and role-playing games (RTS and RPG). Mapped layers provide composers with a powerful and nimble scoring tool. Visit the book's web page to hear samples of mapped layers (www.FocalPress.com/cw/Thomas). Listen to each layer independently, then listen to the transition example to hear how seamlessly and subtly the music transitions from one layer to the next.

Additive Layers

While mapped layers crossfade from one layer to the next, additive layers begin with a foundational music track playing and add a new layer to the score for each new game state. In some ways it is a simpler model than the mapped layering system, yet it can be equally effective. This technique works well for first-person shooters (FPS) and action/ adventure games.

Additive layers may be thought of as a multi-track session of stems. Consider a four-layer example with game states of exploration, danger, combat and intense action with corresponding music stems or layers. Only one stem is active for exploration. When danger is detected in the game level, a second stem is activated and begins playing. Combat triggers a third stem added to playback. Intense action sequences bring in the fourth stem.

Now the full arrangement is playing.

Thoughtful approaches to the composition of each layer will allow each to stand on its own merits, feeling like a complete and adequate part of the score for its game state. Adding layers is a bit like making music loops. It can be done poorly with great ease! It is much more difficult to do masterfully so that each layer is composed as an independent and sufficient musical statement in the score.

Technical Considerations

All of the technical considerations relating to loops discussed in Chapter 4 apply here. Each track in music layers, whether mapped or additive, must be cut to identical, frame-accurate lengths. When synchronizing more than one piece of music in a loop, each track must begin at precisely the same point of origin and terminate on the same SMPTE frame number. Otherwise, drift in alignment between the various tracks will occur. This precision editing should be done after the music is mixed.

Music Sets

Music sets are based on the classical principle of theme and variation. Often used within an intro block, *music sets* begin with a single piece of thematic music followed by short snippets of variations on the theme. Each variation may be performed by a solo instrument taken from the palette of the first piece. Increasing intervals of silence between each playback may be coded to gently expand the scope .

Once the player became engaged in combat, the third layer was added. Often this is where I would use the most aggressive rhythmic elements of the score—marcato strings, brass stabs, woodwind flourishes, and either big pounding percussion or busy hand percussion, but not both.

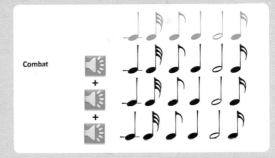

Finally, when the gameplay required intense action in the score, the fourth layer was added. Often this is where I brought in motifs and other kinds of thematic content, to add importance to the scene, rather than busy-ness. It was a lesson I learned along the way, as unfortunately many of the earlier levels sounded crowded rather than epic when the final layer kicked in. Some lessons, no matter how much we would wish otherwise, only come through on-the-job training!

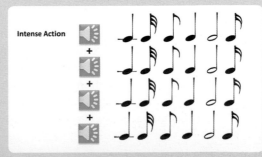

Music Sets

Intro Piece
– Tonal Center
– Signature (melody, harmony, rhythm, etc.)
– Instrumental Palette

Variation Group 1
Variation_Gtr1_01
Variation_Gtr1_02
Variation_Gtr1_03
Variation_Gtr1_04

–
–
–

Variation_Gtr1_20

Variation Group 2
Variation_Obo2_01
Variation_Obo2_02
Variation_Obo2_03
Variation_Obo2_04

–
–
–

Variation_Obo2_20

The introductory piece of music plays only once when the player first enters the level or area. It establishes the tonal center, thematic content and instrumental palette for this entire block of scoring. Numerous short variations on the theme, typically fifteen to thirty seconds in length, are performed by at least two different instruments (or groups of instruments) from the palette. These variations are gathered into groups or sets, where they are played back at random, first drawing from one bank, then from the other, back and forth for as long as the game state remains active. This is effective at keeping the player in the mood established by the introduction, yet still allows room for the soundscape to breathe.

Music sets can deliver hours of cohesive, non-repetitive music score in-game. They are particularly effective for adventure games where large blocks of gameplay involve small quests, puzzles, crafting, conversations, etc., within a limited area. Music sets can be expanded to include theme and variations for day and night options, faction possession options, or any other alternative state the game needs to define for the player. The figure below illustrates a game level where day and night variants need different musical treatments in the score. For the Day Set, the introductory music includes guitar and oboe in its palette. Twenty variations of the Day theme are performed on the guitar with twenty variations of the theme performed on the oboe. Each is placed in its respective set. The intro music for the Night Set includes piano and flute in its palette, so variations are made using these two instruments. For the Day game state, the Day introduction first plays to launch gameplay. After it concludes, the variants from Day Sets 1 and 2 fade in and out, picked at random and alternating between the two sets of variants. The Night Set follows the same pattern.

Music Sets

Music sets can be expanded to provide theme and variations for day and night, faction possession, etc.

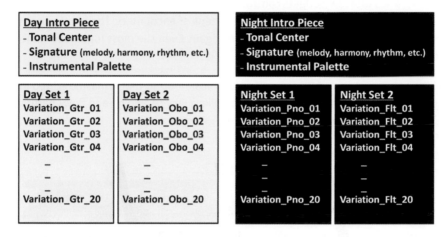

Day Intro Piece	Night Intro Piece
- **Tonal Center**	- **Tonal Center**
- **Signature** (melody, harmony, rhythm, etc.)	- **Signature** (melody, harmony, rhythm, etc.)
- **Instrumental Palette**	- **Instrumental Palette**

Day Set 1	Day Set 2	Night Set 1	Night Set 2
Variation_Gtr_01	Variation_Obo_01	Variation_Pno_01	Variation_Flt_01
Variation_Gtr_02	Variation_Obo_02	Variation_Pno_02	Variation_Flt_02
Variation_Gtr_03	Variation_Obo_03	Variation_Pno_03	Variation_Flt_03
Variation_Gtr_04	Variation_Obo_04	Variation_Pno_04	Variation_Flt_04
–	–	–	–
–	–	–	–
–	–	–	–
Variation_Gtr_20	Variation_Obo_20	Variation_Pno_20	Variation_Flt_20

Here's a quick tip for quickly and affordably generating the variant sets. If live musicians are used to record the thematic introduction, the composer should book at least two musicians who are competent and comfortable improvising. After the session is complete for the thematic introduction, have the selected musicians remain and improvise short variations on the theme. With just a bit of direction from the composer, most musicians who excel at improvisation will be able to generate dozens of useful variants.

Technical Considerations

Each recorded variant should be edited so that it fades in and fades out smoothly and naturally. Variants seem to work well if their playback level is several db lower than the introductory track. A little bit of added reverb is helpful as well. Music files should use a naming convention that makes it easy to organize them into their respective sets. This helps the composer keep track of a growing number of assets, and also helps in the scripting.

Swappable Chunks

Often games with low budgets contract for a single loop of combat music per game level, even though each level may have dozens of encounters. The player ends up hearing the same opening bars again and again. Even the most ingenious combat music will soon grow tiresome.

This can be ameliorated by composing the music loop so that it may be edited into several discrete chunks, each which sounds like a new beginning and flows naturally into the rest of the music track.

To illustrate, consider a music loop composed so that it could believably begin at any one of four different points in the track. A music loop is by definition a piece of music whose end dovetails back into its beginning, resulting in a seamless and potentially never-ending track. Therefore, if the loop is divided into four chunks, the music could begin with any one of them. As long as the chunks play back in proper sequence, the music will sound natural to the player.

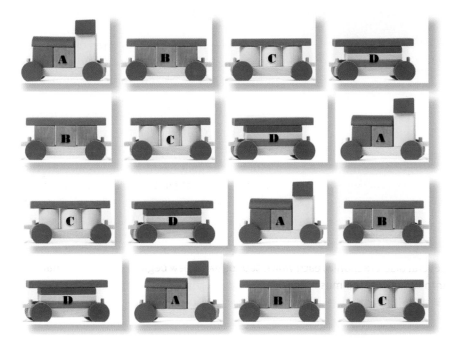

Now, instead of a single combat loop that always grabs the player's attention with the same few notes, the score delivers the impression of variety with four completely "different" music tracks. The beginning is what draws the most attention. Changing the beginning will change the player's perception of the score. This technique helps the player avoid annoyance, saves the developer money and makes the composer look good.

Technical Considerations

The entire combat track should be recorded in a single playthrough or mixed from the entire sequence, rather than taking each chunk on its own. This allows room ambience and mix effects to carry naturally across edit points. Each new chunk should be cut at a zero crossing to avoid pops and clicks. Testing is advisable after dividing the combat track into chunks. Simply reassemble the various chunks in proper order, with each possible combination, and listen to a complete playback of the combat track. If each sequence of chunks sounds natural and clean, then the editing is successful. If not, check for reverb wash, effects bleed, note flams or other small imperfections at the start point or transition points. Some experimentation with sliding the edit points slightly earlier or later should resolve the problem.

PEEK BEHIND THE CURTAIN

Music Stems and Sleight of Hand

In the Disney game, *Ghosts of Mistwood*, the music budget was so small that it provided for only a single three-minute music loop. To best leverage the developer's budget, I built a music design that utilized four different versions of the same music track based on different stem combinations, decreasing volume levels and increased intervals of silence. The resulting score brought players into the experience with the full track, then gradually eased the music into the background until an eventual hand-off to sound effects was complete. Later, when players crossed the threshold of an important milestone, the music cycle would start up again. Simple and subtle, but quite effective in leveraging a tiny budget into a reasonably serviceable game score.

ADDITIONAL TOOLS

The effective use of silence is often overlooked in game scores. Wall-to-wall music is rarely desirable in a video game, as few games (if any) would have the resources to provide enough diversity and relevance in such a relentless score to avoid ear fatigue. On the other hand, a game score that breathes is refreshing. There is a part of the brain that is continually trying to interpret the content and meaning of any music being played (see Chapter 0, "The Language of Music Scoring"). Allowing for silence rests that part of the mind, making any remaining uses of music that much more meaningful to the experience.

Mixing levels also impact the effectiveness of a score. Music played loudly will command attention while music played subliminally can function with subtlety without crowding the soundscape. The effective targeting of mix levels across various score components can have a dramatic impact on the score's dramatic impact!

Effects processing can enrich components of the score in a mix but can also alter the player's perception of music in the game.

SUMMARY

Composers may increase the scope and complexity of their scores by multiplying scoring blocks and connectors. They may also use theme and variations, music layers and optional choices within each scoring block for added score flexibility and richness. Interior pathing organizes and manages these additional pieces of music within each scoring block.

Music layers are stacks of synchronized music tracks within a single scoring block. They allow the score to respond instantaneously and seamlessly to changes in the game state with minimal coding support. Music layers turn traditional scoring on end, taking advantage of the *x*-axis and the *y*-axis to move the score up and down in response to changes in the dramatic arc of the game experience.

Four specific techniques were examined: mapped layers, additive layers, music sets and swappable chunks. Mapped layers are stacks of music tracks, each written to a composition map which synchronizes key musical components like harmony, rhythm, melody and palette. As game states change, mapped layers crossfade from one piece of music to the next, providing the illusion of a single through-composed score. Additive layers build upon one another as game states change, acting more like stems from a single composition. Yet each layer may be composed in such a way as to feel complete on its own. Music sets operate on the principle of theme and variation, beginning with an introductory theme and then pulling from two or more sets of variation tracks to provide potentially hours of non-repetitive, cohesive music coverage for a game area. Swappable chunks bring needed variety to combat loops by dividing a piece of music into multiple chunks, each of which sounds like the beginning of a music cue. They are played back in sequential order, multiplying the perceived variety in the combat music score.

Additional tools such as silence, mix levels and effects processing were touched upon. These tools are also available to score composers to bring utility to the video game score.

This is not a comprehensive list of advanced techniques by any measure. Even as this book is being written, new techniques and innovations in music design are continually springing up, reshaping the landscape of best practices and possibilities. Engaging in a detailed study of these and other techniques will both educate and inspire the creative mind. In the continually evolving craft of video game development, today's students will become tomorrow's pioneers. Grasping current techniques is important. Sparking innovation may be even more important. Today's methods are only the beginning.

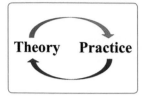

Theory Practice

APPLIED LEARNING

1. Define interior pathing and illustrate one example of it.

2. Describe music layers and how they differ from traditional scoring models.

3. Create a two-layer music map to address game states of adventure and fighting. Using the map, compose a music loop for each game state. Record both tracks and edit them so that they synchronize perfectly, loop successfully and can be crossfaded seamlessly at any time. Test the results and write a summary of what was learned.

4. Build a looping music block with three additive layers to underscore game states of exploration, danger and combat. Record and edit each layer. Test the results and summarize perceived pros and cons of this technique.

5. Create a music set using a one-minute introduction and twelve short variations, six each on two different instruments. Test a mock-up using intervals of about fifteen seconds between each music file.

6. Compose a one-minute combat loop which could be successfully edited into three chunks, any of which could serve as the beginning of a loop. Record and mix the loop, then cut it into three different pieces. Test a mock-up of each version of the loop.

REFERENCES

1.   http://medicalxpress.com/news/2013-11-glial-menagerie-simple-staggering-complexity.html.

PROCESSES

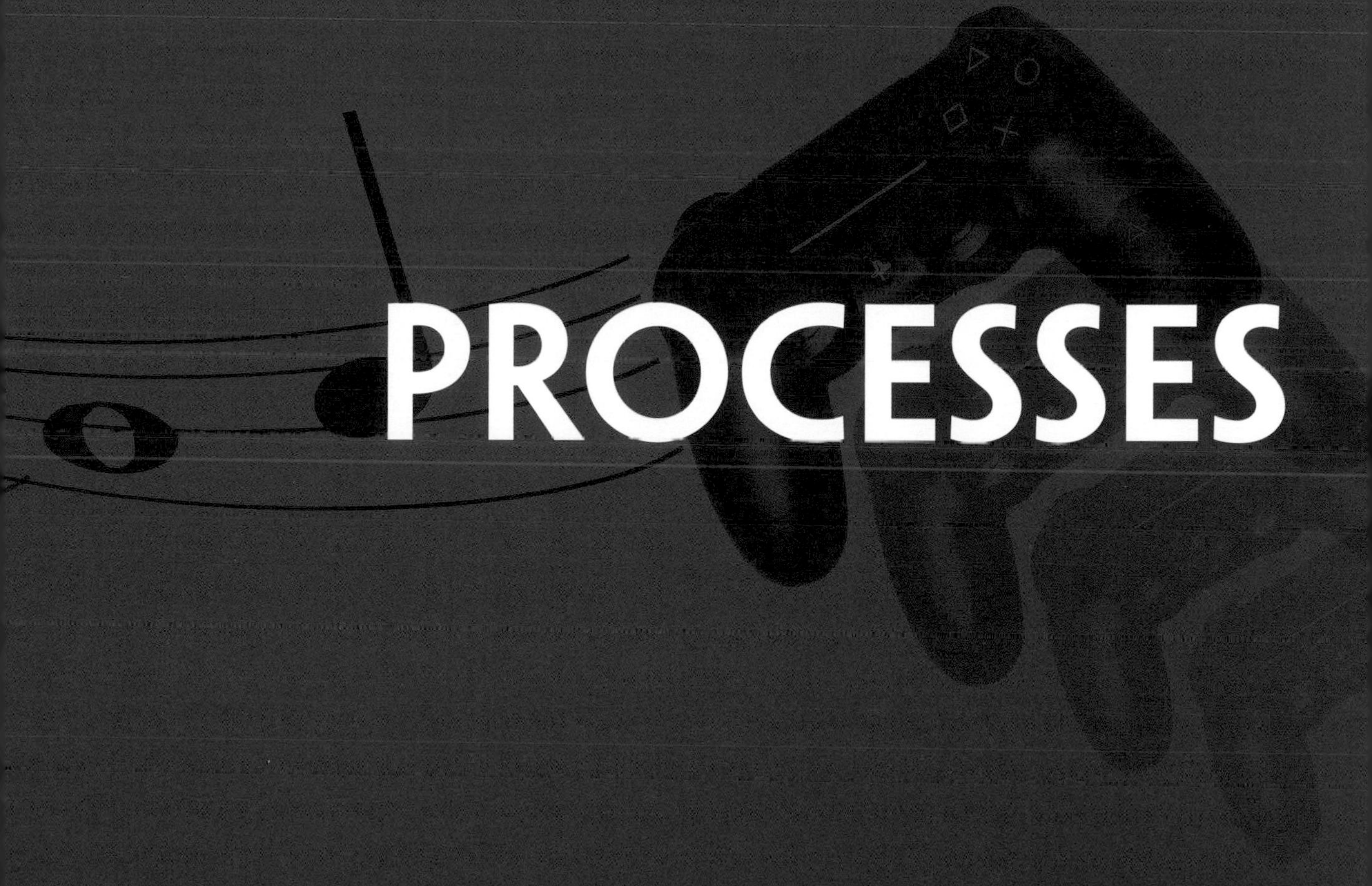

CHAPTER 6
THE PROCESS OF MUSIC COMPOSITION

And from this chasm, with ceaseless turmoil seething … a mighty fountain! [1]

Successful video game composers will write a staggering amount of music over the course of their careers. A single console game may require dozens of original compositions. MMOs can launch with several hours of music. Composers need an effective process in place for generating creative ideas. They also need an efficient pipeline to quickly progress their ideas from blank page to finished score. These disparate tasks all fall under the broad heading of music composition.

Music composition is the process whereby consciously selected musical elements are combined into a new and complete whole—a new original work of music which can be audibly expressed. It is a germinating and sifting process where creativity intersects with principles, tools, judgment, skill and decision.

It is important to note that musical compositions differ from sound recordings. A musical composition is an underlying work of authorship. It may be recorded many times by different performers. A musical composition is an intellectual property, whereas sound recordings are tangible assets. The difference between the two may be thought of as analogous to the differences between a script and a finished movie, or like the difference between a character design and the animation of that character in a game.

Music composition for a video game can involve thousands of large and small decisions, each of which contributes to the

COMPOSITION VS. RECORDING

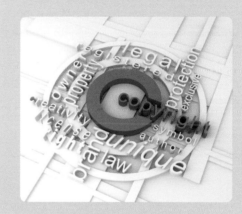

From the United States Copyright Office: "A *musical composition* consists of music … and may be in the form of notated copy (for example, sheet music) … A *sound recording* results from the fixation of a series of musical, spoken, or other sounds." [2] This chapter will address the process of music composition, where the end product is a performable score (whether performed live or electronically). The subsequent process of music production, where the end product is a sound recording, will be explored in the next chapter.

final character of the score. All of these myriad decisions may be loosely categorized under three headings—*organization, creativity* and *crafting*.

ORGANIZATION

Alert composers quickly learn the value of taking time at the beginning of a new video game score to get organized. Taking a few key steps to prepare will optimize the composer's time, efforts and energy over the course of the composition cycle, drastically improving the odds that a better score will emerge at the end. Please consider these following six areas of organization—*music design, cue list, genre selection, scoring palette template, signature targeting* and *scheduling*.

Music Design

Recalling Chapter 3, a **music design** is a comprehensive plan which outlines the purposes, methodologies and logistics for all uses of music within a video game. Taking time at the outset of a score to think through and flesh out an intelligent music design is an obvious first step, as all other facets of the score flow from the music design document. Composers should ensure that all perceived music needs of the game are addressed in this foundational document. Remember also that a music design is an evolving document, so allow some provision for changes as new parts of the design come online while the game's development unfolds.

Cue List

Once the music design is complete, composers should generate a list of music cues needed for the game. A **music cue** is a broad term used to denote any piece of music composed to interact with a given part of the game world.[3] Identifying music cues distills a music design into a list of actionable compositions, including their type (loop, stinger, layer, etc.) and anticipated length.

Using the cue list, composers can also generate a tracking chart like the one on the right, complete with columns for work-in-progress submission dates, client feedback notes, revision delivery dates and final approval dates. This kind of tracking chart can be a life-saver, especially when tackling a large score where dozens of music cues may be required.

Music Cues	Date WIP sent	Client Feedback	Date revision(s) sent	Date approved
Main Theme (2 min)	13-Mar	approved		15-Mar
Menu 1 (90 sec loop)	16-Mar	approved		18-Mar
Menu 2 (45 sec loop)	16-Mar	too busy and melodic	27-Mar	2-Apr
Play Game 1 (15 sec stinger)	27-Mar	approved		2-Apr
Play Game 2 (15 sec stinger)	27-Mar	approved		2-Apr
Exploration 1 (3 min, 3 layered loop)	27-Mar	layer 2 lacks definition	5-Apr	6-Apr
Exploration 2 (3 min, 3 layered loop)	27-Mar	approved		2-Apr
Exploration 3 (3 min, 3 layered loop)	3-Apr	don't like; start over	10-Apr	14-Apr
Exploration 4 (3 min, 3 layered loop)	3-Apr	layer 3 not punchy enough	10-Apr; more hvy perc	19-Apr
Exploration 5 (3 min, 3 layered loop)	3-Apr	layer 1 too amorphous	10-Apr	14-Apr
Exploration 6 (2 min, 3 layered loop)	10-Apr	approved		14 Apr
Exploration 7 (2 min, 3 layered loop)	10-Apr	approved		14-Apr
Exploration 8 (2 min, 3 layered loop)	17-Apr	approved		19-Apr
Transition 1 (15 sec)	17-Apr	approved		19-Apr
Transition 2 (15 sec)	17 Apr	approved		19-Apr
Transition 3 (15 sec)	17-Apr	approved		19-Apr
Transition 4 (15 sec)	17-Apr	approved		19-Apr
Combat 1 (2 min swappable chunk loop)	17-Apr	approved		19-Apr
Combat 2 (2 min swappable chunk loop)	24-Apr	approved		29-Apr
Combat 3 (2 min swappable chunk loop)	24-Apr	bad trans 2nd, 3rd chunks	1-May	10-May
Combat 4 (2 min swappable chunk loop)	24-Apr	approved		29-Apr
Surprise Stinger 1 (10 sec)	24-Apr	approved		29-Apr
Surprise Stinger 2 (10 sec)	24-Apr	approved		29-Apr
Surprise Stinger 3 (10 sec)	1-May	approved		15-May
Surprise Stinger 4 (10 sec)	1-May	replace echo synth sound	8-May	15-May
Surprise Stinger 5 (10 sec)	1-May	approved		15-May
Surprise Stinger 6 (10 sec)	1-May	approved		15-May
Victory 1 (10 sec stinger)	1-May	sounds cheesy	8-May	15-May
Victory 2 (10 sec stinger)	1-May	stronger theme statement	8-May	15-May
Victory 3 (10 sec stinger)	8-May	approved		15-May
Defeat 1 (10 sec stinger)	8-May	approved		15-May
Defeat 2 (10 sec stinger)	8-May	approved		15-May
Defeat 3 (10 sec stinger)	8-May	approved		15-May

GUEST LECTURE
THE SCORING PALETTE
TEMPLATE

Jeff Broadbent (*Planetside,
Transformers, Into the Storm*)

At the start of a project, setting up an appropriate scoring template is an important part of bringing creative focus and efficiency to the process. When I begin a game score, I start by brainstorming what instruments and sonic colors I would like to use. I generally start by writing out the various instrument categories I may use, such as strings, brass, winds, exotic/world instruments, electronic/synthetic instruments, percussion, etc. Then within each of these categories I will define what articulations and patches I may use—such as string marcato, horn legato lines, various types of drums, ideas for synth patches, etc. I will generally write these ideas out in a Word document so I can easily add or delete items. I will do this for each cue I compose.

After assembling a basic blueprint for the sonic colors/instruments I will use, I open up my DAW and begin to assemble a template. I will load up orchestral patches at this time. However, for more sonically creative instruments such as percussion and synthesizers, I will assemble the patches as I compose, as this allows me to try out different patches that will sit better in the mix.

Genre Selection

Genres offer the composer an effective shortcut in communicating with an audience. Selecting a genre is like choosing a recipe of musical ingredients from among palette, orchestration, harmony, rhythm and melody—ingredients whose combination is known to yield a distinctive and serviceable flavor. Often the game development team will dictate the genre to the composer, although the degree of specificity can vary widely. For example, an audio director may ask the composer to deliver a funky fusion score blending the rhythmic sophistication of Pat Matheny with the harmonic language of Earth, Wind and Fire and the instrumental palette of Parliament-Funkadelic. The composer may have no idea what that sounds like yet, but in terms of direction, that's pretty specific. On the other hand, a producer may ask for music that just sounds "really epic", giving the composer more freedom to select an appropriate genre. As an aside, sometimes groundbreaking games will allow the composer an opportunity to really push the boundaries of an existing genre, or approach a new genre altogether. In any case, making a genre selection up front helps the composer narrow the focus sufficiently to progress to the next step of the organizing process, which is setting up the composition palette.

Scoring Palette Template

The *palette* of a score is defined as the collection of tonal colors and sonic textures utilized in that score. All genres suggest a palette, or at least the bare bones of a palette, which gives composers a framework for their creativity. Setting up the palette in a workable template for the composer tends to take shape in one of two ways. Sometimes a composer will set up their template on a score sheet for pencil and paper composition. A score sheet will list all the instruments in the palette, ranging from strings at the bottom, through percussion and choir, then brass and finally woodwinds at the top.

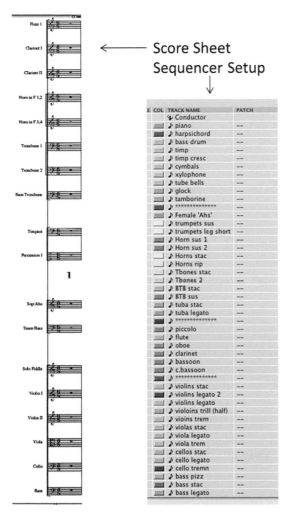

← Score Sheet
Sequencer Setup ↓

For efficiency in mixing I like to route different instrument categories (such as strings and percussion) to buses or multi-instruments to allow for group mixing control (such as volume automation). I generally have a couple of different reverbs available through aux sends to apply to the various instruments. Often I will use a hall reverb for strings/brass/choir, and a plate reverb (or another reverb with a shorter decay time) for percussion, synths and other elements that will be closer and more up front in the mix.

Another technique I employ when setting up a scoring template is using markers to designate different sections of the cue. For example, I will use markers to specify various formal sections of the cue I am working on, such as A1, A2, Theme 1, Breakdown, etc. This use of markers allows me to give formal organization to the cue—to have a "bird's eye view" of how I will organize the cue compositionally. I will often do this when I am setting up the template, before I actually start composing, much in the same way an artist will create a basic outline sketch before filling in the colors.

Partly because the video game industry is a technology-saturated workplace, pencil and paper composers are rare in the industry. The more common way to set up a scoring palette template

GUEST LECTURE
SCORE SIGNATURES AND THE CREATIVE PROCESS

Marty O'Donnell (*Destiny, Halo, Myth*)

Music should be memorable. Robert Schumann famously said, "In order to compose, all you need to do is remember a tune that nobody else has thought of."

Memorable music seems to follow some simple rules. There is a strong melody that feels familiar and new at the same time. It tells the listener a personal story. Most strong melodies contain one or more of the following traits: they are singable, have an interesting shape, one low point and one high point, are built out of asymmetrical phrases, and are both rhythmically predictable and yet surprising at the same time. If you hear something you like, analyze why you think it's effective. Try this: take a melody that you think is great and try to make it ordinary. That can teach you a lot.

Some works of art feel so inspired and elevated that artists could think they had divine help! Even though I believe that humans are made in the image of God, I don't think it would be fair to attribute any specific and likely mediocre piece of music that I've written to the Creator, no matter how inspired I feel. And I don't have a personal Muse.

The reality is much more mundane and, at least in my case, not all that complicated. The following are some general principles of mine that guide the way I think about and approach music composition.

Music should be evocative. Music stirs emotions. I vividly remember moments from my childhood

is with a computer-based composition program, also known as a sequencing program. Sequencing programs add a new track for each component of the score palette, accessing correlated internal or external sounds which can be triggered from a connected MIDI controller. This gives composers instant aural feedback on their work in progress.

Whether setting up for pencil and paper, or building a template on screen, either of these approaches make all the colors and textures of the selected palette readily available to the composer, offering a focused playground where the composer's creativity can have free and efficient reign.

Score Signature

Every score needs a signature of some kind, something that sets it apart from the crowd. This can be a memorable theme, motif or riff. A signature sound may come from an innovative mixing approach, a definitive palette or unusual harmonies. Many composers find it useful to identify in advance what kind of signature they want to target for the score. Will there be a melodic theme quoted in the menu, cinematics, transitions and tags? Perhaps all combat loops will include a common rhythmic motif. Should all defeat stingers feature a female vocal? The possibilities are many. Targeting how to put a signature on the score is one more way to focus the composer's efforts during score development.

Scheduling

There is an old saying that nothing inspires like a deadline. Whether that is an axiom or hyperbole, it is nevertheless important to schedule all music cues to be written for the score across the available dates. This helps composers plan their score development, allocating certain minutes of score to certain days. A well-planned schedule also helps composers see when they are getting behind, and helps them plan where to make up the lost time. Here is the schedule from one of the author's video game scores.

May + June						
	Music Design	Music Design	Scoring Palette Setup	Main Theme	Main Theme	Cue 1 Loop
SUNDAY	MONDAY	TUESDAY	WEDNESDAY	THURSDAY	FRIDAY	SATURDAY
	Cue 2 Loop	Cue 3 Loop	Cue 4 (3 layers)	Cue 5 (3 layers)	Cue 6 (3 layers)	Cue 7 Loop Cue 8 Stinger Cue 9 Stinger
	Cue 10 Loop Cue 11 Stinger Cue 12 Stinger	Cue 13 Loop Cue 14 Stinger Cue 15 Stinger Cue 16 Stinger	Cue 17 Loop Cue 18 Stinger Cue 19 Stinger	Cue 20 Cinematic Cue 21 Cinematic Cue 22 Cinematic Cue 23 Cinematic	Cue 24 Stinger Cue 25 Loop Cue 26 Stinger	Layback & Orchestration
	Layback & Orchestration	Layback & Orchestration	Live Recording	Live Recording	Editing	Editing
	Mixing	Mixing	Mixing	Mixing	Mixing	Formatting, Archiving, Delivery

This score required about forty minutes of music (including the three layered cues), and involved live recording sessions with choir, strings and brass sections. Note that only fourteen days were allotted to compose. If the composer works six days each week, the required average output is three minutes of new music each day. Absolutely doable, as long as the composer keeps up with the schedule.

However, composers who start writing music without a roadmap may find themselves in a very difficult situation. Even on a small score with a tight deadline like this, it is easy to see how missing even a day or two of writing can lead to a logjam of backlog. Having to play catch up while racing toward a delivery date can multiply anxiety instead of creativity. The quality of work tends to drop substantially as the composer rushes from one cue to the next, possibly even missing deadlines. Such unprofessionalism can cost a composer his

when listening to or playing a piece of music evoked some strong, unexpected emotion in me. Hearing the song "Ghost Riders in the Sky" or listening to the soundtrack album to *Ben Hur* my father brought home transported me over and over again. That "stirring" is still the most important moment for me in listening to or creating music even to this day. I don't believe that any of us create in a vacuum, but rather everything we make comes from a complex mix of our past experiences.

So, at the earliest stages of composition I'm trying to discover that "something" that provokes an emotional response. I trust this initial feeling and I try to make certain that I keep the elements that evoked that feeling all the way through to final production.

The underlying music, in its simplest form, is the composition. The melody, rhythm, harmony and structure that make up pieces of music are the elements the composer needs to control and understand. Bach's Art of Fugue or the sketchbooks of Beethoven are pure compositions. The magic is there even before those pieces are realized by performance.

Sometimes, after hours of repetitive practice or days sitting in a studio behind a computer screen, the composition loses the underlying magic to move me. If the power to move me was present during the initial creation stage, I trust that the music will still have the power to move others once they hear it after it is produced.

How do I come up with something that will evoke a desired emotional response using the language of music scoring? First of all I need some idea of the emotions I'm hoping to evoke. I want to know what sort of emotional journey the listener will take. In scoring a film sequence or an encounter in a game, I'll watch footage without music, feel the emotions that are already present and think about how music can enhance or compliment them.

Music should be well crafted. Each composer has their own preferences and influences and needs to find their own voice as they hone their skills. Tonality and atonality are both important to my process.

Why be exclusively in one camp or another? I prefer to think about harmonizing melodies with other melodies in the manner of sixteenth-century counterpoint (where two or more concurrent melodic lines play in juxtaposition to one another). This can be done with as few as two or three voices, where each voice needs to follow similar melodic rules and is strong enough to stand on its own as melody. This horizontal approach can give me a vertical harmonic structure that might be more interesting than simple homophony. The times when I take a homophonic approach (chords with melody) I'll adjust voice leading to be more contrapuntal. This usually involves finding passing tones, suspensions, oblique and contrary motion in the inner voices to make the basic piece more compelling and less predictable.

Rhythmically, I like to find a "feel" that is satisfying. An underlying pulse can be an extremely useful device for propelling music forward. If I find I've written something rhythmically predictable I'll look for syncopation or insert or subtract extra beats. When a piece of music is more ambient, an underlying pulse isn't as important, and simply playing with dynamics and color changes can be incredibly evocative. Also, don't get trapped by the click track! It's a useful tool but the history of music and emotion also contains "feel" and rubato.

Structure shouldn't be predictable. Repetition, variation and surprise are tools to be used and controlled. A great piece of music seems to follow an inner logic that is almost inevitable, yet at the same time takes the listener on a journey they didn't see coming.

My advice is study music and music theory of all kinds: classical, jazz, pop and music from other cultures, and keep remembering what drew you to music in the first place. The music that thrilled me in my youth was just the beginning. I've atteempted to grow my tastes over the years without abandoning my past. Just because I enjoy caviar today doesn't mean I can't enjoy good ol' mac'n'cheese.

Remember and embrace what initially excited you about music. Learn your craft. Find your voice. Keep growing as long as you're alive.

or her shot at the next gig. And in today's crowded marketplace, oversupplied with young and hungry composers as it is, this can torpedo an otherwise promising career.

Creating a workable writing schedule is simple. Sticking with the schedule requires some discipline, but it is manageable. Along with the other organizational choices discussed in this section, scheduling can be a powerful tool in the composer's arsenal. With this kind of organization up front, the composer is ready to dive into the real creative work of the music scoring process.

CREATIVITY

The act of creation is a wonder, leaving admiration and bewilderment in its wake. Where do great musical ideas come from? Even for veteran composers, some aspects of the creative process remain stubbornly shrouded in mystery. And yet, somehow the most successful composers deliver scores for game after game across a track record that can span decades. How do they do it?

Aspiring video game composers are not the only people interested in understanding the creative process. Philosophers and neuroscientists have also pondered and dissected the issue. Certainly some combination of processes is occurring in the human brain which unleashes creativity in artistic individuals. But what are those processes? And more importantly, how can they be learned?

Immersion

Many successful video game composers find that the best way to tap into a creative state is to immerse themselves in a new project as thoroughly as possible. Studio walls can be plastered with screen shots, concept art and high resolution marketing graphics from the game. Game designs and scripts can be pored over and internalized. Demos and vertical slices of the game can be played. Cinematics can be watched again and again, soaking in the myriad details brought together by the game's art and design teams.

The primary purpose for such saturation is to quickly bring the composer to an acquired, intuitive feel for the world about to be scored. This kind of *acquired intuition* will enable the composer to sense when the music is the right fit, even the perfect fit. Or conversely, to sense when it's wrong so that wayward tracks can be discarded.

Immersion is most successful when composers are able to tap deeply into their own imagination. There really is no trick, technique or technology that can rival the human imagination. Composers should continually nurture their imaginations. Nurture the imagination and, in exchange, it can nurture a successful career in music for many years to come.

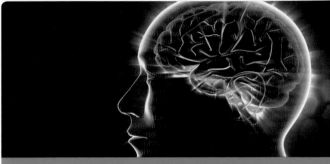

GUEST LECTURE
STUDYING CREATIVITY

Nancy C. Andreasen (*The Creating Brain: The Neuroscience of Genius*)

Nancy Andreasen, in her thought-provoking book, *The Creating Brain: The Neuroscience of Genius*, argues that creativity is an exceptionally rare and transcendent trait which can only be understood by studying those so endowed.

"Creativity is not a dimensional trait. Rather it is a characteristic of rare, unique and unusual individuals. Rather than being at the extreme end of a continuous bell curve that represents the normal population (as high intelligence is), the capacity for creativity is a discontinuous trait or group of traits that occur uniquely in a few extremely gifted individuals … Quite literally, creativity is a "gift" divinely bestowed from God or occurring as a near-miraculous biological or social accident … Creativity can be studied successfully only by focusing on highly gifted people—people who have an established track record of being creative in some field, such as music."[4]

Following on from Dr. Andreasen's conclusions, it would seem that the best way to learn about creativity in video game music is to study successful video game composers—specifically those with a proven track record of consistent creativity over time.

PEEK BEHIND THE CURTAIN

Immersion and Inspiration

I have been composing music for more than forty years. During that time my creative process has gone through a number of evolutionary stages. However, in 2005 I made a discovery which sent a seismic tremor through my craft. It happened during a particularly frustrating and fruitless block of time spent noodling at the keyboard, trying to come up with something cool for *Peter Jackson's King Kong*. I had to create music for a Tyrannosaurus Rex bursting upon the scene and surprising the player's character, then chasing that character up a narrow ravine. Nothing I came up with sounded good to me. In frustration, I finally got up and left so I could clear my head.

At the time, my studio was situated in the forested Sierra foothills outside Yosemite National Park in central California. I had a second-floor deck just outside the studio overlooking the forest, so I went out there to cool off. There was a gentle breeze blowing, which caused the tops of the trees to sway slowly back and forth. As I became lost in thought, I looked off in the distance and noticed two trees swaying in opposite directions as the wind momentarily moved them apart. I thought, "That's exactly what it would look like if a T-Rex was forcing its way through those trees." I followed that train of thought and imagined a path of trees being pushed apart moving steadily in my direction. "Yes," I thought, "It would be just like that if a dinosaur was on the move and getting closer to me." Soon, I was imagining the growing thunder of footfalls on the forest floor. My heartbeat actually ticked up a notch or two.

Now I had completely given myself to the scenario. I imagined the crashing of branches coming ever nearer, the shaking of the ground nearly toppling me from my feet, and then finally, the trees right in front of me bursting apart with the thrust of the predator's head, beady eyes drilling through me with the hot breath of

As a practical side note, it is also important to keep in mind that the music score will need to successfully coexist with other immersive components in the audio track, including sound effects, ambience and dialog. Some sounds just don't play well with others. For example, marcato strings may collide with automatic weapons fire. Racing game engines dominate the mid-range, so composers need to build out the bottom and top. Sustained brass may work well under a military helicopter, while most other musical gestures simply get bludgeoned. Imagining the full sonic spectrum of the experience, including sound effects, dialog and ambience, can help the composer target a complementary scoring approach.

Inspiration

Sometimes the imagination needs a jump start. Beyond immersion in the project itself, turning to outside sources of inspiration can also be an effective way to bring ideas to the composer's mind. Scoring literature is rife with brilliance. Listening to great music from current or past masters can often provide a spark. Being out in nature may be another way to open the mind to musical ideas. Appreciating works of art, sculpture, movies, theater, fine cuisine or anything else that stirs a person's intrinsic aesthetic appreciation can help. Nobuo Uematsu (*Final Fantasy*) once remarked during an interview at the Game Developers Conference in San Francisco that taking a bath sometimes opens his mind to new musical ideas. Some people say their best ideas come in the shower, or when they wake up in the middle of the night.

There are many ways to open the mind and catalyze creative input. Each composer can find the sources of inspiration that work best for them and cultivate them.

CRAFTING

The English poet Walter Savage Landor wrote, "Music is God's gift to man, the only art of Heaven given to earth." Many would agree that musical inspiration is a gift. Whether germinating in the rich imaginative soil of the human brain or originating from something more mystical in nature, most composers refer to certain "aha" moments in the process of composing a score as inspiration. But inspiration rarely covers the entirety of a music score. Usually inspiration comes in the form of a thematic idea, clarity about a motif or some novel approach to an old problem. Like a raw gem on the jeweler's bench, it must be cut, polished, fitted and placed in the right setting. This post-inspiration part of the music scoring process is referred to as crafting. Some would say that's where the real blood, sweat and tears are found. As Billy Joel once said, "I love having written, but I hate writing."[5]

Crafting the score includes many of the principles and tools discussed throughout this book. It relies on conventional principles and toolsets of music scoring. It draws from distinguishing principles of video game scoring and uses methods pulled from both basic and advanced music design. But since this chapter is focused on process, please consider the following four areas of process in exploring music score craftsmanship—*building a composition, making mock-ups, revisions* and *approvals.*

its nostrils in my face. I could almost see the serrated inner edges of the beast's off-color teeth. By this time, I was actually feeling panic. And that's when it happened.

I started to hear music in my mind. Music that was a perfect fit for what I was feeling. I heard the pounding of tribal drums, the dynamic stabs of cimbasso and bass trombones with tremolos in the double bass and cello. I heard the cacophony of trumpets desperately climbing over each other and violins racing to a crescendo. The French horns snarled down a half-step with the woodwinds caught in a dissonant duel. This music reflected exactly what I was feeling!

I rushed back to the studio and began playing parts into my sequencing program. It was almost like lifting an arrangement from a CD—I would listen as the music played back in my mind, then play in the parts I was hearing. It was such a rush. When I finished transcribing, I only had the first thirty seconds of music or so. But honestly, that's all I needed. Craft, instincts and experience could take over from there. I just needed the right start.

From that day forward I have tried to approach each score much like a method actor. I imagine myself totally immersed in the scenario I am scoring, complete with all the sights, sounds, smells, excitement, adrenaline—whatever I can conjure up. The more vividly I can imagine the situation, the more likely the right emotions from my own heart will start to percolate. And the more intimately and powerfully I can experience the emotions of the scene, the more likely I'll begin to hear fitting music in my mind. And that's all I need to get rolling, just that initial gem of inspiration.

GUEST LECTURE
INSPIRATION AND
THE CREATIVE PROCESS

Garry Schyman (*Bioshock Infinite, Dante's Inferno, Bioshock*)

I was recently asked where my inspiration came from when composing. My answer surprised my interviewer—'deadlines!'—thus admitting that fear was one of my greatest inspirations! After the shock and perhaps disappointment, I pointed out the value of deadlines in focusing the mind on the need to write music NOW and not tomorrow. Once that is achieved the process starts in earnest. Creative activity once initiated tends to supply the answers I need when finding what note comes next. Therefore the very act of starting and searching for musical solutions helps me to be creative. I therefore love deadlines as they usually (when not too truncated) are my friend when I am scoring a game or film.

Sometimes when stuck I will listen to other composers' music. Sometimes just a simple juxtaposition of notes suggests something really interesting to me that in the end sounds nothing like what I was listing to. I also have generated a book of my own unique twelve-tone rows that I sometimes go to for a place to start. Stravinsky once said (paraphrased here) that if offered the entire keyboard of notes to compose with he was stymied and overwhelmed with choices and thus not able to begin writing. However, if given just two notes and told to start writing he could begin immediately.

Building the Composition

Imagine that day ten on the scoring schedule has arrived, showing a two-minute combat cue as the day's work. The composer opens the scoring template, names the new file, and after some immersion in the game world, has a flash of inspiration. A two-bar pulsing riff in the cellos comes to mind, doubled with bass clarinet and distorted bass guitar. Cool.

But what now? The cue needs to be two minutes long. How does a composer turn two bars of inspiration into two minutes of engaging underscore? There are several approaches that successful composers have developed. Here are two of the most common.

One method is to sketch first, then come back and color in the details later. With this approach, the composer sketches out the broad strokes of the entire two-minute cue. Chord changes, tempo changes, meter changes, melodic statements, all fundamental lines and curves of the cue are determined in their most basic form. This allows the composer to consider the contour of the cue in its entirety, making any desired changes in a quick and simple way, prior to investing the time demanded for orchestration or arrangement.

As a sketch artist uses a pencil, so the composer may use a piano, a string patch, a guitar, a bass line or some other sound to create a complete framework for the composition from beginning to end. Polyphonic instruments are preferable for most scores because they allow for the expression of harmonic content. But bass lines or groove loops may also be effective sketching tools for certain kinds of scoring approaches. Whatever tool allows the composer to convey the essence of the cue quickly and simply, that is the right tool for this job.

There are some benefits to the "sketch now, color later" method, even beyond saving time. If a cue works at an evocative emotional level as a single instrument sketch, odds are the composer is onto something really good. It will only get better with the right orchestration and production. Alternatively, if the sketch fails to deliver the right emotional response, revisions are probably in order. In the same way that it is difficult to make a good movie from a bad script, cool sounds and impressive orchestration can never completely compensate for poor writing.

That always struck me as critical and I try to find the metaphoric "two notes" so I can start. I sometimes use Slonimsky's *Thesaurus of Scales and Melodic Patterns* which can be a font of ideas—again with the Stravinsky idea of just getting those first couple of notes out so you can start. I just need an idea that attracts me, that sucks me in and makes me want to compose music using that idea.

Once I begin writing, all kinds of ideas pop and suggest themselves. So I start writing, often with my first idea or perhaps second. I may later abandon it, but at least I have started. If I feel I am on to something, I can send it to my director or audio professional to evaluate. If they like it too, then I am on to something and I have done the most difficult part—starting! As I have said above, starting is critical because, once achieved, ideas flow as the music suggests what comes next.

In Malcolm Gladwell's book *Outliers* the author suggests it takes 10,000 hours to become really good at something. I do not have a single technique for writing cues that I can depend on every time I work, but I do have quite a bit of technique that has comes via university study (degree in Music Composition from USC), private study with some great composers, as well as endless private score study and listening to works of the great composers, both classical and soundtrack composers. But what is most critical is that I have spent thousands of hours writing and rewriting music, perfecting cues and compositions, gaining confidence and judgment. Nothing is more important than knowing when you have written something that is lame and you need to change it or rewrite the cue. That judgment comes with years of experience and listening to good music and being able to properly second guess yourself as to whether you are really on to something or have simply started a piece of music and are reluctant to abandon a dead end. Thus building technique through study and composing helps me compose "intuitively", but on the shoulders of an enormous amount of work over the years.

The mock-up. Some composers are annoyed or find mocking the music up to be a time-consuming distraction, but to the contrary I find that it helps me. I have a lot of samples and can make music sound very convincing using the latest technology. This is not only critical for the folks I work for who need to hear the music as convincingly as can be portrayed to properly evaluate how effective it will be in the film or game, but it inspires me to hear the music. When stuck I often go back to the beginning of the cue and play it over and over to the point where I left off until the music suggests something to me, or tells me where it needs to go to support the scene or the game at that moment. Here technique mixed with years of thinking about and writing music, along with good old-fashioned creative intuition, is my source for inspiration.

Finally I visualize the music. When stuck I often get away from my musical setup or piano and take a walk, lie down on the sofa and close my eyes and visualize what comes next. Before doing so it is critical to inspire myself with the material I am working on. Whether it is a scene from a film or cinematic I am scoring or a portion of the game that I am writing a loop for, I watch it over and over, have discussions with the creative partners on the project as to what is really going on during this scoring moment and then get away and visualize what I need to do for the score. This can be very affective for me. When really stuck I will often visualize the musical challenge just before I go to sleep. I can't tell you how many times the answer comes first thing in the morning once I start writing. Just love the human brain! Our best friend when it comes to creating music.

Another approach is to complete the cue in vertical slices, section by section. In this case, a composer builds the cue as a series of fully orchestrated or arranged segments, one complete section after another. For example, the first six measures will be completely finished before starting on the next eight-measure section, and so on. This approach allows the composer to define all parameters of the score as he or she progresses through the composition, hearing a near-finished product as it comes to life, one section at a time.

One benefit to this approach is that it enables composers to capture all facets of their imagination or inspiration as they go. If the composer hears all parts of a section in their mind, this approach allows them to seize the moment of inspiration in its entirety. Another benefit is the enhanced adrenaline level that hearing a completed section generally stirs in the composer. It really is fun to hear a piece of music come into full-blown focus right from the start, though this can also be a danger, as love for orchestration choices or ear-candy sounds may overpower the composer's judgment of the innate quality of the music without such bells and whistles. Another benefit to the vertical slice approach is that listening back to the completed section repeatedly may vividly suggest ideas to the mind for further development.

The author has utilized both approaches and finds them both effective methods. Composers are encouraged to experiment with these and other approaches to determine what works best for enriching their own creative process.

One side note while discussing building the composition. Most composers are passionate about their work, and may lose all track of time, surroundings and bodily function when in their writing zone. In spite of this, there is one piece of continual housekeeping that must never fall off the radar. Save early and often! If there are any kinds of auto-save routines that can be turned on in the sequencing program, turn them on! If a composer needs a sign or alarm as a reminder, make it happen! Truly, there are few moments of frustration so intense as the moment where a computer locks up or the power flicks off, erasing hours of inspiration and hard work. One video game composer famously had a sign in his studio, prominently and forcefully displayed:

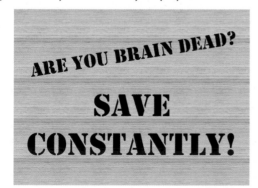

ARE YOU BRAIN DEAD?

SAVE CONSTANTLY!

GUEST LECTURE
MY CREATIVE PROCESS

Tom Salta
(*Halo, H.A.W.X., Prince of Persia*)

When I observe my own process for creating a score to a game, I notice that I typically go through various stages. It usually starts with "The Blank Slate" (often referred to as the "Blank Canvas" or "Blue Sky") when I first get word of a project. This is when I typically procrastinate and have the most fear and doubt in myself. Most all creatives dread this stage.

I call the second stage "Dipping the Toe in the Water". This happens when I know I really *should* start working so I don't run out of time later. During this process, I often start creating initial ideas that just "come to me". The best version of this is when I go through various sounds and libraries and come across something that inspires me to create an idea. Then I will put a simple idea down. Once I feel the initial idea is communicated and I feel like I can build upon it, but I really don't want to spend the time, I'll move onto a blank session and keep going through new sounds. If I'm on a roll, I might create many ideas in a row like this … and this will often be the basis for cues I develop later.

Phase three is "Getting into the Meat of It". No more random experimenting … the clock is ticking and now I need to take a close look at the level documents and start thinking about an approach. When in doubt, start from the beginning. I still collect various ideas that might come to me at various times, whether it be in the supermarket or driving. I will sing or hum an idea into a voice recording app on my phone. Then I can email it to myself and save it in an ideas folder.

The remaining phases get increasingly specific, putting the music into context or figuring out ways to simulate it when there is no footage available. Eventually I enter into "Panic Mode" or ideally "Controlled Panic Mode" when we're weeks away from the end. At this point, any live sessions need to be scheduled and all the music has to be written and prepared. After this stage everything gets recorded and then I go into final production and mix mode. Since I always mix my own music, I can be very efficient and tweak right up to the very end.

GUEST LECTURE
MOCK-UPS

Rodney Gates, Guerilla Games

The importance of high-quality mock-ups is at an all-time high. A composer needs not only to be skilled at writing and orchestrating the music itself, but they must also be skilled MIDI orchestrators as well. Getting there can require a great deal of patience and skill to coax the very best performances out of the mock-up. Although massaging complex articulation key-switching and continuous controller data can definitely slow the process of writing, it will always deliver a much better listening experience and realism for the music.

Mock-ups

Directors and producers who are paying out large or small sums of money to composers generally want to hear how the score is coming along. They want work-in-progress samples so they can decide if the score will meet their expectations or not. A *mock-up* is a digital realization of a music cue in the score. Instrumental and/or vocal parts play back through digital samples, virtual instruments or synthesizers. It is generally not fully mixed or inclusive of live instruments or vocals. Mock-ups are generally not yet considered completed music tracks.

Having said that, the mock-up should offer a reasonable representation of what the final cue is going to sound like. More than a sketch, a good mock-up allows the client to hear the composition, orchestration, embellishments, and many of the effects planned for the score. The better the mock-up, the easier it is for a client (who may have no musical training) to render their opinion about the content and direction of the score. The best mock-ups leave very little to the imagination.

To that end, composers should consider investing in the highest quality digital samples and virtual instruments available. The marketplace for virtual instruments is constantly churning, so composers new to the scene will find great benefit in reaching out to current professionals at conferences, through social media or in Guild forums to learn what are the best current samples for orchestral instruments, urban beats, big band, rock guitars, and so on. The next chapter will survey the current crop of top samples libraries, but only as of the date of this publication.

A level of expertise in audio production is also important for composers to develop. While great sounds will not turn mediocre music into gold, a mock-up that sounds bad due to poor engineering can effectively disguise or even neutralize an otherwise fine piece of music. Learning basic audio engineering skills and following best practices will ensure the delivery of a mock-up that puts the music in the best possible light.

Revisions

Henry Mancini, a successful film composer of a bygone era, wisely quipped, "Don't fall in love with every note you write."[6] So true, but what a challenge for passionate, creative artists! Composers may slave over a composition, expending tremendous energy to immerse themselves in a game level, conjure up emotions, reach for inspiration, work and rework a sketch, build a full orchestration, obsess over details of the mock-up, and then submit their work-in-progress with high hopes and fingers crossed. By this time, they may have fallen in love indeed—not just with every note but with every fader move and sample tweak and reverb splash in the cue.

If the mock-up *sounds* like MIDI, with the instruments running all over one another like a pipe organ, it will undeniably sound fake, and the piece may be rejected outright.

Here are some best practices that I feel are important when writing for virtual playback:

- Write to the samples you have. Do not force them to perform other articulations if they were not covered in the recording process.
- If you're not using wet libraries with the recording space present in the samples, be careful setting up your delays and reverbs.
- Learn the basics of audio engineering if you haven't already. Then you will most likely avoid issues such as unprofessional delivery formats, gain structure problems that can lead to clipping and distortion, or muddy mixes due to lack of experience using plug-ins and/or hardware processors effectively. There are a lot of people jumping on computers to write these days without learning basic signal flow, and it shows.

The current crop of libraries sound much better than their predecessors due to the fact that many are mixed and mastered by seasoned professionals, as well as the fact that they are recorded "wet" to capture the sound of the room or scoring stage when applicable.

Having said all that, sometimes a single live player added to a sequence of samples can really bring the piece to life and make it all work. I know when a composer has hit the nail on the head when all of these elements come together universally: the piece hits us emotionally, fits the game wonderfully and sounds fantastic because it is well produced and executed.

GUEST LECTURE
UNDERSTANDING AND
RESPONDING TO CLIENTS

Penka Kouneva
(*Transformers, Prince of Persia*)

About client feedback. One of the most important tasks media composers will ever learn (over a lifetime) is to interpret and implement the client's feedback. Yes, often it's inane or inarticulate but it's our job to "read minds", listen very closely, and try our very best to implement whatever is requested, into meaningful musical revisions that ultimately deliver what the client wants.

It's not a skill learned overnight and it's not a skill you can learn just from a book. Only through real-life collaborations and experiences can this become second nature. This is why collaborative experiences are so important and students should be encouraged to work with one another, express feedback, learn to listen and discern what their collaborators want.

In spite of all this focused effort, sometimes the client just won't like something about the music. In fact, they may not like anything about it. Sometimes the client asks for revisions. Sometimes they will reject a piece of music entirely. Mancini's quote was born from just such a reality of the composing business. But do not fret. Revisions are an inevitable part of doing business in the video game industry. Every composer has been there.

If the composer is fortunate, the client will be able to articulate exactly what they don't like in the submission, sometimes even offering specific musical ideas for the next version. When this occurs, the wise composer will respond humbly, thanking the client for their patience and insight. With specific and actionable notes from the client, changes can be effected as requested, likely resulting in approval on the next submission.

It is more challenging when a client lacks the musical understanding required to articulate their reservations. Telling a composer something like, "It needs to be more … um, you know … more purple …" is not just a joke in a textbook. That kind of vague feedback is more common than one might think. One of the most critical skills a composer can acquire is the ability to understand and respond effectively to a client's concerns.

Ferreting out the real objections in such a case is not easy. A client may know exactly what they don't like, but may lack the language to communicate specifics. In such cases, the composer needs to use their best communication skills to query the client. Here are some questions composers can use to open the dialogue. Remember that the goal is to help clients recognize and identify what they would like to hear differently:

- *Were there some parts of the music that you liked?* This question helps the client start to think through the cue in components, rather than as a single entity. It causes the client to refocus on the good things in the cue first, turning them toward a positive view of the composer. This question also helps the composer recognize which musical sections or components in the score are working well. Digging a little deeper can uncover whether there is a particular sound, progression, beat or combination that really resonates with the client. Make note of any such insights for future reference.

- *At what point in the music did you hear something that you didn't like?* This question reinforces looking at the cue in components, rather than in its entirety. Identifying a single component of a cue that needs revising saves time and energy, especially when compared to the alternative of starting from scratch. Additionally, leading the client to point out a specific part of the cue they don't like will help the composer understand if there is a particular sound, melodic turn or some other musical component that is rubbing the client the wrong way. This could also be made note of for future reference.

- *What emotion(s) did you want the music to evoke?* Sometimes revisiting the original purpose for a music cue can bring greater clarity and focus to the composer's efforts. If the client wants to evoke poignancy and the music is simply sad, then the composer can revise the cue by quoting from a relevant theme, or working in some appropriate harmonic language—such as a dissonance cadencing to a major, then resolving down to minor. And so on. Gaining clarity about the client's emotional objective will often suggest musical solutions.

- *Do you have any reference music that hits the target for you?* Asking for a reference track can offer the composer a peek into the client's musical perceptions, revealing what the client thinks is a good fit for a particular part of the game. It may be instantly clear, upon hearing the reference, what the client wants. Sometimes though, it will be more confusing than ever. In those cases, simply follow up with the client, asking as many questions as needed to understand what positive attributes the client feels are being conveyed in the reference track.

GUEST LECTURE
HUMBLE ATTITUDE

Josh Aker (*Infinity Blade, Shadow Complex, Undertow*)

I remember my first composing gig. It went something like this:

Friend: Josh, you're a composer, right?

Me: Yes. (*I'd never composed anything in my life. I was merely an aspiring composer.*)

Friend: Great! I work for a production company. We're making a documentary and we're looking for a composer to score it. We'll pay you $500.

Me: Hmmm. Yeah, I can probably discount my fee and make that work. (*In my head—AWESOME!!!!*)

I set out to compose what I'm certain will be the best music they'll ever hear … EVER. And if they hear it and don't agree I'll let them know they're wrong. A few weeks pass, I deliver the music, they pay me, all is well. And then my friend approaches me.

Friend: Josh, let me talk to you for a second.

Me: Yeah, what's up?

Friend: Just wanted to tell you something as a friend.

My red flags are up. I'm ready to disagree with whatever he says.

Never be afraid to engage a client in such queries. The more useful information a composer can acquire from their client about desired musical style, purpose, sound, feel, color, etc., the easier it will be to hit the right target.

Ultimately the composer's job is to realize the client's vision, ideally to a degree which surpasses expectations. The best inspiration comes with the best information. And the best information generally emerges only through taking time for good communication with the client.

Approvals

From an artistically pure perspective, a piece of music may never be truly finished. But at some point, the composer simply must stop working on it. One optimal point for conclusion is when the client gives their approval.

It is important that composers develop a system for tracking approvals. This matters for at least three different reasons. (1) Most music agreements include language which requires explicit approval from the publisher or developer before final payment can be tendered. Therefore, tracking approvals leads to getting paid. (2) There are rare occasions when a client may come back and ask for additional revisions after a previous approval has already been given. This can cause problems if the composer has recorded live overdubs, mixed the cue or is tied up in another project. In such cases, most composers will do all they can to make the requested revisions but should not be liable for extra costs of rerecording, remixing or putting off another client. Tracking approvals offers a paper trail of proof should the client try to push those expenses back to the composer. (3) There is a strong intrinsic feeling of satisfaction when checking off the approval box on their cue list. Tracking approvals keeps the endorphins flowing.

SUMMARY

There is process behind every act of creation. Music composition is no different. Various composers may approach it from different vantage points, but each engages in a flow that leads from a blank page to a finished score. The process of composing music includes *organization, creativity* and *crafting.*

Getting organized at the start of a video game scoring project involves music design, generating a cue list, selecting the right genre, setting up a scoring palette template, targeting musical signatures in the score and scheduling necessary tasks across the time available. These steps can save hours and headaches during the score and offer a competitive advantage over the long run.

Creativity is a rare and beautiful gift. Studying successfully creative people offers insights into the creative process. Some composers harness the creative power of their imagination through emotional immersion in the game world. Some listen to other great works of music for inspiration. Deadlines provide the impetus for some composers to distill their creative ideas into tangible form.

Composers bring craftsmanship to bear in building their musical composition, delivering good mock-ups, making necessary revisions and gaining approval for their scores. Some composers will sketch out their score ideas first, then fill in detail later. Others prefer to create full-blown versions of the score one section at a time. Both have advantages. Remember to save early and save

Friend: Listen … your music was fine and all …

My teeth are gritting—only fine?!

Friend: … but you were really hard to work with. You don't take criticism well and you're very cocky. If we're paying you, then you should give us what we want. And honestly I'm not sure we'd hire you again.

There's more to the story. But the take-home is this—I swallowed my pride and since that time I've only heard from my clients that they enjoy our working relationship.

I'm certain my friend's honest words saved my career right from the beginning.

often. Revisions are a necessary part of the score development process. Good questions from the composer can help the client better articulate any needed changes. Remember to track client approvals. It's how most composers ultimately get paid. It feels great to be a finisher.

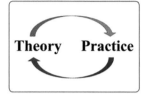

APPLIED LEARNING

1. 1. Using the music design created at the end of Chapter 3, build a cue list and tracking chart.

2. In any sequencing program, set up a scoring palette template appropriate for scoring in a hybrid electronic/orchestral genre.

3. Plan out a reasonable scoring schedule based on the cue list generated in #1 above.

4. Practice mental/emotional/sensory immersion with the following scene:

What kinds of input are available to the five senses? What sorts of emotions does the scene evoke? Imagine and describe fitting music for such a scene. Compose a piece of music that fits this description.

5. Listen to FPS score samples from three different composers. Using their work as a source of inspiration, create an original thirty-second combat cue.

6. Create a mock-up recording using the music composed in #4 or #5 above. Share it with a friend or colleague and ask them to find at least two things they would like to hear differently. Revise the music accordingly.

REFERENCES

1.   From the poem "Kubla Khan" by Samuel Taylor Coleridge. www.poetryfoundation.org/poem/173247.

2.   http://www.copyright.gov/circs/circ56a.pdf.

3.   Royal S. Brown, *Overtones and Undertones: Reading Film Music* (Oakland, CA: University of California Press, 1994), p. 50.

4.   Nancy C. Andreasen, *The Creating Brain: The Neuroscience of Genius* (New York and Washington, DC: Dana Press, 2005).

5.   http://www.nytimes.com/2013/05/26/magazine/billy-joel-on-not-working-and-not-giving-up-drinking.html?pagewanted=all&_r=0.

6.   http://www.navyband.navy.mil/article_arranger.shtml.

CHAPTER 7

CHAPTER 7
THE PROCESS OF MUSIC PRODUCTION

Chase perfection.[1]

Music production is the process through which compositions are brought to life sonically and affixed in a recorded medium. It is an elucidation process, where the highest possible interpretation of a composer's vision is pursued. Expressiveness in performance, sonic richness, creativity and clarity—all aspects of production are exploited to enhance the aesthetic prowess and evocative impact of the composer's creation. As production wraps, the resulting audio file is not only a billable deliverable to the game developer, but a fixed messenger of the composer's creativity to all the world. This process includes *selecting sounds, layback (including tempo map and click track), sheet music prep, tracking, editing, mixing, mastering* and *format conversion*. Audio scripting or other software deliverables will be addressed in Chapter 8 on implementation.

PRODUCING A TRIPLE-A SCORE

This chapter will take readers through the process of a big budget game music score, complete with both live and virtual elements. Thus every step of music production which score composers may likely face during their careers will be addressed. It is hoped that this approach is relevant to smaller budget scores as well, since most music production pipelines follow a similar path. While less elaborate productions may skip some intermittent steps along the way, the remaining steps can be applied to any score production.

Selecting Sounds

Composers are always searching for better sounds to realize their vision. This is as true of past masters as it is of contemporary vanguards. As a preponderance of video game composers create much of their music using digital samples and virtual instruments, a few guidelines may be helpful to empower composers in making the best choices for their sound sources.

Composers should be very demanding in their quest for sounds. Good enough isn't really good enough. Keep in mind that whatever sounds a composer selects during production, those sounds will represent the composer's music to the world, possibly for years to come. There should be no compromise, no shortcuts, no casual Fridays when it comes to scrutinizing sounds. If a string patch sounds cheesy, it must be replaced. If a percussion hit is weak, it has to go. With so many outstanding options available on the market there is no excuse for settling on second-rate sound sources.

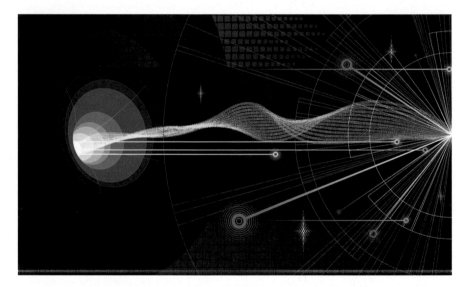

Sound Sourcing

High quality sound sources can be expensive, so it may be useful to consider some suggestions on how to build a good core library. Most scores will require some or all of the following sounds: *strings, percussion, brass, woodwinds, piano, choir, guitars, ethnic instruments* and *synthesizers*. Specialized genre scores may require less common instruments, but there are sound sources available for most of those as well. Almost any instrument or musical sound known to man has probably been sampled by someone. But for the purposes of this section, only a library of core sounds will be explored. Keep in mind that new sound sources are constantly being released, so consider the following survey as a time capsule from the date of publication.

Strings

There are a number of excellent strings libraries available, each of which offer certain advantages. For example, Symphobia has one of the more useable staccato string sounds in the business. Hollywood Strings does a terrific job handling legato lines. Cinematic Strings 2 excels in its ease of use, with all articulations accessible from a single patch. Some of the best string libraries include EWQL Hollywood Strings, Symphobia I and II, LA Scoring Strings, EWQL Symphonic Orchestra, Cinematic Strings I and II and Vienna Appassionata and Dimension Strings.

Since no single library excels at everything, composers are encouraged to visit the websites of each, listen to the audio demos, read reviews and make their own judgment about which would be the best investment for their core library. Eventually, most professional composers will grow their collection to include several string libraries. Since strings form the backbone of the cinematic sound, beginning composers are encouraged to invest in at least one top quality string library if they hope to be competitive.

Percussion

After great-sounding strings, killer percussion is probably the next most important component of a competitive core library. Orchestral percussion, Taiko drums, ethnic percussion and hybrid hits are among the most common sounds game composers are called upon to use. The timpani from Spitfire Audio's Definitive Percussion has a truly epic sound, while 8Dio's Taiko Ensemble offers a more aggressive edge than comparable libraries. Damage by Heavyocity includes a range of useful effects that bring a modern edge to its hybrid samples. For a wide-ranging, all-purpose percussion library, composers might consider Hans Zimmer Percussion Volume 1. And for a good selection of drum kit sounds, take a listen to Ministry of Rock 2 from EW.

There are literally thousands of percussion libraries available. Sifting through them all would take weeks. Try an Internet search for "Best percussion libraries" and read recommendations on composer forums, library roundups, and audio enthusiast sites. That may help narrow the search to a more manageable level.

Brass

Historically, brass has been difficult to replicate well with samples. Trumpets have been especially problematic. But both Trumpet Corps from the British Modular

Library and Hollywood Brass from EWQL do an admirable job with the sound and articulation control of their trumpet sounds. There are a number of solid horn and trombone libraries available, among them CineBrass Pro and several from VSL. Sample Modeling also has several brass offerings. Personal research and lots of comparative listening, as always, are in order.

Woodwinds

Berlin Woodwinds from Orchestral Tools is a solid choice for an all-in-one woodwind collection. Westgate Studios offers a number of à la carte woodwind libraries. Their Oboe Section is a particular standout.

Piano

Production Grand by Production Voices has a sparkling clean acoustic grand sound. Synthogy's Ivory II Steinway Concert D Grand offers a more weighty resonance. Other options to research include the Acoustic Samples Piano Collection, Steinberg's The Grand 3 and the Pianos Virtual Instrument from EWQL.

Choir

Requiem Pro from 8Dio with its word building feature is an epic choir ensemble that sounds great and is intuitive to use, though the low end is weak. Soundiron's Olympus Symphonic Choir collection also has powerful word building features with a closer, more defined sound. Other options to investigate would include Storm Choir from Strezov Sampling and VSL's Vienna Choir.

Guitars

Vir2 Instruments, Orange Tree Samples and Ilya Efimov Productions all offer a variety of excellent acoustic and electric guitar sample libraries. Cinematic Guitars by Sample Logic is good for atmospheric effects and Ministry of Rock I and II from EW are decent guitar starter libraries.

Ethnic Instruments

Ilya Efimov has a nice collection of world woodwind instruments, including the duduk, hulusi and zhaleika. These have deep layers of dynamic and articulation samples which allow for flexible and lifelike performance emulation. They also possess a rich, warm sound that is rare to find in ethnic libraries. EW offers two libraries that have been making the rounds for years, Silk and RA. These also include some ethnic winds but add stringed instruments and world percussion. They have proven quite useable, but be aware that some samples sound a little thin. Ethno World 5 from Best Service offers an encyclopedic collection of world instruments and voices, but there is a brittleness to the sound that may not appeal to some composers. Also the limited depth of the sample sets and specificity of riffs may limit the usefulness for some parts of the library.

Synthesizers

There may be even more virtual synths on the market than percussion libraries, not to mention outboard and standalone synthesizers, both analog and digital. A person could disappear for days browsing through every specialized soft synth and V.I. on the market. But for a composer's core library, at least four multi-purpose synths deserve a closer look: Zebra from U-he, Absynth 5 from Native Instruments, Omnisphere 2 from Spectrasonics and Alchemy by Camel Audio. Each offers intuitive interfaces, loads of great samples and powerful shaping tools to vary and control the sounds.

With any category of sample library, the composer's top priorities should be the quality of the sound and the expressive capabilities of each virtual instrument. It should be pointed out that mastering an instrument's expressive capabilities may take a significant investment of time. Even outstanding samples from the best libraries will only sound as good as the composer's selection, performance and editing of appropriate articulations, dynamics and phrasing. In many respects, mastering a given virtual instrument is akin to learning to play any other instrument. Guidance, experimentation and practice are required to obtain proficiency.

Websites for all of the libraries listed above have audio demos posted for perusal so composers can hear for themselves. Reviews and forum discussions abound where conversations rage back and forth on the respective pros and cons of each library, including their ease of use and expressive capacity. Time spent researching available options is definitely worth the effort.

Extensive and ongoing ear training will also help composers become increasingly astute judges of sample quality. Constant listening to the best-sounding game soundtracks, film soundtracks, trailer scores and pop tunes will acquaint the ear with the most engaging of contemporary entertainment sounds. Always make note of sounds that strike a resonant chord and stir the creative imagination. Track them down, isolate them, listen to what they do and how they do it. Time and energy

GUEST LECTURE
THE SYNERGY OF CROSS-POLLINATION

Nancy C. Andreasen (*The Creating Brain: The Neuroscience of Genius*)

Art in Florence was created in studios or shops run by master artists and populated by multiple-talented young men. Everyone examined what others were doing. They looked within their own shops, but also at the work of others. They looked at the new creations of their contemporaries, getting ideas about the development of new techniques. They also studied what others of an earlier generation had done. In art alone the city was filled with men of genius, bouncing ideas back and forth and borrowing what was best. Add to that the philosophers, poets, and politicians—it was an astonishingly rich congregation of human beings, who created social networks that cross-fertilized one another and opened avenues from which new ideas could emerge.[2]

spent training the ears is an investment that will pay big dividends again and again.

A similar paradigm exists among the best video game composers in the business today. The annual Game Developers Conference offers listening sessions for both amateurs and professionals to showcase their work. Lively discussions follow in hallways, restaurants, clubs and parties late into the night. Each year the Game Audio Network Guild Awards offers members the opportunity to listen to the latest work of the top composers in the business. All nominated scores are instantly available at the click of a button. Listening to the composition and production chops underscoring these top picks offers a rich education for the ears.

Layback

Layback refers to the process of recording virtual sounds from a sequencing program into a digital audio workstation for additional production. Most sequencing programs generate streams of MIDI data that trigger internal and/or external sound sources anew each time the sequence plays. Layback captures the playback of those sound sources into a DAW as digital audio files. It is useful to note that the MIDI and DAW functions may be handled by two different pieces of software, even two different computers. Or they may be wrapped into a single program on the same machine. Whatever the format differences, layback achieves the same purpose of generating digital audio files.

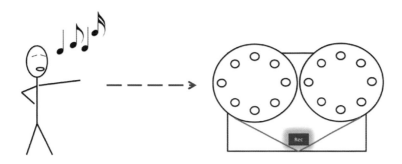

For old schoolers, it may be clarifying to think of the MIDI program as generating a performance, while the DAW serves as a recording machine which captures the performance.

In a pressurized environment, such as when handling a large score under a tight deadline, some shortcuts may have occurred in the composition phase. Perhaps parts weren't played in as cleanly as needed, or with the best-sounding samples, or with the best dynamic shaping. It happens. Since the main tasks during composition are to distill ideas and arrive at client approval, a tight deadline may force a composer to pull out some time-saving tricks just to get the musical ideas out there and approved. However, during layback, many of these shortcuts will be exposed and must be fixed. Sloppy performances have to be cleaned up. Substandard sounds have to be replaced. Every part of the virtual score has to be raised to its highest quality bar. Good enough never is good enough. Chasing perfection is what the best video game composers must be about.

A next step during layback is to generate a ***tempo map***. This is a stream of MIDI data containing information about the tempo, meter, key and markers in the composition, including any variations (rubato, ritard, changing meters, etc.). If using different programs for sequencing and layback, the tempo map is generated in the MIDI program and imported into the DAW. Once imported, the DAW file is set for perfectly synchronized recording with the MIDI file. On a practical note, if working with two different programs, be sure that the frame rates and SMPTE start times for both the MIDI file and the DAW file are the same, including any count-off measures or offsets.

Some studio configurations allow for all virtual files to track into the DAW simultaneously. Others allow for only a few tracks at a time. Whatever a composer's particular setup, the heart of the layback process is locking the MIDI and DAW programs together, then pushing record on the DAW while the MIDI data plays back in frame-accurate sync. This level of accuracy is especially important if the system is restricted to a limited number of tracks concurrently and must perform multiple passes to capture all parts.

Again, while laying back each part, the composer should do everything possible to ensure the highest attainable quality of each recorded track. Record at the highest sample rate and deepest bit depths that are practical. The higher the sample rate, the more accurately a wave form can be captured, since sample rate refers to how many times per second a sample is taken (like a snapshot) of a given waveform. The deeper the bit depth, the more detailed the sample of the waveform can be (think higher resolution snapshot). Composers should also provide for the highest quality signal path affordable. This includes any digital converters, word clocks, pre-amps or interfaces involved in the audio chain. Jitter, distortion and truncating digital bits can all affect sonic quality, costing the composer transparency, sheen and other ear tickling intangibles that are so desirable in the best recordings. And of course, do not allow any clipping or any unintended distortion of the signal.

The composer also needs to generate a click track. A **click track** is a metronome-like recording of each beat in the composition, generally including two measures of count-off, which plays in sync with the tempo track discussed previously.

Click tracks are essential when recording any live overdubs. Click tracks given musicians an audible time reference so they can synchronize their real-time performances to pre-recorded tracks. Clicks can also be helpful for lining up parts in editing and visualizing beats in mixing. Many DAWs have click-generating functions built in, which makes things easy. Lacking that, clicks can alternatively be generated from a MIDI program or even played in from a keyboard or percussion controller.

Sheet Music Preparation

Often running concurrently with composition, and sometimes stretching into the layback phase of production, is the preparation of sheet music files for the score. Sometimes simply called *music prep*, this step involves making legible transcriptions of any component of the recorded score that will need to be performed live. Composers looking for any live additions to their music will need to complete sheet music prep at some level. This can be as simple as making a chord chart for a studio musician, or as complex as stacks of printed and bound sheet music books for an orchestra. Many video game composers will experience both extremes.

Some composers do their own music prep. Others farm out the task to a third-party specialist. Since many steps are the same with either approach, this section will follow the process taken when a composer contracts an outside music preparer for a full orchestral/choral score.

The composer generates a clean MIDI file which contains all of the musical parts to be transcribed, plus tempo map information. A clean MIDI file has been stripped of extraneous data (such as key switching), has been scrutinized for accuracy and is ready to send out for music prep. When getting a MIDI file ready for music prep, the following checklist may be useful:

Organizing a MIDI File for Sheet Music Prep

1. Remove any plug-ins and virtual instruments.

2. Change any single note triggers (woodwind flourish, guitar lick, etc.) to actual notes.

3. Quantize performances to desired note values for sheet music. Include note durations, as well.

4. Break sectional parts down into individual parts.

5. (Optional) Combine tracks with different articulations of the same instrument into a single track.

6. Order and name MIDI tracks to conform with traditional score layout.

7. Double check everything.

8. Save as music prep MIDI file.

1. Any plug-ins or virtual tracks, etc. that don't contain note information will need to be extracted from the file.

2. Many composers utilize music loops or samples containing riffs, lines or flourishes in their mock-ups. But any single MIDI event that triggers samples of multiple notes or loops will need to be changed to capture the actual notes the live player(s) will perform. Of course, the original samples and loops can also be recorded during layback for mix support or backup.

3. If all notes are quantized to their desired performance value, the chances for a smooth and error-free translation into music prep increases substantially. With quantizing, it's important to notate not only when a musician starts playing a note, but also when they should stop playing the note. So note durations deserve a look too.

4. When getting ideas down, many composers will play certain parts on a single MIDI track as a chord block. For example, they may play in brass parts like a piano, using both hands to play several parts simultaneously. Parts thus inputted should be separated, placing their respective individual instrument parts on individual tracks—tuba, trombones, horns, trumpets, etc. It is not generally necessary to split individual sections apart in the MIDI files, such as Horn 1, Horn 2, Horn 3 and so on. But each set of like instruments should be split apart into separate tracks in the MIDI file.

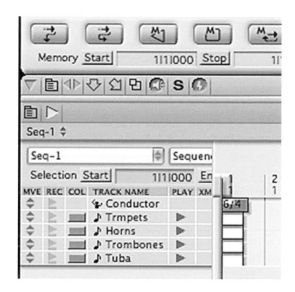

In those cases where a composer does send a MIDI file with all string parts on one track, all brass on one track, woodwinds on one track, etc., then the sheet music preparer takes on the additional role of an orchestrator, taking the composer's piano chord score and distributing the various parts across the appropriate instruments in the orchestra.

5. At the opposite extreme, a composer may also have generated several MIDI tracks for a single part. As an example, consider a first violin part requiring legato, staccato, forte, piano, marcato and *sul tasto* in the same piece of music. These different kinds of articulations may all be handled by different samples with their own MIDI track. The composer may consolidate these onto a single track for Violin 1. On the other hand, some orchestrators actually prefer the exact opposite. Some would rather have each articulation broken out into a separate track, so it's important to clarify this preference at the outset.

GUEST LECTURE
SHEET MUSIC PREPARATION

Paul Taylor (*Rift, Lord of the Rings Online, Dead Space*)

A composer typically sends me a standard MIDI file and audio of the approved cue. My responsibility is to accurately convey his or her intentions onto the full score. At times this may require reworking of the MIDI to make it more "orchestra friendly", at other times the tracks (parts) are laid out concisely and my main focus is on preparing the score and parts to be optimally readable, with all necessary markings. The composer then checks over the full score, makes suggestions or comments, and the parts are extracted from the finalized score. The parts get sorted out for each individual musician and we're ready to record.

In school we were taught that 90 percent correct on a test would earn an "A", maybe an "A-minus". When preparing parts for a recording session? Ninety-nine percent would be an "F", a dismal, never-get-hired-again failure.

Absolute precision in every aspect of the musicians' parts is essential to best utilize the valuable time of the live players. Even when the parts are spot-on, the players will ask questions or request clarifications. Every question that can be predicted and clarified on the parts ahead of time could mean the chance to get that perfect take.

6. Using standard conventions for naming and order helps the transfer process proceed more quickly and accurately. Traditional orchestral layout, from top to bottom, generally proceeds with woodwinds, brass, pitched percussion, unpitched percussion, harp, piano, choir and finally strings. Within each group, individual instruments are listed from top to bottom in pitch order, highest at the top. For example, the strings are laid out with first violin at the top, followed by second violin, viola, cello and double bass.

7. It is vital to review the cleaned MIDI file to ensure that all notes are accounted for and accurately represented. Almost without exception, some error or omission will be discovered. Such errors are almost inevitable when dealing with potentially thousands upon thousands of points of MIDI data.

8. When saving the clean MIDI file for music prep, select a different naming convention so that the original MIDI file used for layback isn't overwritten. One never knows when a return to the layback session may be required by client changes or to retrieve missing data. Some composers set up separate folders for the various versions of the MIDI file as it moves through composition and production. For example: Composition_Combat01_v1 becomes Layback_Combat01_v1, which then becomes MusicPrep_Combat01_v1, etc. Making and keeping several points of fallback is like setting belaying ropes in place for a climber further and further up a slope.

Having prepared a clean MIDI file, the composer must also convey basic articulation information to the sheet music preparer. A list of initial notes, such as these, helps the process along:

```
WW
mm 16-17, clarinet;  hairpin (cresc < > decresc) across both measures
mm 32-33, flute;  hard flutter

BRASS
m 25;  cresc
m 52;  2 beat cresc from mp < f
mm 62-64;  little cresc toward end of each measure
m 65;  big cresc at end of measure
m 66;  sfz on downbeat

Mandolin – gentle strumming tremolo on m 13, m 14 beats 4-6, and m 23
Guitar – please indicate rolled chords at mm 13, 19 beat 4, 23, 27, 31, 35 and 36

STRINGS
mm 5-6;  pizz in the celli
mm 7-10;  mockup violas sounds uneven;  should be straight 16th notes
mm 7-10;  violins sul tasto;  ms 10 cresc and add tremolo
mm 28-29;  violins and violas sul tasto
mm 30-33;  tremolo in violins only
```

The composer should also send the music preparer an audio file of the mock-up, such as an mp3. Some music preparers also like to receive stems: woodwinds, brass, percussion, harp/piano, choir, strings, effects, etc. Combined with the composer's initial notes, the MIDI and mp3 files give the music preparer everything they need to begin an accurate transcription of the composer's musical ideas.

Once an initial score is prepared, the composer will review a copy of the sheet music and make note of any additional revisions required. Often in this review stage, the composer becomes more aware of where many expression and articulation markings would be useful. These notes are conveyed to the music preparer (see the example at right) until the sheet music contains all the necessary information for a successful recording.

The process continues until the sheet music accurately reflects the composer's intentions. Here are the first two pages of a completed and approved PDF from one of the author's scores.

Clarity ensures the composer can get the interpretation he or she needs, and maximize the amount of music successfully recorded in the allotted time. Clarity and accuracy are *everything*.

My first job with Chance Thomas was a big one. *Peter Jackson's King Kong* had seventy minutes of music to be recorded with full orchestra—strings, brass, woodwinds, harp and percussion. Great action cues, *lots* of notes. Some composers meticulously go over my scores, others look them over in broader strokes. Chance is definitely one of the more meticulous types! After many days of recording he said to me in frustration, "Even through all our filters, one wrong note got through." My response? "Well, we'll just have to do better next time!"

```
WW
mm 8 - - flutes, decr.
mm 17-18 - - flutes;  slur 3 note figure beginning with 8th notes
mm 22-23 - - whistle & flute;  make beat 2 of m 22 staccato, rephrase slurs
m 26 - - whislte and flute;  make beat 1 staccato
mm 29-30 - - whistle & flute;  make beat 2 of m 29 staccato, rephrase slurs
m 35 - - whistle & flute;  extend slur to cover half note
m 37 - - whistle & flute;  make beat 5 staccato
m 38 - - whistle and flute;  make both notes of beat 4 staccato, rephrase slurs
m 39 - - flute only; make beat 5 staccato

BRASS
m 4-10 - - bones;  have bone 2 col bone 1 thru m 10 beat 4
mm 5-6;  horns & bones;  slur 3 note figure beginning with 8th notes
mm 9-10 - - horns & bones;  slur 3 note figure beginning with 8th notes
mm 12-20 - - bones;  have bone 2 col bone 1 beginning at m 12 beat 5
m 14 - - trumpet;  accent beat 1
mm 17-18 - - all brass;  note figure beginning with 8th notes
m 58;  bones;  accent beat 1

STRINGS
mm 3-6 - - all strings;  remove accent on beat 6
m 8 - - all strings; remove accents beats 5 & 6
m 9 - - all strings; remove accent beat 6
m 11 - - all strings; remove accents beats 3 & 6
m 12 - - all strings; remove accent beat 3
m 14 - - 1st violins only; beat 6 add slurred 8th note between D4 and E4
m 29 - - fiddle;  phrasing is slur first 3 notes, nest 2 notes, next 5 notes, last 2
m 34 - - fiddle; remove slur
m 35 - - fiddle;  extend slur to cover half note
m 36 - - fiddle;  remove slur
m 60 - - celli;  enter this measure, doubling bass
m 77 - - all strings;  remove accent on beat 6
```

Tracking

With the best possible sounds laid back and all music prep complete, the composer now brings the score's DAW files and sheet music to the recording stage to begin the tracking process. *Tracking* describes the process of recording any live component in the composer's score. This may be as simple as recording a single electric guitar part directly into the DAW, or as complex as tracking multiple orchestral and choral sections in different acoustic spaces across several cities.

A band, orchestra and/or choir may be recorded all at once in a large acoustic space, or tracked in separate sections one at a time. There are certainly benefits and drawbacks to each. Recording a large group requires an equally large acoustic space. This is both a benefit and a drawback. The benefit is that top engineers have

identified most of the really beautiful-sounding large orchestral rooms in the world. Recording in one of these spaces practically ensures a beautiful sound to the room. But these spaces are very costly to rent, not to mention the audio equipment and engineers that come along as part of the deal. Having all the musicians in the room together has both benefits and drawbacks as well. On the positive side, as Chuck Doud of SCEA once quipped, "They can really get the room hummin'!"[3] There is a powerful and beautiful sound that happens when everyone in a group is playing their part correctly and in sync with everyone else in a large recording space. It creates the sound everyone loves from classic film scores and great classical music catalogs. On the down side, it is expensive to hire enough musicians to acquire that sound. And one bad player can hold the entire orchestral session hostage. Many composers can tell the tale of having seventy or more musicians on the scoring stage who all sound amazing, except for one horn player who can't quite play the part in tune. (Not picking on horn players in particular, just using them as a random example. Could be a tuba player. Or an oboe player.) Thousands of dollars in musician and studio fees per hour have been wasted by a few players who couldn't get the part.

Alternatively, recording an orchestra in sections one at a time also has benefits and drawbacks. Continuing the horn player example, maybe the musician only needs a few more runs at the part to get it down. How much more cost effective to do that with six horn players on the stage than with a ninety-piece orchestra sitting there? Recording in sections also gives the composer tremendous flexibility and control during the editing and mixing phases of production. If a string line is late against the brass when tracking an entire orchestra, that's the way it remains. But if recorded in sections, the lagging part can easily be edited to sit right in the pocket where it's needed. Recording in sections also allows the composer to utilize fewer musicians and smaller recording rooms. Many composers will take a small string section and record several passes playing the same part over and over. This is called stacking. Some engineers will set up different mic pairs in the room for each subsequent recording, in order to vary the sound of each stack. This must be done with great skill and scientific accuracy (or luck), in order to avoid phase cancellation or other electronic or acoustic anomalies. Sometimes this approach can deliver a big, live sound, similar to the sound of a full orchestra in a large space. But often it merely results in the sound of a small section playing super intensely.

Many composers will blend smaller live sections with samples of larger sections and work wizardry with reverbs and early reflections to achieve the bigger sound. Because large music production budgets are rare in the video game industry, composers will likely have many opportunities to work on this skill.

One question facing the composer is whether to personally conduct the orchestra on the sound stage or produce the session from inside the control room booth. Conducting one's own music with a live orchestra can be fun and fulfilling. And a composer with genuine conducting skills may draw out a highly expressive performance from the group. Conducting also makes for great publicity photos. However, many composers have related a sad tale that goes something like this: after the rush of conducting, when returning to their studio with the finished tracks, they face both surprise and disappointment because the recording does not sound nearly as good as it felt when they were on the podium. It is difficult to exercise the degree of fine-tuned listening necessary to produce an exquisite recording while waving a baton and leading the musicians in an orchestra. There are so many stimuli. For that reason, many composers will hire an experienced professional to conduct while they produce the score from the control room, listening critically to each take and offering focused feedback and direction through the talk-back to the conductor and musicians. This approach often leads to a more well-produced score with better tracks and fewer surprises.

Session manner is important as well. Remember that musicians are people with emotions, ambitions and creativity of their own. A large recording studio with dozens of musicians on the sound stage can be a pressure cooker for the composer.

Dollars can disappear at a staggering rate. But it is important for composers to take time to greet musicians, chat during breaks and help them feel comfortable and energized about the session. Musicians appreciate genuine compliments. They also appreciate good direction when asking for a different take. If the composer is able to articulate in precise musical terms what needs to be done differently, it helps the musicians target their energy, keeping their focus up. Too many times just asking musicians to "do it again" with no accompanying musical direction saps vitality and dilutes focus. It can drain the positive energy right out of a session. Some good humor is helpful too.

It is important for musicians to understand any protocol for the session. For example, if the composer does not want people checking their smartphones or reading a book between takes, that should be explained at the outset. If silence is required between takes, that should be emphasized. With a large group, this becomes increasingly important since critical headphone communication often occurs in these moments between the composer, the conductor, engineers and musicians.

Many sessions are set up to begin on the hour, with a ten-minute break after fifty minutes of recording. If the group is in the middle of a take, or on the verge of mastering a difficult passage, most groups will agree to some flexibility with the break time. Sometimes a composer will provide snacks and beverages for the musicians during their breaks. They tend to like that.

PEEK BEHIND THE CURTAIN

Recording Studio Atmosphere

The recording studio is my playground. But it's also my workplace. I like to show up early and check things out. I'll look over the mic placement and trade ideas with the recording engineers. I like to meet the musicians as they come in, learn their names and find out something about each one. I keep a list of everyone's name at the producer's desk when I'm running a session. When pointing out an exceptional take, asking for changes or soliciting input, it helps to call on people by name. I like to take a few minutes at the beginning of the session to explain the project. I try to convey what's interesting, challenging or inspiring about the project to give the musicians an angle from which they can approach the score. I also like to leave room for creative input. Sometimes a suggestion or question will come up which leads to some new insight or direction that improves the recording. I don't care where great ideas come from. They don't have to be mine, I just want great ideas in my scores. I really do love and admire studio musicians. And oh! How I need them! I need them to be enthused and engaged and plugged into all the intangibles of the music in order to bring out the very best. I need their creativity and their passion and their focus and their brilliant execution. We do work hard in the studio. Anyone who has done a tracking or mixing session with me can attest to how hard I push when pursuing a great-sounding score. But we also have a good time. A well-timed joke can work wonders in the studio. And great performances ultimately make everyone happy.

Editing

After tracking all of the live components of the score, music enters the editing phase of production. This is where entrances, exits and punches are smoothed out. Wayward sounds are isolated and removed. Takes are scrutinized for expression, accuracy and blend. Different takes may be edited together to create the best possible performance of a part. Timing errors can be corrected. Undesirable pitch imperfections can be addressed. Versatile DAWs such as Pro Tools are most effective for this kind of work.

The most common tasks in editing include cleaning up the session, lining up timings and piecing the best parts of different takes together into a new take. Tracks generally need some cleaning following a recording session. There may be studio noises prior to the start of the take, such as a bass player's bow hitting a music stand, a guitarist checking a tuning or a soprano clearing her throat. Digital tracks can be peeled back to the start of the first performed note, erasing all prior extraneous noises. It is common to write a short fade-in at the entrance of any note, so that the noise floor rises smoothly and imperceptibly. Tacit stretches between and after takes should also be cleaned out with similar fades written on entrance and exit points. Sometimes when tracking, only one part of a phrase will need to be replaced. In this case, the engineer will start the DAW at some point prior to the needed change. Musicians will perform right along with the pre-recorded tracks. When the moment for the needed change arrives, the engineer pushes the record button, and recording begins from that point. This technique, called punching in, may result in an abrupt or jarring transition in the sound. During editing, the old and new takes are crossfaded with each other, resulting in a single smooth phrase. The punch becomes imperceptible.

Lining up timings so that all instruments play together in the pocket is crucial. Even slightly irregular differences in rhythmic alignment can steal the life out of a groove, pulse or drive. One editing trick is to isolate whichever element of the score is really driving the groove correctly. It may be a loop or a percussion track. Look at the track against a grid view using at least a sixteenth note resolution. Certain beats will hit right on the grid, but some may consistently land slightly behind or ahead of the grid.

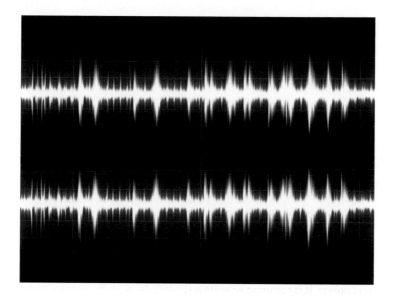

This is what gives that particular groove its push or pull. The live elements of the score can be dragged around as needed to match these push and pull points. It is surprising how a lackluster feel suddenly jumps to life when timing errors are corrected through savvy editing.

Intonation, phrasing, and other intangibles are captured with slight differences from take to take. Scrutinizing various takes of a given line can reveal nuances that may be more or less desirable. Deftly piecing together the best bits from each take can elevate the final result significantly. Narada Michael Waldon produced blockbuster recordings for Whitney Houston and Maria Carey in the 1980s and 1990s. At a songwriting conference in the early 90s, Narada told the audience that most people are not able to articulate when some aspect of a recording is slightly out of tune. But they can feel it. More importantly, they can feel it when the recording is perfectly in tune. That finely tuned sonority draws people in. He described recording dozens of takes of Mariah Carey singing her songs, then editing together one syllable from this take and one syllable from that take, until the final edited vocal performance sounded perfect in every way.[4]

One word of caution about editing. Editing can be like plastic surgery for the score. Done tastefully and with great skill, it can restore damage and enhance the musicality of a recording. If taken too far, it can create an artificial sense of sterility or vacuousness. When done clumsily it can even warp the music into a misshapen oddity.

GUEST LECTURE
MIXING

Bobby Owsinski,
The Mixing Engineer's Handbook

Most great mixers think in three dimensions. They think, "Tall, deep and wide," which means to make sure that all the frequencies are represented; make sure there's depth to the mix, then give it some stereo dimension as well.

Every piece of modern music ... has six main elements to a great mix. They are:

- Balance—the volume level relationship between musical elements
- Panorama—placing a musical element in the sound field
- Frequency Range—having all frequencies properly represented
- Dimension—adding ambience to a musical element
- Dynamics—controlling the volume envelopes of a track or instrument
- Interest—making the mix special.[5]

The reference point can come from ... listening to what other first engineers do, or simply by comparing your mix to some CDs, recordings or [other audio formats] that you know and consider to be of high fidelity.

Mixing

The mixing phase is the last stop for any significant altering of the score. *Mixing* blends all of the disparate music tracks of a given cue into a single, polished musical statement. It involves balancing levels, adjusting EQ, panning and effects processing.

Mixing is an art form in its own right. With an expertly crafted mix, much can be accomplished to bring sparkle and magic to a score. Anything that sounded great after tracking can be enhanced with good mixing. Through the application of interesting effects, new facets of delight can be introduced into the music. Dialing key frequencies in (or out) can bring greater lucidity to an orchestration and clarify foreground, color, accompaniment and background components. Great mixing will shine a spotlight on those parts that are most important and most impressive in a score. Mixing can shape the soundscape of a tune like a sculptor shapes clay into a fine work of art.

On the other hand, a film composer once told a group of master class students, "I have never been satisfied with a mix of my music."[6] Because mixing is the final step for many composers, it represents a moment of finality, where ambition finally grinds to a halt against reality. The original, lofty gem of inspiration has now been cut, crafted, set and polished. Unrealized hopes and expectations from any prior stage—composition, sound selection, layback, tracking and editing—become glaringly obvious here. Bad writing, dated sounds, poorly engineered recordings and amateur performances can never be fixed in the mix. That which is good can certainly be enhanced. But understanding that mixing never replaces quality production in the earlier phases cannot be emphasized enough.

Regardless, mixing can be magical. If the team has worked hard through all phases of production and produced outstanding material, mixing can make a great score sound even better. Here are a few principles that will help video game composers get the best value from their mixes.

- *Aim high*. Contract with the most exceptional, experienced and creative mixing artist possible. Listen to the best-sounding scores and find out who mixed them. Track the mixers down and find out about their rates and availability. Don't be surprised to find that top mixers can cost upwards of a thousand dollars per day. Great mixers aren't limited to soundtrack work either. It can be profitable to work with top mixers from other genres as well. The cross-pollination between genres can generate unexpectedly creative results.
- *Patience*. Mixes in the beginning stages can sound terrible. Sounds are being isolated, balances are out of whack and all kinds of experimentation may be taking place. Be patient with the early stages of the mix. Give mixing artists time to do their work. It is often useful to sit down with the mixer at the beginning of the day to outline a vision and share reference materials, then leave for several hours. By the time the composer returns, there is generally enough progress that the mixer has settled into a direction and the composer can start giving useful feedback.
- *Don't settle*. If a mix leaves you feeling flat, don't hesitate to ask for a different approach. The more specific the feedback, the better.
- *Authority*. If the composer has contracted the mixer, then the composer is the client and

GUEST LECTURE
THE MIXING MYTH

Graham Cochraine, founder of *The Recording Revolution*

Graham Cochraine, founder of the popular recording blog *The Recording Revolution*, makes the point that composers should have high expectations and demand more from the tracking stage of production. He says:

"Pretend like the mixing phase doesn't exist … Before you begin recording you need to think like a producer and know what sounds you want to create in the studio. Once you have that sonic landscape in mind, it's time to make it happen with the tools at your disposal. If upon first listen back your track sounds lackluster, you know one thing and one thing only: you're not done [tracking]. In fact, you should never sign off on your tracks for mixing until they sound great and you are really pleased … Slow down your recording sessions and take the time to really get the sounds you hear in your head."[7]

the client is always king. This means that the composer has every right to direct the mix. Never hesitate to point out something that doesn't sound right. If part of the mix is bothersome now, chances are it will be even more bothersome later. Remember that it is the composer's vision on behalf of the game developer which is being realized. Thus, the composer has every right and obligation to communicate that vision and guide its realization. Of course, common courtesy, tact and a good studio manner are essential. Especially if the composer is pushing creative boundaries and experimenting with new approaches, a cheerful disposition and respectful demeanor will go a long way toward minimizing frustration and help the mixing artist feel like a collaborator.

Mastering

A primary purpose of score mastering is to fashion a consistent sound across the wide breadth of music cues in the score. *Mastering* involves standardizing the perceived loudness and tonality of the score from one cue to the next. That doesn't mean that an exploratory cue should necessarily peg the meters like a combat track. Rather, all tracks of a common function should play at a consistent level. Also, any differences between categories of score should be mastered to play back as intended.

Another purpose of mastering is to put a final sheen on the music production. Picture a beautiful sports car with a dazzling paint job. Mastering is like adding that final coat of wax to really bring out the shine on the car. Mastering engineers utilize high resolution equalization, compression and limiting to achieve these purposes.

Not all mastering engineers are created equal. As in all other aspects of production, there are mastering masters and mastering wannabes, with every gradation in between. If budgets allow, composers are encouraged to pursue mastering engineers who have worked on the best-sounding

CREATIVE AND PRODUCTION PIPELINES

Many publishers create clear separation between "creative" work and "production" work. Often there will be two budget streams, one specifically for composers (based on a per minute rate, deliverables, etc.) and a second budget dealing with production, live recording, mixing, editing and mastering. "It's rare," says Paul Lipson, Senior Audio Director at Microsoft, "that we ask a composer to manage the production side, but rather state preferences while the publisher manages the logistics, budgets, and schedule." Large publishers may also take complete ownership of the technical side of the pipeline. Lipson continues, "Format conversion is almost never asked of the composer, as we usually need high quality masters—and then our internal integrators and technical audio directors decide on engine optimization, codecs, and how to integrate the audio to spec. We handle all of this on the dev side."

scores possible. When budgets are smaller, consider giving a new mastering engineer an opportunity. Some are willing to master a single track for free so composers can judge the quality of their work. It certainly never hurts to ask.

Format Conversion

As the final step in the production process, composers may need to convert their high resolution WAV audio files to the specific format needed for implementation in the game. Popular codecs include AAC, MP3, WMV, OGG VORBIS and CAF. Each codec includes variants that affect file size, sound quality and CPU demands. One minute of uncompressed, 24 bit stereo music at 44.1 kHz requires about 16 MB of storage. There is virtually no hit on the CPU to play an uncompressed audio file and the sound quality is outstanding. The same file compressed as a 128 kbps OGG file won't sound nearly as good and will hit the processor harder to decompress the file. But the memory footprint drops to under 1 MB per minute. Sound effects, dialog, game art, animation and cinematics all require lots of storage space and processor bandwidth. The battle for space and processor turf is a continual struggle. Courteously fighting for the highest quality music file format, balanced against the overall objectives of the game, is a vital concern for video game composers.

It may also possible to use different compression specs for different categories of music. For example, combat music may not need to play back at the same quality standard as menu music or exploration music. Wherever the music is most exposed, that is where the highest quality compression should be used. Where music may be buried under a cacophony of sound effects, smaller footprint compressions may be used.

Beware of simply turning the process over to someone without expertise in audio, perhaps a junior level programmer on the dev team. They tend not to think through nuances of format conversion for music and may simply squash the entire score into the smallest footprint possible, which can wreak havoc on the sound quality. Nothing is worse than pouring immense time and energy into composing and producing a fabulous-sounding score, only to have it reduced to tinny warbling through an unnecessarily aggressive compression codec. The resulting bad translation can be miles away from what the composer intended.

Finding the right balance between the competing priorities of sound quality, file size and processing load is the key to successfully navigating this final stage of game music production. Don't be afraid to go to bat for higher quality sound where it really matters. Players and reviewers who appreciate great game music (and there are legions of them) will be thankful.

It may be helpful for composers to create a spreadsheet to track the various components of production. The example below also includes columns to track progress through iterations and approvals in the composition process. Such organization can save time and headaches.

Track Title	V1	V2	V3	apprvd	music prep	layback	tracked	edited	mixed	edited	format	delivery
battle_01	x	N/A	N/A	x	x	x	x	x	x	x	x	x
battle_01_end	x	N/A	N/A	x	N/A	x	N/A	x	x	x	x	x
battle_02	x	x	N/A	x	x	x	x	x	x	x	x	x
battle_02_end	x	N/A	N/A	x	N/A	x	N/A	x	x	x	x	x
battle_03	x	N/A	N/A	x	x	x	x	x	x	x	x	x
battle_03_end	x	N/A	N/A	x	N/A	x	N/A	x	x	x	x	x
countdown	x	N/A	N/A	x	x	x	x	x	x	x	x	x
dead	x	x	x	x	x	x	x	x	x	x	x	x
dire_lose	x	N/A	N/A	x	N/A	x	N/A	x	x	x	x	x
ganked_lg	x	N/A	N/A	x	N/A	x	N/A	x	x	x	x	x
ganked_med	x	N/A	N/A	x	N/A	x	N/A	x	x	x	x	x
ganked_sm	x	N/A	N/A	x	N/A	x	N/A	x	x	x	x	x
laning_01	x	N/A	N/A	x	x	x	x	x	x	x	x	x
laning_02	x	N/A	N/A	x	x	x	x	x	x	x	x	x
laning_03	x	x	x	x	x	x	x	x	x	x	x	x
dead_buyback	x	x	N/A	x	x	x	x	x	x	x	x	x
radiant_lose	x	N/A	N/A	x	N/A	x	N/A	x	x	x	x	x
respawn	x	N/A	N/A	x	x	x	x	x	x	x	x	x
roshan	x	N/A	N/A	x	x	x	x	x	x	x	x	x
smoke	x	N/A	N/A	x	N/A	x	N/A	x	x	x	x	x
smoke_end	x	x	x	x	N/A	x	N/A	x	x	x	x	x
smoke_hero_end	x	N/A	N/A	x	N/A	x	N/A	x	x	x	x	x
ui_hero_select V2	x	N/A	N/A	*	x	x	x	x	x	x	x	x
ui_main V2	x	N/A	N/A	x	x	x	x	x	x	x	x	x
ui_startup	x	N/A	N/A	x	x	x	x	x	x	x	x	x
victory_dire	x	N/A	N/A	x	x	x	x	x	x	x	x	x
victory_radiant	x	N/A	N/A	x	N/A	x	N/A	x	x	x	x	x

SUMMARY

Music production is the process through which compositions are brought to life sonically and affixed in a recorded medium. This process includes *selecting sounds, layback (including tempo map and click track), sheet music prep, tracking, editing, mixing, mastering* and *format conversion*. Composers should build a core library from the best-sounding samples and most expressive virtual instruments available. Extensive research and ongoing ear training will help. Layback transfers MIDI information to digital audio. Tempo maps and click tracks are also generated during this part of the process.

Clean MIDI files, mp3 mock-ups and some initial articulation and expression notes get sheet music preparation off on the right footing. Tracking captures any live components of the score. Composers should carefully consider the respective pros and cons of various tracking options, including session size and whether or not to conduct. Careful attention should be given to obtain the highest possible quality performances and recordings. With tasteful editing, discrepancies may be corrected and nuances plumbed to piece together the most impactful and expressive tracks possible.

Mixing brings all the individual elements of a score together and melds them into a complete whole. Mixing brings perspective, focus, sparkle and shine to great recordings but cannot compensate for shortcomings in earlier phases of production. Mastering evens out the perceived loudness of a score and brings a final layer of polish to the sound through high resolution equalization, compression and limiting. Format conversion puts the file into game-ready files, balancing the competing priorities of sound quality, file size and processor load.

APPLIED LEARNING

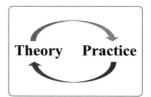

1. Research five commercially available orchestral percussion libraries. List the pros and cons of each.

2. Using the revised score mock-up completed in #6 of the Applied Learning section from the previous chapter, generate a tempo map and click track.

3. Continuing from #2 above, layback all the virtual parts as audio files into a DAW.

4. Select at least one part in the score mock-up to perform live from #2 above. Have a peer create the sheet music for this part using the processes described in this chapter.

5. Produce a recording session to track the part selected in #4 above.

6. Edit the performance to create the most impactful and expressive track possible.

7. Have a colleague mix the piece being produced for this chapter. Follow the guidelines in the text to guide the mixer to achieve your vision.

8. See that the final mix is run through a mastering pass. Adjust the EQ and use compression to optimize the sound of the recording.

9. Convert the mastered music file into three different mp3 formats: 64 kbps, 128 kbps and 256 kbps. Describe the differences in sound quality and file size. If possible, have a software engineer run the files through a game engine, such as Unity, and note the difference in processing bandwidth required for each.

REFERENCES

1. From the Vince Lobardi quote: "Perfection is not attainable; but if we chase perfection we can catch excellence."

2. Nancy C. Andreasen, *The Creating Brain: The Neuroscience of Genius* (New York: Dana Press, 2005).

3. Personal comment made to author at GDC.

4. Author was in attendance and heard the speech.

5. Bobby Owsinski, *The Mixing Engineer's Handbook* (Vallejo, CA: Mix Books, 1999).

6. Author was in attendance and heard the comment. From Merrill Jenson at BYU commercial music master class, January 9, 2014.

7. Audio blog: http://therecordingrevolution.com/2014/02/24/stop-leaving-stuff-for-the-mixing-phase/.

CHAPTER 8

THE PROCESS OF MUSIC IMPLEMENTATION

The best laid schemes o' mice and men, oft go astray ....[1]

The promised joy of a brilliantly devised music design can disintegrate into vaporware without effective music implementation. So much potential, so many magical moments in a game have been dashed to pieces simply because music files were never implemented as designed. To drive the point further, consider that every principle, method, practice and process addressed in this book can be reduced to total irrelevance for the player, without proper music implementation. Yes, implementation is the all-powerful bottleneck through which all else must pass!

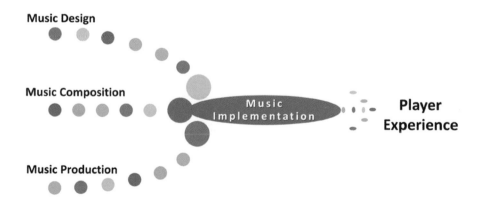

It is ironic that a process so far removed from traditional music scoring—for instance there is no listing for "implementation" in the *Grove* or *Oxford* dictionaries of music—can have such a dramatic impact on the player's musical experience. Thus the importance for video game composers to understand and claim their role in the implementation process.

GUEST LECTURE
OVERSEEING MUSIC
IMPLEMENTATION

Brian Schmidt
(President, Game Audio Network Guild)

One of the key differences between linear media (film, TV, etc.) and games is *integration and implementation,* the process of putting the music into the game itself. Because games are inherently non-linear, the process is not at all straightforward, and needs to be overseen (or ideally performed directly) by the person on the team who best understands the music and how it fits into the game's narrative. That person is *always* the composer.

Abdicating that responsibility to the programmer would be like composing and recording all the cues for a movie still in production, throwing the finished cues onto an FTP site, and hoping that someone else on the team decides to put the music in the right place.

Music implementation describes the series of actions through which music assets are deployed to react with and respond to various triggers in the game's coding. Assets, deployment, triggering, coding ... this sounds more like software engineering than music school. Thus, many video game composers passively check out after music production, delivering all music tracks as contracted and trusting programmers to determine how music should work within the game experience. Does that raise a red flag for anyone?

Without question, someone who understands music scoring should have a hand—a *strong* hand—in steering the music score's implementation in a game. Who better to offer that guiding hand than the score's composer? Yet surprisingly, many video game composers simply relinquish that power, that responsibility, by turning implementation blindly over to the programming team. As a result, composers often cringe when their game comes out and the music implementation bears little resemblance to their original music design.

Video game composers should be loath to give away the right to oversee integration of their music in a game. Decide now to remain involved through each step of implementation. The risk/reward ratio is just too high to do otherwise.

Don't give away your right t

Yet there remains this fact. For many aspiring video game composers, music implementation is a black hole of uncertainty. Even for some veterans, it remains the great question mark in the game scoring equation. Humans tend to fear or avoid the unknown. But understanding even basic steps of implementation can shine a light into this particular black hole, revealing it to not be a black hole at all. Rather, it is a workshop of wonder, where powerful moments of gameplay magic are forged.

One final caveat before diving in. Video games populate a staggering array of devices. A current Wikipedia article on gaming consoles lists nearly two hundred different machines.[2] Add to that total various kinds of personal computers, mobile phones and toys—all of which have slightly different hardware and software requirements—and the landscape can get overwhelming in a hurry. Thus an exhaustive plumbing of each device's details will not be attempted. As always in this text, the preferred approach is to offer an understanding of common principles which apply universally, malleable to tweaking as needed for individual cases as change and circumstance warrant throughout the composer's career.

To begin, this chapter will examine six basic steps of music implementation. For those who aspire to higher technical prowess, a subsequent section on advanced music implementation will follow.

BASIC STEPS OF MUSIC IMPLEMENTATION

There are several common steps involved in most music implementations. These include determining the *signal path*, setting up a *naming convention*, connecting music files to *hooks and triggers* in the game code, specifying *playback behavior*, *testing* and *mixing*.

Signal Path

The term **signal path** should be familiar to most score composers. It is a term that comes from audio production, describing the flow of an audio signal from its source through various processes and finally to an output. In traditional music production, some sounds may be generated from virtual instruments, some may come from outboard hardware synthesizers and still others from live recordings. These disparate signal sources flow through channels of a mixing console (hardware or software), reverbs and delays, EQs, limiters and other kinds of processing. In the end, all the paths converge into the stereo or surround output buses.

Similarly in a game's audio flow, there are various sources from which a music file can originate and different paths through which it can course before finding its way to the player's headphones or speaker array. Thus a first step in the implementation process is determining from which source the music file should originate in the game.

There are three primary sources to consider. In the game's audio flow, music files can originate from: (1) the game's memory, (2) an internal storage source like a drive or (3) an external storage source like a disk, cartridge or cloud server. An office furniture analogy may be helpful.

The game's memory (RAM) is like the top surface of a desk. The rows of drawers surrounding the desk are analogous to internal storage sources. External sources may be compared to large bookshelves or file cabinets sitting behind the desk. Each source offers particular kinds of beneficial functionality and other kinds of limitations.

Consider the table-top analogy first. Whatever items are needed for the present task are brought onto a desk's surface for *quick* and *frequent* access. Similarly, the game's memory loads and stores temporary data for the current game level or game state. This may include artwork, animation, code, sound effects, dialog and music. Internal memory is a relatively small and crowded space, with many assets competing for a share of the table top.

Deciding which, if any, music files to source from the game's memory depends primarily on whether the files are small and if they will be needed *quickly* and *frequently* in the loaded game state. For example, a stinger may fit each of those criteria and could be assigned to sit on the desk's surface, loaded into the game's memory.

On the other hand, long background music tracks are oversized by comparison to other file types in the game. Overwhelming the game's memory with full-length layers of long, looping music files would be a poor use of the desk top. Nor is it necessary, as other and better options exist.

Consider next a gaming system's internal storage, such as a disk or drive. Internal storage may be compared to rows of drawers surrounding the desk. This is where most game assets reside, loaded into these drawers and tucked away until needed on the desk top. It is a good place for music assets to sit which require layering, stacking and crossfading. Most game systems can pull multiple streams of audio simultaneously from internal drives, buffering them into the memory small pieces at a time, discarding them as they are used up and buffering the next chunks. It's like pulling a couple of papers at a time from the open drawers to the desk top for reading, then shuffling them off to make space for the next ones. Most music assets for advanced music designs should be loaded here.

The last location to consider is external storage. External storage may be compared to file cabinets and shelves sitting behind the desk. These are game CDs, DVDs, cartridges, cards or cloud servers. Much content from these sources will be used to fill up the desk drawers or, in other words, loaded into the gaming system's internal storage. But some assets remain on the shelves, accessible even in external storage. For example, a game level requiring only a single track of background music can easily stream directly from the disc. This could be compared to having an iPod docked on top of the file cabinet, with Bluetooth speakers on the desk playing songs back one at a time.

It should be easy by now to recognize the high value of a well-conceived music design. Understanding the logistics of the music score for each game state will help composers determine the best place of origin for each music track in the signal path, whether internal memory, internal storage or external storage.

Naming Conventions

There may be hundreds of music files in a video game. Blithely naming the files from 001 to 999 may not be the best way to keep track of the score, as there will be thousands of other files in the game from art, animation, programming and sound design teams. On the other hand, using flowery descriptive file names such as *Glorious Destiny Fulfilled* and *Anarchy Among the Towers* is not especially useful either. Good naming conventions empower anyone on the project to instantly acquire a basic understanding of the file's type and purpose.

The importance of such conventions becomes clear when considering any of the following scenarios. If a composer quits the project or gets fired halfway through, a logical naming convention will enable the next person to more easily pick up the pieces and go on. If there's a bug in a certain part of the game (there are always bugs), a straightforward naming convention will help troubleshooters quickly identify and isolate relevant files. A systematized naming convention will also offer a handy framework for keeping files organized. Long-running MMOs may contain millions of files. Keeping them organized would be unmanageable without an intelligent system of file names.

So what does a good naming convention look like? A good naming convention will include such details as file category, file function, game location (or other identifier), item number (if there are several in a similar group), version number and file type. Consider the following table.

Category	Function	Identifier(s)	Item #	Version	Type
Music	Exploration	Cosmodrome/Loop	03	v2	Oggvorbis

Mus_Expl_Cosmo_Lp_03_v2.ogg

Imagine that this represents a music file used for exploring the Cosmodrome in *Destiny*. It is a looping music file, the third of five such looping files used for exploration in the area. After some initial revisions, this is the composer's second version of the loop, delivered as an Oggvorbis file. All of that information is packed into a single file name, providing the dev team with a rich snapshot of data in a short string of abbreviations and numbers.

Using this table as a guide, composers can derive similar naming conventions for music in their own projects. Here is an example from *Dinosaurs 3D*: "**Mus_Fight_Raptor_Lp_06_vFnl_Perc.mp3**". What information can be gleaned about this file, just by looking at its name? "**Mus_**": for starters, it is a music file, not a line of narration, a shader effect or an interface graphic. "**Fight_Raptor_**": this music file is used to underscore a velociraptor fight. "**Lp_06_**": it is a looping music file, the sixth such loop for fighting Velociraptors in the game. "**vFnl_**": after any previous revisions, this is the final approved version of the music. "**Perc**": it is a percussion stem only, rather than a mix of the full arrangement. "**.mp3**": the track has been rendered as an mp3 file.

Notice how many important details are revealed instantly about the file, just by looking at its name. Thus, after determining the signal path for a given piece of music, a second step in the implementation process is to set up an effective naming convention for each music file.

Triggers and Hooks

Music in the game has to be told when to start, stop, transition to another track and so on. These logistics will have been planned out while building the game's music design. Connecting the appropriate music files to the game's code is the next step in the process. Programmers on the development team do this by adding triggers for music and creating music hooks in the game code. Without getting overly technical, **hooks** and **triggers** are small pieces of ancillary code which open the game to recognize and respond to designated actions, event occurrences or changing variables set in motion by a player's actions.

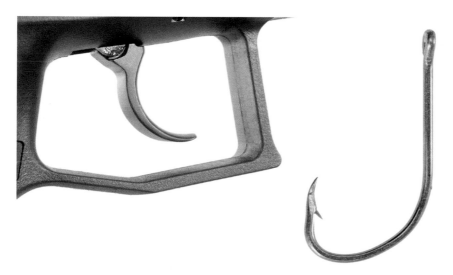

A simple example would be starting the game. The game code may include a trigger that launches a menu music file as soon as the player presses "start". A slightly more complex example might apply for an ambient music set when the player enters a magical forest. The game code for loading the forest level may also include a hook for additional audio coding governing playback of an ambient music set's intro piece and subsequent variants.

It is not the composer's job to write these lines of programming language. But it is the composer's job to communicate clearly and specifically to the engineering team when and where all such music triggers and hooks are needed in the game. This can take on a number of different scenarios. In the best case, a composer will work directly with an audio programmer on the dev team, or other software engineer dedicated to overseeing music implementation throughout the entire game. In another desirable scenario, the composer works closely with an audio director or audio lead on the team, who in turn works with the engineering team to get the right triggers and hooks in place. A worst case scenario would be sending assets blindly over to the developer.

Playback Behavior

With hooks and triggers in place, the next step for the composer is to specify the playback behavior for each music track. *Playback behavior* gets into the nitty-gritty of how coding will handle a given music file. Will it be looped? Will it play once and terminate? Will it fade in? If so, how long is the fade-in? Will it play in sync with other tracks in a layered system? Many of these questions will have ready answers listed in the composer's music design document.

To illustrate, return for a moment to the *Winter Frog Crossing* example from Chapter 3. Recall the gameplay where the player has to move the frog across the road. Here are the relevant sections of the music design document from that specific group of game states:

- *Crossing the Road*—loop Road Crossing layered tracks, randomly choose one, two or three layers for music bed, always play melody, play one of the stingers per crossing for near misses.
- *Slipping*—300 ms pitch bend of tracks a half step up and back (or down and back) randomly in real-time on slipping.
- *Hit by Car*—play one shot of stinger on getting hit, simultaneous 300 ms fade out of Road Crossing tracks.

It is at this stage of implementation that all the pieces of the puzzle really start coming together. Knowing where the music files are located, what they are named, which triggers and hooks they attach to and desired behaviors for each, the composer is now in a position to deliver comprehensive and useful implementation notes to the engineering team, guiding their efforts to unlock the score's potential inside the game. Implementation notes for the *Winter Frog Crossing* music score segments above might look like this.

Game State	File Location	File Name(s)	Trigger/Hook	Behavior
Crossing Road	SD card	Mus_Cross_Layer_Lp_01_ogg Mus_Cross_Layer_Lp_02_ogg Mus_Cross_Layer_Lp_03_ogg Mus_Cross_Layer_Lp_04_ogg	Trigger is frog entering road; hook music code from the event code that moves frog onto the road.	Set up layered looping with these 4 files, under these conditions: —Start and loop all 4 files in sync —Mute layers 1, 2, 3 randomly —Allow no muting as a possibility —Retrigger behavior as loop repeats —Continue looping until one of these disruptive events occurs: —Frog slips —Car hits frog —Frog reaches other side. —When the disruptive event occurs, transition music behavior to matching description in next tables below.
Near Miss	Memory	Mus_NrMiss_Stngr_01_ogg Mus_NrMiss_Stngr_02_ogg Mus_NrMiss_Stngr_03_ogg	Trigger from car entering frog buffer.	Randomly play one of the 3 stinger music files.

Game State	File Location	File Name(s)	Trigger/Hook	Behavior
Frog slips	SD card	Mus_Cross_Layer_Lp_01_ogg Mus_Cross_Layer_Lp_02_ogg Mus_Cross_Layer_Lp_03_ogg Mus_Cross_Layer_Lp_04_ogg	Trigger is frog slipping; hook music code from event code that triggers slipping animation.	Apply pitch bend to all files currently looping. Define bend as a half step (100 cents) linear shift and return occurring in 300 ms. Randomly select 100 cents above or below original pitch for each instance.

Game State	File Location	File Name(s)	Trigger/Hook	Behavior
Car hits frog	Memory	Mus_Hit_Stngr_01_ogg	Trigger from car collision with frog.	Play stinger file one time.
	SD card	Mus_Cross_Layer_Lp_01_ogg Mus_Cross_Layer_Lp_02_ogg Mus_Cross_Layer_Lp_03_ogg Mus_Cross_Layer_Lp_04_ogg	Trigger from car collision with frog.	Simultaneous to stinger playback, fade out all files currently looping. Make fade out 300 ms.

None of the above is written in C#, C++, Python or any number of other popular game coding languages. But the information in each table *is* written in language that software engineers can clearly understand. These implementation notes provide all the relevant information necessary for the engineering team to do its job and write code enabling the composer's music to play back as intended.

Play Testing

Video game composers should play test the games they have been scoring. During the implementation process, the composer should play through areas in the game where music has been implemented. "Isn't it enough," some protest, "to prepare and deliver all these tables of implementation notes we've just been reading about?" In a word, no. If there's one constant in the universe, it is that even "best laid plans" often go astray. The only way to ensure that the music is working correctly is to play through each section and listen. No one else on the team can possibly know the composer's intentions as well as the composer.

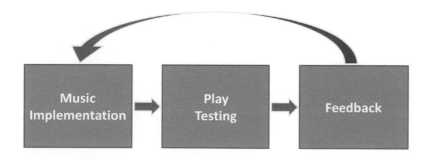

GUEST LECTURE
HOW TO REPORT BUGS
EFFECTIVELY

Simon Tatham,
Professional Programmer

The first aim of a bug report is to let the programmer see the failure with their own eyes. If you can't be with them to make it fail in front of them, give them detailed instructions so that they can make it fail for themselves. In case the first aim doesn't succeed, and the programmer *can't* see it failing themselves, the second aim of a bug report is to describe what went wrong. Describe everything in detail. State what you saw, and also state what you expected to see. Write down the error messages, *especially* if they have numbers included.

By all means try to diagnose the fault yourself if you think you can, but if you do, you should still report the symptoms as well. Be ready to provide extra information if the programmer needs it. If they didn't need it, they wouldn't be asking for it. They aren't being deliberately awkward. Have version numbers [of the game build] at your fingertips, because they will probably be needed.

Write clearly. Say what you mean, and make sure it can't be misinterpreted. Above all, *be precise*. Programmers like precision. [3]

When errors or undesirable surprises are found, the composer relays the problem back to the team. With most developers this process can be formalized through a bug tracking system. Often the dev team will have a dedicated software program which tracks problems, or bugs, in the game and assigns each problem to a member of the team responsible for fixing it. This is a best case scenario for the composer in terms of efficiency and accountability. As the composer is given access to the team's bug tracking software, formal bug reports can be generated within the system.

The next best method of providing feedback is for the composer to generate an independent bug report and send it to the audio programmer or audio director who has been the composer's primary source of interface with the team. The composer's bug report should include all relevant data. Report what happened. Describe what was *supposed* to happen. Include any steps necessary to repeat or reproduce the problem. Attach the original implementation notes and, if necessary, point out any clarifications or modifications of previous instructions given. Use as much clarity and precision as possible. Ask for an estimated turnaround time, so the composer can retest the issue.

Mixing

In the last chapter, music mixing was defined as blending disparate music tracks into a single, polished musical statement. But when discussing music implementation, mixing takes on a slightly different meaning. In this context, *mixing* encompasses all the audio components in a game (dialog/narrative, sound effects/ambience and music), balancing each one against the other in a way that most effectively complements gameplay.

Mixing sound effects and ambience in the game may involve tremendous sophistication, including real-time 3D panning, dynamic EQ, occlusions, signal processing, etc. However, with the game's music score, most processing choices are already baked-in during production. Most games use the music score as emotional subcontext, playing in the background. In the case of surround systems, the music generally plays from the front left and front right speakers, sometimes adding reverb from the score into the back left and back right speakers. Stereo systems typically deliver music across the left and right channels. There are more complex game music mixes here and there, of course. And some of those exceptions, when pulled off, can be exceptional. But from the composer's perspective, the key responsibility to attend to during the game's audio mix is to make sure the music doesn't lose emotional impact by getting stomped on and buried by sound and narrative.

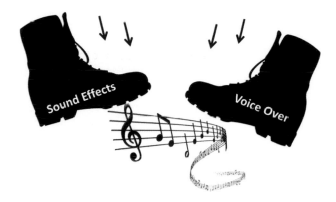

ADVANCED MUSIC IMPLEMENTATION

For more technically wired composers, there are advanced avenues of implementation to be explored as well. Sophisticated middleware programs, so named because they bridge the traditional gap between composing and coding, put more control over implementation directly into the hands of music makers. Dev teams still create hooks for the middleware, but once the software hooks are in place, the composer is empowered to build and test music behaviors independently, without relying on an external coder.

As of this writing, the two juggernauts of the audio middleware world are Wwise from Audiokinetic and FMOD from Firelight Technologies. Both are capable of delivering a wide range of music behaviors, ranging from simple looping to complex music reconstruction based on algorithms. Each is available for free download and experimentation. Both update regularly to interface with the newest versions of

audiokinetic®

GUEST LECTURE
GENERATIVE MUSIC ARRANGING IN WWISE

Guy Whitmore
(*Peggle 2, Bejeweled 3, Fable 2*)

In *Peggle 2* every sound you hear is perfectly tuned, in harmony with every other sound, every musical phrase, everything you do. It is, in essence, a symphony. And it is all created in real-time, adjusting on the fly to your every action, automatically, by the Wwise engine. Says Whitmore,

"[Wwise] is an algorithmic arranger, based on the gameplay. It is taking all those elements and rearranging them in real time … A lot of the rhythmic power and logic happens right in [Wwise], which makes it easier for the programmers. They're just sending these very simple state calls or switches, logic calls, that we interpolate … We assign what music should play at any given point in time, based on those calls."

It's basically a script, giving Wwise different options for different circumstances. Once the game is running, the engine takes control, playing music according to the script, then improvising based on variations. Wwise is simply selecting musical segments from its library, layering them over the sections of music already playing, perfectly in synch with the beat and in the proper key. It is one of those things that, when you hear it, sounds natural.[5]

all popular gaming systems. Basic tutorials in both programs are available on the book's website (www.FocalPress.com/cw/Thomas). A wide range of more advanced tutorials are available online from the developers, as well as a number of third-party experts.

Looping Options

Using these tools, a three and a half minute music track can be programmed to do much more than play through and start over. Consider the following music file:

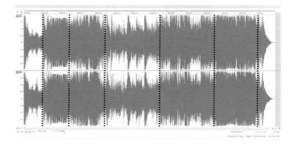

From the shape of the waveform itself, it appears that this piece of music is structured in sections. That is exactly the case, as the piece includes an intro, a combat loop, a theme statement, a transition section, a second combat loop, a boss combat loop and a tag.

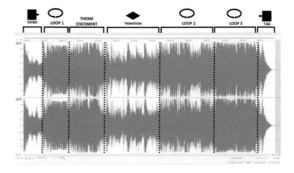

Each section could be broken out as an individual music file for building-block deployment. Or, using sophisticated looping functionality available in middleware, the composer could specify a number of sequential behaviors. For example, a new game state triggers the start of the music file. The intro plays once, then flows directly into loop 1. Loop 1 continues during combat until the player wins. After winning, the music continues through a single statement of the theme. Then the transition section follows, playing straight through into a second combat loop. The second loop continues until the game state changes again, moving onto the third combat loop. As combat concludes, the music flows directly into the tag and concludes.

As complex as this sounds, its functionality is within the reach of any composer. Using an example in FMOD, the composer sets up markers for each section, three "nested" loops and a brief script for each game state.

Generative Music Possibilities

Moving beyond looping—way, *way* beyond looping—lies many a technically minded composer's holy grail of generative music. Brian Eno famously defined generative music as "compositions which change every time they're played as the systems behind them introduce some sort of randomness."[4] Video game composers might modify that definition. For them, *generative music* is music which changes relevantly each time it's played, as the underlying systems detect musically significant game state changes.

GUEST LECTURE
GENERATIVE MUSIC CREATION IN FMOD

Stephan Schütze
(*Flight of the Bumble Bee, Barnyard, Polar Express*)

One of the principal purposes of audio middleware is to provide functionality that would otherwise require significant programmer time to implement. I am currently creating the music system for a game project that, without a middleware solution, would have taken weeks to months of a programmer's schedule and cost many thousands of dollars to create.

As far as I know, the kind of music system I set out to create has never been attempted before. I spent months designing the music system for the game before I even started working with sound files. The process has involved a lot of trial and error as I test the boundaries of what is possible and what sounds good. This system assembles music down to the note level, so the design needs to allow the composer to edit and adapt at each level without having to rebuild the entire project each time.

To create this system I used a feature available in FMOD Studio called a Reference Event. Events in Studio are used to produce sounds. A Reference Event is unique in that each instance of the Event serves as a kind of copy of the original. Any changes made to the source Event are reflected in all instances of the Reference Event.

195

For example, to create a drum rhythm, I create an Event containing a single drum strike. Then, every time I want a drum note, I use a Reference Event that refers back to the original single drum strike.

This means that if I create four Reference Events to make a four-note drum pattern, I can easily adjust it when required. If I decide that each of the four notes is too loud, I simply adjust the original Event, and all instances of the reference event update automatically. I can make changes to individual Reference Events without affecting the others, but any changes to the original Event are reflected across all related Reference Events.

In creating the drum rhythms, the individual notes themselves are tuned to maximize resource efficiency. Minor randomization of pitch and volume can reduce the sense of repetition when using the same sound file. Randomizing frequency-based levels with a simple three-band EQ module improves this effect significantly.

Beyond randomization, it is actually possible to simulate a range of velocity effects with the same type of effect module. A drum strike at fortissimo can actually be modified to simulate lesser velocity notes. The difference between a fortissimo strike and a mezzo piano strike is more than just volume. By reducing the high and mid-frequency content of the sound you can reduce the hard, sharp edge of the sound. By increasing the low frequency content and reducing the overall volume it is possible to modify a single fortissimo strike so that you can create *ff*, *mf*, *mp* and even *p* notes from a single sound file. This process does not work perfectly for all instrument sounds, and the values you use for a drum may be very different than the values you use for a harp, but the concept is sound.

So, this system takes a single sound file and, where necessary, alters the values of pitch, volume and frequency weighting and places it on a timeline with a tempo and time signature. Combining this with other notes means you can create complex rhythms.

Guy Whitmore's work on *Peggle 2* won a Game Audio Network Guild Award for Best Interactive Score in 2014. Utilizing the scripting capabilities within Wwise, he was able to define parameters for selecting pieces of the score's arrangement based on specific gameplay events. The result is a score that flows with the player's decisions with such fluidity and responsiveness, it feels as if it were through-composed to the player's actions.

Stephan Schütze is another technically minded composer who has learned to exploit the power of middleware. For his work on a recent game, Stephan utilized the functionality available in FMOD to design a music score that unfolds anew each time the game is played, responding to micro-level changes in player behavior, stitching together a newly relevant and responsive score each time.

Proprietary Software

Many of the bigger video game publishers have devised proprietary software which their development teams use to implement music in their games. Electronic Arts, Sony PlayStation and Square Enix are three examples of such publishers. While freelance composers are not always given direct access to these programs, the respective in-house audio teams generally have enough experience with the proprietary tools to handle some very ambitious processes.

Sometimes a developer will build music software specifically for a given title or franchise. If this is the case, composers may need to work directly with a senior engineer responsible for overseeing the game's code. This can create a bottleneck of its own. Top engineers are always working on tasks of the highest importance to the game's critical path. Sophisticated music implementation is rarely considered part of a game's critical path. It can be difficult to get the attention of these top programmers, let alone their time. But dogged persistence, persuasiveness and creative problem solving from the composer can help break open the bottleneck, sometimes resulting in pioneering achievements.

SUMMARY

There are a number of paths implementation can take. Many development studios use proprietary systems to deploy their music assets in the game. Other developers use third-party programs which composers can access through the dev's audio team or learn on their own. Because the game industry is continually courting and developing new technologies, additional paths will continue to evolve in the years yet to come. Just as understanding principles of signal flow in audio production equip the educated to successfully find their way through successive generations of new gear, so too an understanding of implementation principles will help guide composers through myriad implementation processes, adjusting to variations as needed on the fly.

Music implementation has a staggering impact on the way a game's music is experienced by the player. Composers are encouraged in the strongest possible terms to remain on a project through completion of the implementation process. Basic steps of implementation include determining a *signal path*, setting up a good *naming convention*, connecting music files to *hooks and triggers* in the game's code, specifying *playback behavior*, play *testing* and *mixing*.

Even the start time of each note can have minute randomization applied so the start of each note may be delayed by a few milliseconds. The end result is that an eight-bar rhythm pattern will play, but with enough variation of each note that, even when set to looping, the eight bars do not sound like an eight-bar phrase set to loop. They sound like eight bars of music being performed repeatedly as if a human was performing them, as each note is subtly unique and the overall timing is less than computer perfect.

This music system combines an eight-bar drum phrase, with other eight-bar drum phrases based on the data provided by the game. Tempo or stylistic changes and even instrument choices can all change dynamically on a beat to match the actions occurring in the game. The drum lines are then layered with bass, melody and chord harmonies. These are all created at the note level, but are designed to layer together and change dynamically when needed. Individual layers can change, so a consistent drum rhythm can play while key changes occur in the chord layers, or melodic content can change from one instrument to another. The entire musical score can adapt on a beat to provide underscoring for the events of the game, support the narrative and enhance the player's experience as they play through the game.

The non-linear nature of games means that it is impossible for the composer to predict how a player will act and what thematic material will best support the narrative at any particular time. This method of composition/implementation or *"complementation"* is a natural progression of the skills needed to create content for interactive projects. Even better, the system does this without intensive programmer time, and minimizing the use of resources for music. The result is dynamic, responsive, resource-friendly music on any platform.

This entire field is very new and the possibilities for future composers are incredible and exciting!

GUEST LECTURE
EA TOOLS AND INTERACTIVE MUSIC IN SSX

Gordon Durity
(SSX, Madden Football 25, NHL 14)

For SSX we wanted to have user music remixed on the fly based on gameplay, akin to a "virtual DJ". DSP processes such as beat detect, filters, simple delays, interpolating delay lines and amplitude modulation are possible and controlled by event and parameter data coming from the game and processed through the music context system. The end result was a very satisfying experience of having the players' music remixed based purely on how they play the game and what mode they're in.

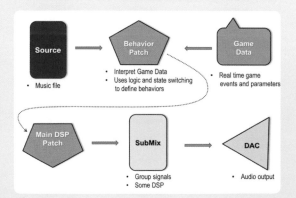

Short music files needed quickly and frequently may be effectively loaded into the game's internal memory. Most music files, especially those required by advanced music designs, are loaded into a game's internal storage where they are cached as needed, pieces at a time, in and out of memory. Some music files can remain in external storage, streamed for playback one at a time.

Good naming conventions should convey a file's category, function, game location (or other identifier), item number, version number and file type. These should be represented in a brief string of abbreviations and numbers. Music files connect to the game through hooks and triggers added by the dev's programming team. Specific music behaviors defined in the game's music design are conveyed by the composer through implementation notes, often aided by the tables included in this chapter. The effectiveness of implemented hooks, triggers and behaviors should always be verified through play testing by the composer, with revisions communicated as clearly as possible. Composers are encouraged to weigh in on the game's audio mix as well, to ensure that the score's impact is not lost.

More advanced options are available to composers through third-party middleware programs and in-house implementation software, whether generalized tools or custom designed. In all cases, composers are encouraged to approach the implementation challenge with determination, creativity and the highest possible standards.

APPLIED LEARNING

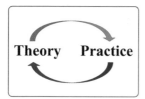

1. Recommend a signal path source, whether internal memory, internal storage or external storage, for each music file in a single level, as required by the music design created in Applied Learning question #2 in Chapter 3.

2. Play any level of any game, and identify any piece of music in that game level. Fill out a naming convention summary table for that music. Create a file name that fulfills the key functions of naming conventions, as outlined in this chapter.

3. Working with a programming student or game developer, specify any needed triggers or hooks for the music files in #1 above.

4. Create music implementation notes for each music file in #1 above using the implementation table format in this chapter.

5. If three of the music files from #1 above were not playing back properly, what would an effective bug report look like? Write this report.

6. Download the FMOD and Wwise client programs: http://www.fmod.org/download/ and https://www.audiokinetic.com/downloads/. Explore. Experiment. Play!

All of these behaviors were achieved using our in-house audio tools. Game data for jumps, velocity, vector, tricks, etc., would inform a Behavior Patch, triggering DSP chains for EQ filter sweeping, band pass or notch filtering, delays, modulation, distortion, pitch changes, you name it. Whatever effects we felt would make the player feel the action as they were living it in-game, in real-time, that was the chain we set up inside our tools.

7. Using the online tutorials on the book's website (www.FocalPress.com/cw/Thomas), learn how to execute the following functions in FMOD and Wwise:

   a. Play a music file.

   b. Loop a music file.

   c. Set up an additive three-layered loop. Fade in and fade out layers on triggers.

   d. Set up and play a nested loop.

   e. Create the following, with smooth transitions between each scoring block:

   Intro block—Three-layered loop—Nested loop—Tag block.

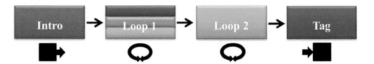

REFERENCES

1. Robert Burns, poem "To a Mouse" (1785), Stanza 7. New English interpretation from original Scots.

2. http://en.wikipedia.org/wiki/List_of_video_game_consoles.

3. http://www.chiark.greenend.org.uk/~sgtatham/bugs.html.

4. http://www.wired.co.uk/news/archive/2012-09-28/brian-eno-peter-chilvers-scape.

5. http://www.polygon.com/features/2013/12/11/5174562/making-peggle-2.

BUSINESS

CHAPTER 9
TUNING UP FOR BUSINESS

All organizations are perfectly designed to get the results they are getting.[1]

There is an iconic sound that fills the soul of every classical music lover with anticipation. It is a sound made by all orchestras across the world prior to beginning a concert. It is the sound of musicians bringing their disparate instruments into alignment, each making their own great or small adjustments so that all parts will play in perfect tune one with another. It is unabashedly cacophonous. But even amid the chaos, one senses an awakening of the tuned resonances, the upper harmonics, the sympathetic vibrations, the sheer emotive power of finely tuned voices soon to fill the hall. Yes, there is a growing hint of inevitable purposing in this familiar sound. The clamor subsides. The dissonance dissolves. A stillness settles in. The orchestra is tuned up. It's time for the performance to begin.

So it is with the education of aspiring video game composers. Students collect disparate pieces of preparation scattered across the disciplines of music, art, language, science, philosophy, math, psychology, marketing, accounting, economics, management and technology. The learning can seem disorderly, irrelevant, even cacophonous at first. But inevitably, almost imperceptibly, each piece of the puzzle finds its proper place. The clamor subsides. Dissonances dissolve. A confidence settles in. The composer is tuned up. It's time for the performance to begin.

This chapter surveys many of the scattered components which must be gathered and tuned for a prosperous, long-term career as a video game composer. The vantage point is that of a successful freelancer. This is a broad view which may include some details not applicable to every composer in every circumstance. Not to worry. Underlying principles are portable and can be extracted for application to any number of differing situations.

THE PUZZLE

Tuning up for business is like completing a puzzle. There are so many pieces to figure out. At times, it looks like some pieces don't fit anywhere at all. Yet, there seems to be an inevitable tug toward synthesis in human intelligence. The longer the mind focuses on the puzzle, the more time spent fitting one piece with another, the longer and more thoughtfully a person chips away at the problem … the more likely each piece will find its proper place. Finally the big picture emerges. All puzzles yield to persistent effort.

PUZZLE PIECES

As many young schoolchildren know, solving a puzzle becomes easier once the corner and edge pieces are in place. For the composer's business, such framework pieces would include the *workplace, storefront, back office, community, skillset* and *personal character*. Each category will be examined along with its several components.

Workplace

Every composer needs a place to work and tools to work with. Startup capital and a plan for periodic reinvestment will be needed. At the minimum, a composer will need a computer hosting a pro-grade sequencing/DAW program, a core collection of quality sound sources (see Chapter 7) and a pair of studio-grade headphones. Initial capital for such a system will range between $2,000 and $3,500. This is a paltry sum of money compared to the startup costs of most businesses. Little wonder that *USA TODAY* reported composers and music directors as the third fastest growing job category in America.[2]

As the composer's business starts to generate income, upgrading to the next level of tools may be desirable. Common next steps include more and better sound sources, a diversity of audio shaping plugins and higher computing power. An $8,000 budget could provide a powerful computing tower and monitor, three to five new virtual instruments and a dozen high quality DSP plugins. The composer may also want to hear music played back in a room, rather than just through headphones. This requires amplification, speakers, stands and possibly a mixer. Prices for most powered monitoring speakers range from $150 to $10,000 each. Costs for project studio mixing consoles range between $1,000 and $20,000. Looking down the road, high end speakers can run north of $20,000 apiece, with top recording studio consoles reaching into six and seven figures. Every kind of addition to functionality, quality and quantity will require software and/or hardware purchases and upgrades. Each level of upgrade should be planned judiciously based on a strategic business need or opportunity, rather than upgrading because of gear lust, envy or sales pressure.

Now consider the work space itself. Composing requires imagination, focused listening, acoustic clarity and long hours. Ideally the work space will be spacious, quiet, acoustically treated, aesthetically pleasing and comfortable. Meeting these requirements puts the composer in the best possible situation to be successful.

But costs for suitable spaces can be a considerable road block. Composers just starting their careers may live in a small apartment and lack funding for an external studio. Where dollars fall short, ingenuity must make up the difference. There is certainly precedent for this in the game industry. For example, Darren Korb famously turned the closet in his one-bedroom apartment into a recording studio for *Bastion*. The score was composed in his bedroom. Guitars, ukulele, bass and voice were all recorded in his closet, surrounded by clothes and bedding to provide a measure of dampening and isolation. *Bastion*'s music struck a chord with fans and media alike, becoming a popular and critical hit.

By contrast, the music score for *Infamous: Second Son* was created at Sony PlayStation's state of the art sound studio in Foster City. The room is floated for sonic isolation. It is spacious, acoustically sound, silently air conditioned and wired for any possibility. Beyond all that, it looks really cool. The music from *Infamous: Second Son* has also generated rave reviews.

GUEST LECTURE
AVOIDING THE UPGRADE TRAP

Adam Gubman
(*Bejeweled, Super Hero Squad, Just Dance*)

I was dirt poor when I first started out. I'd buy McD's cheeseburgers when they had the nickel deals and save them in the fridge. I had Top Ramen for dinner every other meal and whatever frozen things I could find at the gas station. I was teaching while dreaming of a career in music. The little money I had certainly couldn't go towards gear.

With my old PC running Cakewalk and an all-in-one sample library, I had to focus on production skills, great arrangements and mixing. I had to put extra effort into making sure my work had the utmost integrity, diminishing the focus on my lack of quality gear. I learned that I could do great work even without top tier equipment, gradually upgrading as my budget allowed and business needs dictated.

I've now got more than 600 game titles under my belt. I continue to invest some of my earned income back into my studio (as any composer should), but only if I feel that the purchase provides enough character and flexibility to warrant reuse. I don't view my purchases as toys, but rather as investments that *must* generate a return greater than the purchase price. Otherwise, I won't even consider the purchase.

While these two scores are strikingly different, each of the composers made the best possible use of the work spaces and tools at their disposal. *Infamous: Second Son* could not have come from Darren Korb's apartment. The workspace requirements for that score were too far beyond its reach. But an argument could be made that *Bastion*'s score could not have come from Sony's studio either. The *Bastion* score was conceived, developed and produced within the limitations of the workplace. Perhaps if those limitations hadn't existed, a very different score may have been attempted. In any case, a composer's workplace can wield a shaping influence on the direction and form of the music score. Or to phrase it differently, every workplace is perfectly designed to get the results it gets.

With that in mind, composers need to think carefully about how they want to gear up for business. Between $2,000 and $3,000 can assemble a bare bones setup. An additional $8–10,000 can bring the composer out of the box and up to the next level. But as composers progress in their careers, their tools and work spaces should evolve in the direction that takes them *where they want to go*, helping them grow in their craft and meeting the needs of their existing and targeted clientele. All of this should be done in a balanced, judicious way. There is no need to throw away viable tools just because something new comes out. A screwdriver can still turn a screw, regardless of the color of its handle.

Storefront

Storefront is an old school term left over from brick and mortar days. But it captures the right idea for an important corner piece of a composer's business. The **storefront** presents the composer to the world as he or she wants to be perceived. It ranges from how he dresses in public to what kinds of social media posts she makes.

This includes the composer's website, networking activities, business cards, public relations and formal representation. It may reflect a carefully constructed and cohesive image, or it may be cobbled together completely at random.

The fact is, all composers have a storefront, whether they conscientiously construct one or not. All composers give off an impression of themselves to others, both privately and publicly. The question is whether that impression is what the composer intended. Just as video game scores benefit from a well-conceived music design, so composers will benefit from the deliberate planning and execution of a storefront strategy to ensure that the message being broadcast is accurate, effective and desirable. A composer's storefront strategy may also be referred to as **branding**.

Consider the public websites of two video game composers, Kevin Riepl and Rich Vreeland:

Each website immediately conveys specific impressions about the composer. Browsers would surmise that Kevin's music is dark, heavy and action oriented while Rich makes music that is playful, bouncy and cute. Exploring the music sections of each site proves such first impressions to be true. Both composers have done an excellent job reflecting their musical style in their storefront.

Think of the website as an online sales brochure. Every page can paint a clearer picture of the composer. Every page can move a client closer to a hiring decision. Consider the questions potential clients might ask in their composer search. What games has the composer scored? The website should have a credits section listing the composer's game credits. This could be a text listing or it could include graphics. It could be in chronological order, or listed by popularity. Has the composer won any awards? If so, there should be an awards section on the site. What does the music sound like? Ah yes, the music. This should be the centerpiece of the composer's site.

PEEK BEHIND THE CURTAIN

Showcasing Music on Your Website

When a potential client lands on your website, you want them to find exactly what they want, and to find it quickly. One way to facilitate this is to organize your music by category.

This is the music section of the HUGEsound website. All music samples on the site are organized into useful scoring categories. Clients can instantly find whichever style of music they are looking for at the click of a button. Once a client clicks on a category, for example ACTION, immediately a list of action music cues appears.

The first track begins playing automatically. The category continues playing each track in the list unless another track is clicked. Notice that each music selection is brief. People tend to move quickly while browsing. Each track is edited for maximum

Music should be accessible easily and frequently throughout the site, with at least one section devoted entirely to music samples. These music samples should be well organized, eye-catching and, of course, impressive to the ears.

While fans may listen to everything a composer has ever written from start to finish, busy developers may only listen to the first few seconds of a music sample. If one music sample doesn't grab them right away, the smart composer will have another option instantly accessible. This is a powerful benefit to presenting music samples by category. It takes advantage of human nature. Remember, the primary purpose of having music samples on a website is to move potential clients toward a hiring decision.

All facets of a composer's online presence may be seen in this light. The YouTube channel is another page in the composer's sales brochure. The Facebook Timeline is another page in the composer's sales brochure. The LinkedIn Profile is another page in the composer's sales brochure. IMDB, iTunes, Bandcamp, Soundcloud, Tumblr and other outlets that become relevant to the game industry are just added pages to the composer's sprawling sales brochure. Every part of the online persona can be tuned to reflect the unified messaging that the composer wants the world to receive. Every piece of the online puzzle should be designed to move potential clients one step closer to a hiring decision. The website makes an ideal hub for all online activity, with links to each of the composer's scattered outlets.

Social media deserves some additional scrutiny here. It is important to pay attention to where people gather. It is also important to notice when they migrate to a new gathering place. A noted music agent once spent considerable time and energy setting up an online presence for composers on MySpace just as the target audience had shifted to Facebook. Facebook's younger demographic in turn has embraced Snapchat, Instagram, Tumblr, WhatsApp and others. Twitter has proven to be an effective tool for many composers in reaching game developers. Social media is an important and constantly shifting landscape. It requires the composer's vigilance and periodic reassessment.

YouTube has been one of the more consistent and effective outlets for game music composers to share their work. YouTube makes it easy to upload game levels, cinematics, montages, behind-the-scenes clips, interviews, etc. Hearing the music a composer has scored while watching the accompanying game or cinematic sends the strongest possible message about the composer's competency and effectiveness. Composers are encouraged to create a YouTube channel, populate it with impressive examples of their work, and feature it prominently in their storefront strategy until the next better option comes along. As a reminder, the composer's presence on YouTube and any other social media channels should always include links back to the composer's website.

Another part of the composer's storefront is the business card. At conferences, meetings and other kinds of networking events, a business card is like a personal billboard in miniature. It should broadcast a key selling proposition and include the composer's name and contact information. Every composer needs a business card as part of being well put together. It can be uncomfortable to be caught without one when an important networking moment arrives. In that sense, a business card is like deodorant. Its use is expected. Its absence can be awkward.

impact. You want to put your best foot forward. The music flow should be explosive, showing your best work from one track to the next. After finishing the selected category, the website automatically opens the next category, in this case THEMATIC, and continues playing:

This proved to be a highly effective method for showcasing music to potential clients on the web. It was also cost effective to develop. I was able to prepare the complete design, flow and functionality for the music player on my own. Then I hired a really smart guy to write the back end for me. My out-of-pocket cost was around $250. This was such an intuitive and useful innovation when it came out in 2004 that it was nominated for a G.A.N.G. award in the category of Best Website Audio.

Video game composers should also dress for success. In the game industry, that usually means comfortable—comfortable for the composers and comfortable for those around them. A photo of the *Diablo III* sound and music team is a case in point.

Loose, comfortable, casual is the order of the day. And yet there is always room for individuality. When the author appeared on stage to conduct the Utah Symphony for Video Games Live in 2014, host Tommy Tallarico announced that in all of VGL's history, this was the first time anyone had ever worn a tuxedo. The audience erupted in spontaneous applause. Casual may be the order of the day, but composers should also feel the freedom to be themselves. As with all other aspects of the composer's storefront, personal appearance sends a message.

This messaging will take on a broader reach as the composer engages with the media during interviews and features. These articles can remain on the internet for years, even decades. They typically include pictures, quotes and sometimes samples of the composer's work. As such, they can be powerful messengers for the composer, sometimes reaching thousands or even millions of people. Such publicity is generally considered beneficial, though it can be difficult to pin a definitive value on it. If 20,000 people read an interview but none of them are ever in a position to influence a composer-hiring decision, how valuable was the exposure? It is an unanswerable question, because no one can predict who will read the article and what future actions may be influenced. Some composers hire publicity specialists to drum up articles and interviews for them. Others handle PR themselves. Whatever the case, widespread publicity is part of the composer's extended storefront and should fall under the same strategic scrutiny in presenting his or her image to the world.

A good music agent can also assist the composer in developing, honing and maintaining an effective storefront. Indeed, having an agent sends a message all by itself. In addition, agents have their own storefronts, and joining an agent's stable adds another circle of influence to the composer's reach into the industry.

Back Office

While the storefront helps bring customers in the door, setting up an organized back office will keep those doors open. The back office includes contracts, accounting, tax planning, budgeting and ongoing education. These are the unglamorous underpinnings that keep a composer viable and operating as a business.

Contracts define the understanding between a composer and a client. Key items that might be misinterpreted, misunderstood or unacceptably altered by either party should be addressed in the contract. These range from payment amounts and terms to rights of ownership, usage and publicity. Contracting is so important that a chapter will be devoted to it later on in the book (see Chapter 11). A composer should never start working on a new game score without a good contract in place.

Once the contract is signed by both parties, an invoice is sent to the client for a deposit payment. Free invoice templates are available all over the internet. Alternatively, a composer may design a custom invoice. The best invoice designs are clean, easy to read and contain all the relevant information related to the transaction. These include total contract price, future payments, current amount due, payment currency and where to send it. They may also include some graphic or messaging which reinforces a key selling proposition for the composer. Here is a sample invoice from the author's business.

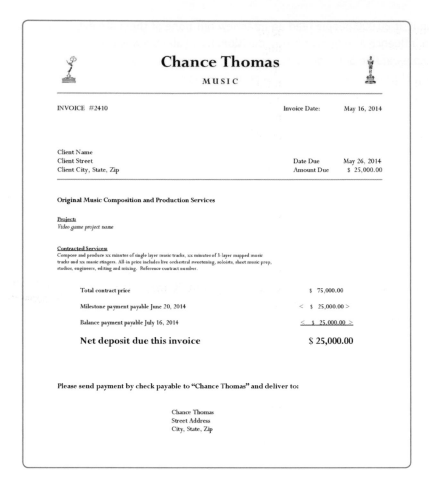

Chance Thomas

MUSIC

INVOICE #2410   Invoice Date: May 16, 2014

Client Name
Client Street   Date Due   May 26, 2014
Client City, State, Zip   Amount Due $ 25,000.00

Original Music Composition and Production Services

Project
Video game project name

Contracted Services
Compose and produce xx minutes of single layer music tracks, xx minutes of 3-layer mapped music
tracks and xx music stingers. All-in price includes live orchestral sweetening, soloists, sheet music prep,
studios, engineers, editing and mixing. Reference contract number.

Total contract price	$ 75,000.00
Milestone payment payable June 20, 2014	< $ 25,000.00 >
Balance payment payable July 16, 2014	< $ 25,000.00 >
Net deposit due this invoice	**$ 25,000.00**

Please send payment by check payable to "Chance Thomas" and deliver to:

Chance Thomas
Street Address
City, State, Zip

The awards images in the header send a strong message without saying a word. The invoice is numbered for easy tracking and record keeping. Current and due dates are listed at the top, along with the amount due. This is a deposit invoice, so the customary thirty-day payment turnaround is shortened to ten days. The body of the invoice contains the project name and a brief description of the relevant services. The contract number or name is also referenced. Total contract price is listed at the top, with future payments listed and subtracted from the total. This particular contract was divided into three payments, a deposit, a milestone and a balance. Each amount is listed for clarity, with the current due balance typed in a bold and enlarged font size. Payment instructions are included at the bottom. The composer's website, phone number and address are all included in the footer of the invoice, not shown here.

Invoices are meant to solicit payment. When payment arrives, the composer needs a banking account to put it in. Some composers incorporate, setting up corporate accounts and tax IDs completely separate from their personal finances. There can be tax incentives and other benefits to this, including transparency, fiscal compartmentalization and protection of personal assets from liability. Other composers operate as self-employed professionals, adding a professional account at their bank or credit union for music-related earnings and expenses.

In either case, income and expenses related to composition must be tracked separately and independently from any other income-producing activities the composer is involved with. This is primarily because of tax laws and obligations which impact the composer annually. But it may also become relevant in other circumstances, such as seeking outside investment, applying for credit or selling the business to a third party. Having a bank account dedicated to the composer's business helps keep that business siloed financially.

Tax obligations come due quarterly for corporations and annually for sole proprietors. But even annual payees may need to make quarterly estimated payments. As a result, a current accounting of income and expenses is required throughout the year. Commercial accounting applications like QuickBooks, Wave, Nola Pro and others are available which provide templates, tutorials and built-in calculators. Composers may also design their own accounting ledgers using Excel, Lotus or other spreadsheet software. Old schoolers may even prefer a bound paper accounting ledger. Many tools are available for recording income and expenses.

There are some key things to consider in tracking the flow of money through the composer's business. Income accounting should include the amount, source and date of all music-related income. Expenses should include the amount, type and date of all music-related expenses. Some expense categories will require additional scrutiny and processing, such as automobile

BUSINESS CREDIT CARD

It may be useful to have a credit card used only for business purchases. This facilitates the separation between personal and business spending. Statements become an effective record and proof of business expenses for tax and accounting purposes.

expenses and home office expenses. Tax law requires calculating the percentage of business use compared to personal use in both cases. Any record-keeping system set up by the composer should take all of these requirements into account.

The composing business is notoriously a feast and famine proposition. Income can be wildly sporadic and arrive in chunks. There can be long dry spells between scoring contracts. Money must be managed very carefully. That generally implies having a budget. Many composers will arrange to pay themselves a consistent and modest sum each month, while client payments stockpile in the business account. This makes things easier for personal or family budgeting as the amount withdrawn for personal use is predictable month after month. If there is a surplus at the end of the year, composers can always give themselves a raise or a bonus.

Regular and recurring business expenses such as internet and phone services, studio space and utilities, contracted purchase payments, insurance and other such items should be planned for and covered in a company budget. An amount should also be set aside for periodic business trips, conferences, advertising and promotion. Big ticket items such as studio upgrades may need to wait for a substantial project to come along. Alternatively, careful planning and patience may allow large enough amounts to accumulate over time.

One word of caution. Debt is depicted in many clip art drawings as crushing, entrapping, binding, squeezing, drowning and otherwise ruining a perfectly good life. It may be better to patiently build up equipment and other aspects of the business as extra income becomes available, rather than taking on unnecessary

debt. Even a high profile, award-winning and lucrative score one year does not necessarily mean the composer will produce an equally lucrative income the following year. The video game business is volatile. Predicting future income may be no more accurate than looking into a wishing well. Fiscal caution is advised, especially when it comes to debt.

One final point of back office discussion is the need for ongoing education. The world changes continually, sometimes chaotically and always unpredictably. Time and sometimes money are needed for regular investment in the composer's evolving quest for knowledge. Knowledge is an enabling power, opening new doors and bringing renewal to the mind. It is the only way the composer will be able to evolve with the changing times. Inertia is the enemy of education. To take it a step further, many people avoid learning new skills and techniques (or even reviewing foundational principles) because of laziness or fear. Fight those vices as if career success depends on it. Because, to one extent or another, it actually does.

Community

A composer's *community* includes those family members, friends, mentors and peers who build up, advise and support the composer. The community, at least as it pertains to this chapter, consists of those people who have the composer's back. Building such a community is important for all businesses, but perhaps especially so for composers. Video game composers spend massive blocks of time working alone in their studios. Yet human beings are social creatures and share a need to belong. A sense of connection to others is critical.

Delivering a new score can feel risky for a composer. It is an act of tremendous vulnerability to put music out there for the world to judge. Rants and flamers abound, and some people love to target creative endeavors for abuse. A cheering section of loyal friends and supporters can go a long way towards making that experience less traumatizing. Composers can be a sensitive lot. Depression and discouragement can surface, especially during periods of unemployment. A community of support can make those bleak periods more bearable.

Community can provide other kinds of assistance which keep a composer in business as well. Requests for help on game audio forums and groups are often answered within the hour. Audio post-mortems offer reams of knowledge and inspiration to attendees. Video game composers cheer for each other at the G.A.N.G. Awards, encourage each other on social media and show genuine appreciation for each other's accomplishments in private emails, visits and calls. Video game industry composers share an unusually open and friendly camaraderie.

Sharing a healthy sense of community does not mean video game composers aren't competitive. On the contrary, video game composers are relentlessly competitive. Everyone wants to deliver the next bar-raising game score. Everyone wants a shot at the next gig. But the author's observation is that the competitive fire driving game composers to higher and higher levels of achievement is tempered by a pervasive culture of good sportsmanship and mutual admiration. Competition takes on the character of "may the best composer win" rather than "winning at all costs".

Professional sources for community connection include the Game Audio Network Guild, the Interactive Audio Special Interest Group, the Academy of Interactive Arts and Sciences, the National Academy of Recording Arts and Sciences, and the Society of Composers and Lyricists. Additionally, video game composers can connect via special interest groups on LinkedIn, Facebook, Twitter and others. Privately hosted forums and email groups have also grown into the fabric of the industry such as the Video Game Musicians mailing list and Overclocked Remix.

One important principle with community building is to go where the people gather. If a professional forum seems dead, don't waste time on it. Find out where people are spending their hang time and build bridges there. Taking advantage of trends and staying with the movement of audiences will help keep the composer's community building efforts on track. At a time when the Game Audio Network Guild site was hopping with traffic, sound designer Richie Nieto built his community by engaging in friendly competition with its leadership. As an early advocate of game music covers, violinist Taylor Davis built a vibrant community on YouTube through continuous content updates, taking time to answer posted comments individually and personally. At the height of its popularity, composer Jeremy Soule built a strong Facebook community by connecting to game music fans, friends and peers through genuine interest in their posts and regular career updates. A balanced blend of professional and personal messaging seems most effective in community building, balancing the composer's self-interest with curiosity and delight toward others in his or her community.

Skillset

Tuning up for business includes taking stock of one's own skillset to ensure readiness to perform. While words like "savvy" and "acumen" describe things that a composer knows, *skillset* refers instead to what a composer can actually do. Here is a skillset checklist applicable to the vast majority of video game composers today. It's a good self-test for those aspiring to join the industry:

- Read music
- Play piano or keyboard (additional instruments too, if possible)
- Operate a computer
- Write music that communicates emotion and effectively underscores onscreen action
- Set up, operate and manipulate virtual instruments, synthesizers and samplers
- Arrange and orchestrate in many styles
- Prepare music designs
- Generate a click track, MIDI map and layback audio tracks in a DAW
- Organize and run a recording session
- Edit digital audio
- Mix music
- Prepare effective implementation notes
- Engage people socially and professionally, in writing and in person
- Speak competently in public
- Manipulate graphics and video
- Use tools to build websites and engage in social media
- Understand and negotiate contracts
- Generate and track necessary business forms and documents
- Maintain accurate accounting records
- Prepare budgets
- Manage budgets, time, relationships and health

GUEST LECTURE
REPUTATION

Warren Buffet, Chairman and CEO, Berkshire Hathaway

It takes twenty years to build a good reputation and five minutes to ruin it. If you think about that you'll do things differently.[4]

Character

The late Neil A. Maxwell, a gifted speaker and spiritual educator, once said, "Some enjoy being a character, letting their eccentricity define their personalities. It is always easier to be a character than to have character! Those with sterling character, always in short supply, are invariably the high-yield and low-maintenance individuals."[3]

No question about it, high-yield/low-maintenance creative partners are highly desirable assets, attractive to any overworked audio director (and they are all overworked). Character matters. Integrity, trustworthiness, cheerfulness, positive outlook, can-do attitude … not only are these the attributes that tend to enhance family and personal life, they are also helpful in business. The video game business, for all its vast reach and financial loftiness, remains a surprisingly small-world industry. Reputations make the rounds quickly. If a composer is difficult to work with, chronically late or under-delivers on promises, word gets around. There is such an enormous oversupply of composers[5] that anyone with a bad reputation is quickly swept aside by the tidal wave of new talent rushing in for their chance to shine. Dishonesty is disastrous in any form. No one wants to work with a person they can't trust. Be very careful about even claiming too much credit on a title. If a composer prints click tracks and tempo maps for another composer's score, they can hardly claim credit for having scored the game. Time and space are always at a premium, but credits should ideally include the composer's specific role on the title.

The other side of the coin is that a sterling reputation breeds repeat business. If a dev team has a great experience working with a composer, they will likely be back again for the next project. They can also spread the word to their colleagues. Video game companies come and go, but their employees often remain in the industry, resurfacing at new studios around the globe. This can help the composer's career grow in unexpected places, as loyalty toward trusted, top performing collaborators is high in the business. A good reputation based on honesty, integrity, professionalism and teamwork can be hard to earn and easy to lose. But the benefits of high personal character are worth their weight in gold.

Winifred Phillips, in her excellent handbook for video game composers, adds that there are several personal qualities that successful industry composers share. They include a love of video games, an enjoyment of the quirky nature of the game industry, a desire to be on the creative frontier, a fearless attitude toward technology, a passion for music composition, the determination of a small business owner, the desire to contribute to a new art form, the spirit of a gambler and the desire to be part of a great team.[6]

Other character traits can be helpful to young composers finding their way in the game industry. A video game composer needs to develop a careful balance between assertiveness and patience. The squeaky wheel gets the oil and all that, but the annoyingly squeaky wheel just gets jettisoned and replaced. There is a clear difference between showing interest and becoming a nuisance. Showing interest includes reaching out, submitting materials, periodic follow-up and finding common ground. It does not mean contacting someone several times a day or several times a week to find out if they liked a demo submission. It is much better to make an introduction then wait for a week

PEEK BEHIND THE CURTAIN

The Virtue of Honesty

Honesty is like playing an instrument. The more we practice, the better we get. Eventually, after practicing honesty for years, a person can become a *virtue*-oso.

During college, I played the piano at ski resorts, country clubs and restaurants. I always set out a tip bowl to supplement my hourly wage. Sometimes people would drop in a five, a ten or a twenty. Sometimes people would drop in loose change. I always counted it afterwards, recorded the exact amount in a ledger and reported every penny on my taxes. Some of my peers thought I was naïve to report my tips. But I was just practicing my honesty so I could get better at it.

or so to see if there is a response. If not, try again. But don't wear out the welcome mat before the door has been opened. Of course, an impassioned composer cares deeply about every contact and is highly motivated to move forward. But the hiring entity may have dozens of high priority challenges to deal with. Most people will respond eventually. When they do, that response can be the start of something wonderful. Don't blow it with impatience.

Another trait of successful video game composers is their tendency to process with both hemispheres of the brain. Traditional psychology theory holds that some people favor the left hemisphere of the brain (logic, organization, analysis) while others favor the right side of the brain (creativity, intuition, emotion). The best video game scores task both sides of the brain, as do the demands of running a viable business.

Successful composers also benefit from a high energy level and strong work ethic. More often than not, music comes at the very end of the game development cycle. Staggering amounts of music are often composed, approved, produced and implemented under brief time constraints. All-nighters are common—yes, common—in the video game industry. The amount of energy required to work at a high level across the creative, technical and business facets of game scoring is extraordinary. A composer with excellent health definitely has an advantage. More about lifestyle management will be explored in Chapter 12.

SUMMARY

In addition to learning the art, craft and technology of video game scoring, composers must also prepare to succeed in business. Cobbling the right components together to launch a viable enterprise can be compared to tuning up an orchestra or completing a puzzle. Key pieces of the process include establishing a *workplace*, setting up a *storefront* and *back office*, building a *community*, ensuring a complete *skillset* and managing personal *character*.

Workplace concerns include tooling up and building out. The storefront encompasses everything visible to the public, with the website in particular serving as a virtual hub. Essential back office activities track and manage the flow of income and expenses. Communities of support are cultivated by balanced efforts to share professionally and take an interest in others. Composers should take stock of their skillset to ensure readiness for the industry. Personal character is critical in building and maintaining relationships of trust with clients and peers.

With vigilant awareness, focus and patience, all of these pieces will find their proper place in the composer's business. There is an inevitability about intelligent human striving. Persistent efforts seem self-adjusting over time, ever-improving toward better and more effective results. Aspiring video game composers don't have to build Rome in a day.

APPLIED LEARNING

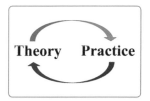

1. Put together an equipment list and itemized budget for a viable starter kit of tools for a video game composer. Total budget cannot exceed $3,000.00.

2. Do the same exercise as #1 above, but with a total budget of $10,000.00.

3. Create a sketch for the home page of your composer website. List ten ways in which this home page reflects the image you want conveyed to the world and why.

4. Lay out a site map for your composer website. Write a brief description of how each component of the website can move prospective clients closer to a hiring decision.

5. Write a statement that defines your social media strategy. Identify five ways in which your social media interactions of the past month have been aligned with this strategy. Identify five ways in which they have not aligned with your strategy statement.

6. Imagine that Sony has hired you to score a new game. The total contract price is $50,000.00, with 35 percent down, a 30 percent milestone six weeks into the project and the final 35 percent balance due on completion. Create an invoice for each payment.

7. Using the accounting template on the book's website (www.FocalPress.com/cw/Thomas), enter data for a simulated month of business activity. Note any profit or loss for that month.

8. Visit the website of each professional association below. Write out the pros and cons of joining each. Make a plan to join the association of your choice.

    a. Game Audio Network Guild, http://www.audiogang.org/

    b. Interactive Audio Special Interest Group, http://www.iasig.org/

    c. Academy of Interactive Arts and Sciences, http://www.interactive.org/

    d. National Academy of Recording Arts and Sciences, http://www.grammy.org/

    e. Society of Composers and Lyricists, https://www.thescl.com/home.

9. Find something you like about a competitor's YouTube video or recent Facebook post (or comparable social media presence). Write a positive comment on their channel or timeline.

10. Using a scale from 0 to 5, rate yourself on each item listed in the video game composer's skillset checklist. Select one area that is lacking and make a plan to improve. Start on the plan immediately.

REFERENCES

1. Tom Northup, *Five Hidden Mistakes CEOs Make* (Brisbane, Australia: Solutions Press, 2008).

2. http://www.usatoday.com/story/money/business/2013/09/02/10-fastest-growing-jobs-in-usa/2750169/.

3. Neal A. Maxwell, *Whom the Lord Loveth* (Salt Lake City: Deseret Books, 2003), p. 13.

4. http://business.time.com/2010/03/01/warren-buffetts-boring-brilliant-wisdom/.

5. http://www.filmmusicmag.com/?p=4746.

6. Winifred Phillips, *A Composer's Guide to Game Music* (Cambridge, MA: MIT Press, 2014), pp. 3–14.

You don't close a sale, you open a relationship.[1]

Arthur H. "Red" Motley was a businessman living in the eastern United States during the Second World War. He was described in *The New York Times* as "the greatest salesman God ever created."[2] He was a seller, a motivator and a successful publisher who made his fortune growing *Parade* magazine from a regional novelty to a weekly circulation of more than ten million copies. Red Motley was something of a celebrity among his peers in the publishing business. But he became universally famous for a string of words he pulled together as a motto. He coined a phrase in the 1940s which entrepreneurs, managers and CEOs from every corner of the business world have been quoting ever since: "Nothing happens until somebody sells something."[3]

Many music school graduates know this all too well. Their minds are percolating with ideas, their work space is ready with new gear and they have all of Chapter 9's puzzle pieces in place. They are ready and waiting to score a hit game. Yet, the phone doesn't ring. The texts don't come. Their email box is empty. No one visits their website. Their music may be edgy, masterful and glorious. But they sit idle, unemployed. What is the problem?

With rare exceptions, today's video game industry will not beat a path to the music school graduate's door. Rather, composers must learn to be hunters and gatherers. They will need to go out and search for their own opportunities. For example, what games will be coming out in a year or two that may need original music? Who are the development teams building those games? Which team members should be contacted about music? Once these opportunities and individuals have been identified, the composer must devise a strategy for gathering them. That means getting meetings, building the relationship and preparing demos. All of these gathering activities should be undertaken with a mindset of opening a relationship, not just closing a sale. The balance of this chapter will explore the kinds of *hunting*

GUEST LECTURE
THE BETTER MOUSETRAP FALLACY

Joel Klebanoff (*BYTE-ing Satire*)

Ralph Waldo Emerson purportedly said: "Build a better mousetrap, and the world will beat a path to your door." The idea is that if you create a better product, a better service, a better system for doing a commercially viable task, then customers will track you down and line up in droves to give you money.

But there are a few problems with this theory:

- Market Awareness—If nobody knows you exist and that you have built a great mousetrap, no one will know there is a path worth beating.
- Actual Needs—If people do not have a mouse problem, they do not need a mousetrap.
- Perceived Needs—People who have mice but are not aware of their existence will not be interested in your mousetrap. Likewise, people who think mice are "the cutest little things" are not good prospects.

and *gathering* activities that can lead to career success—identifying and researching prospects, making initial contact, getting a meeting, following up and pitching for a project.

HUNTING

There are many paths to a prospective gig. Ask twenty different composers how they landed their first game score and they will undoubtedly tell twenty different stories. Nevertheless, those who are consistently successful across many years and long careers have discovered a few quarries in the industry that can be mined repeatedly with predictable results. This section will focus on three of the most fruitful: *finding games, finding developers* and *finding peers*.

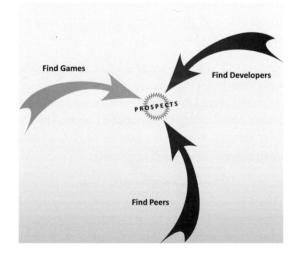

Finding Games

It is a tremendously rewarding experience for composers to write music for a game they love. Thus, one effective way to build a career is to search out and pitch for games the composer wants to work on. Composers with distinctive strengths may also find it profitable to search for upcoming games that portend a good stylistic fit. For example, a composer who specializes in chip tunes might find success by searching for 2D side-scrollers in development. An orchestral composer may want to research fantasy or adventure games coming down the road.

Finding upcoming games early enough in the development process can be tricky. Many publishers keep developing projects under tight wraps, buried under reams of NDAs and secured facilities. The author once worked on an unannounced game whose development studio was accessible only through barred gates, double-locking chambers and revolving, intertwined metal bars protected with changing key card codes!

Nevertheless, there are a few publicly accessible avenues composers can research to find upcoming games. One of the most comprehensive of these sites is the IGN database.

www.ign.com/games/upcoming

Composers can search the IGN database in many different ways thanks to a host of targeting tools. Games can be searched by release date, either in chronological order or in reverse. Games can be searched by platform, with over twenty different platforms listed. Games can be searched by genre—from action games, to casino games, to platformers and so on—with nearly thirty different genre categories to choose from. These can be combined to filter out unwanted options and focus a search toward a desired target. For example, selecting "iPhone" as the platform will

- Definition of Better—Prospects will only buy your product if they agree it is better. Someone who is style conscious may consider a mousetrap that is 10 percent more effective at catching mice but 20 percent less attractive to be inferior. For that prospect, a better mousetrap comes in designer hues.

- The Effort of Beating the Path—Finally, even if customers have real needs, perceive their needs and recognize that your product is better, they still may not beat a path to your door. The effort customers will expend to buy your product depends on their perception of its value and its ease of access. If they believe it offers only a 1 percent improvement over other mousetraps, they likely will not travel through miles of untamed jungle to get to your door. However, they may call a toll-free number if you promise to deliver the mousetrap and install it for them.[4]

return well over a hundred results. But adding a second identifier, such as the genre tag "Puzzle", now returns only eight games. With such a reduced list a composer can more effectively find and research games that look promising. Clicking on any game in the database brings up a brief summary page with information about the game, including its projected release date, developer and publisher.

Many other sites also list games in development, including Wikipedia, MetaCritic, GamesRadar, MMObomb and others. An internet search for "Upcoming Games" will return pages of options to explore. Trolling these sites regularly can enable the vigilant composer to notice when a new game pops up for the first time.

Another way to find new games in the germinating stage is to cultivate relationships with university game development programs. Proposing, designing and building new games is their bread and butter, it is what they do. In fact, it is a requirement for students enrolled in these programs. Thus each school offers composers a guaranteed and consistent source of new games annually, year after year.

A good place to start looking for such academic programs is in the Princeton Review. This regularly updated website maintains a ranked list of top game development programs in the United States and Canada at both undergraduate and graduate levels.

www.princetonreview.com/game-design.aspx

Unfortunately, the Princeton Review lacks the snazzy search engine that IGN's database offers. Clicking on a ranked school only links to the main campus website for that school, so additional research is needed to find information about their game development programs. As an example, the top listed school for a recent year was the University of Southern California. Going straight to Google, a quick internet search for "USC game development" returns "games.usc.edu". This home page is a gold mine of information with links for targeted research about the program, its accomplishments, students and leadership.

Game development conferences offer yet another avenue for finding new games as they percolate into public awareness. GDC, IndieCade, BostonFig, IGF and dozens more offer composers the opportunity to see new games on display and imagine how they might score them. Here is a regularly updated website that lists many of the recurring game conferences around the world, sorted by country.

www.gameconfs.com

Keep in mind that many games being demonstrated at shows like these have music already attached. But it never hurts to ask. Never decide in advance that someone is going to say no. Let them make that decision. Besides, talking with people at each booth about what they have incubating back at the studio may open up other kinds of interesting opportunities.

The key thing is to discover a new game as early in its development cycle as possible. If the game happens to be without an attached composer, often the gig will go to the best candidate who strikes first. This is particularly true with indie and casual games. Typically these kinds of games come from young developers who may not have established connections to a music composer yet. This can be fertile soil for getting in on the ground floor, building relationships and finding key collaborators with whom to grow throughout long careers.

Finding Developers

Like any business, development studios have distinctive cultures, strengths and weaknesses. Composers may find it profitable to research developers in order to locate those that are a good match for the composer's personality, goals and skills. There are a number of effective methods for finding developers, some of which are simply next-step offshoots of the game-finding techniques discussed above. For example, the IGN database lists developers and publishers for most of its games. Clicking on the developer link will open up a summary page about the development studio, including its track record and website.

Conferences are a great way to connect with developers. Featured games will publicize their developers and publishers, who likely have an eager presence at the conference. Finding a developer's booth may be as simple as checking a conference directory or just walking the floor. While it's true that walking the floor at a big conference like E3 or GDC can be a bit overwhelming, having a target in mind and a map in hand can effectively reduce the seemingly infinite options and filter out the noise.

Another approach to finding developers is to focus on geographic regions. For example, a composer living in Austin may want to check out the local scene before reaching out to a major conference across the country or even the other side of the planet. An internet search for "Austin Game Developers" can eventually lead to studio websites, but may require cumbersome sorting through pages of mixed results to find actual studios. Fortunately there is a better way.

GameDevMap.com

GameDevMap is a world map listing video game development studios in most major cities. Red dots indicate cities where developers are located. Clicking on any red dot populates a list of developers located within that city at the bottom of the frame. Company names and websites are listed along with the exact city and state (or province) where each developer is located. GameDevMap is free to use, open to all and instantly accessible.

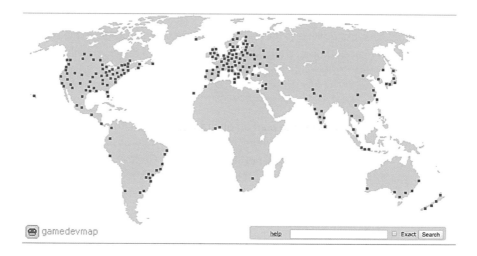

Another option for geo-locating developers is the GameIndustryMap site. This is also free to use but requires registration and password protection. GameIndustryMap's functionality flows out of the GoogleMaps engine and utilizes some of the same conventions.

GameIndustryMaps.com

To use GameIndustryMap, the composer types in the name of any city, state and/or studio. For the hypothetical Austin-based composer cited earlier, entering "Austin" into the search engine reveals a large push pin icon over the city of Austin. Zooming in reveals several more such icons scattered across and around the city.

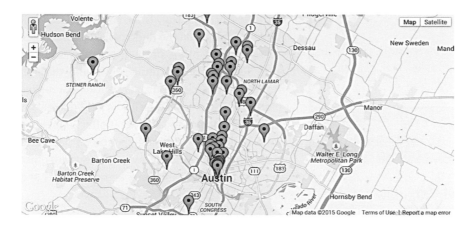

Selecting any of these virtual push pins will bring up an information box listing the developer's name, website, street address, phone number and email contact. The composer can use this info to plan an onsite visit, cold call or pursue further research.

Finding Peers

Another reliable path to prospects is to search for people whose interests and ambitions parallel those of the composer. Video game scoring is a highly creative enterprise. Working with intelligent and talented collaborators who happen to like each other is both fulfilling and fun.

The video game industry thrives on relationships. As a busy colleague once remarked, "It's not what you know, it's who you hug."[5] Some composers go through their entire careers having only a single client who happens to love their work and rehires them loyally and frequently. Finding such a client, a creative collaborator with whom to share the journey of a career, is the video game composer's equivalent to finding the Holy Grail. Josh Aker, composer for the *Infinity Blade* series, refers to these couplings as "sacred pairs".

GUEST LECTURE
SACRED PAIRS

Josh Aker (*Infinity Blade, Shadow Complex, Undertow*)

George Lucas and John Williams. Tim Burton and Danny Elfman. Christopher Nolan and Hans Zimmer. James Cameron and James Horner. J. J. Abrams and Michael Giacchino. The list goes on and on. These director/composer combinations are what I refer to as "sacred pairs". I can think of two very good reasons that they exist: (1) the two individuals that form a sacred pair are more or less equal in the talent they bring to the table, and more importantly, (2) they like working with each other.

Early on in my career as a composer, I was paired up with ChAIR Entertainment, a game development company that was also in its own infancy at the time. I scored their very first game, *Undertow*. We had a mutually positive experience. So they hired me to score their second game, *Shadow Complex*. Again, a mutually positive experience. And then they hired me yet again to score the *Infinity Blade* trilogy, which has now seen over fifty million downloads worldwide. ChAIR Entertainment and I are a sacred pair. We grew up together. We create together. We know what to expect from each other and we value our relationship.

A sacred pair is an extremely fortuitous place for a composer to be. There are literally thousands of budding game developers and filmmakers that will be the ChAIRs, Blizzards, Valves or Christopher Nolans and J. J. Abrams of tomorrow. They're looking to produce their first project and that project is going to need music. Find them, make a relationship, make good music and in the end you just might make your own sacred pair.

In the absence of a Holy Grail, composers can still find a diversity of audio directors, music directors, producers and other peers they enjoy working with. Such peers are frequently found through professional associations, conventions, websites and social media. The Game Audio Network Guild is one professional association that offers numerous opportunities for aspiring game composers to meet and mingle virtually and in person with other composers, sound designers, audio directors and music directors working in video games.

Industry conventions like GDC, E3 and GameSoundCon are invaluable venues for meeting and connecting with peers in the business. Sharing laughs after hours or arguing the finer points of an evocative presentation can generate curiosity, mutual respect and even friendships. Any of these kinds of human connections can potentially lead the composer to work opportunities that are enjoyable and lucrative.

For those without the budget or other means to attend conferences, the internet is the great equalizer. Many developer websites include a tab labeled "team", "people", "company" or something similar on their home page. These are diamond mines of information, often including names of employees, photos, job titles and even brief personality statements or bios. This can lead composers to the audio director or producer they need to contact, with enough key information to help the composer make a friendly initial connection.

Researching people can be as important to a composer's career as researching games, maybe more important. Even if a composer discovers a new game in development that looks promising, that awareness is useless without knowing who to contact and how to reach them. Finding a name is only the beginning. Researching a person's professional background can give the composer an important frame of reference and potential talking points for an initial contact. MobyGames is a great site for this info, with credits listed for nearly everyone working in the game industry. It can help to have a handle on the individual's personality as well. Facebook and other social media outlets are terrific portals for that research. Timeline posts, photos, games, music and movie lists—all of these info bits help cobble together an impression about the prospect's personality.

Finally, the composer needs to acquire the prospect's contact information. LinkedIn is an effective site for professional introductions and a great storage site for people's contact information. Most everyone lists a preferred email address. Some profiles also include personal websites, where additional contact information may be contained. Even as people move from job to job throughout their careers, most will keep their LinkedIn profiles current, updating new contact information as appropriate.

It's important to be good to people. Care about people. Make friendships that last. Cheer genuine

GUEST LECTURE
FINDING PEERS

Richie Nieto (*Assassin's Creed Unity, Tom Clancy's Splinter Cell Blacklist*)

Immersion is a word that we use frequently in game design, but in my opinion it's precisely the key to effective networking. It's not enough to just lurk around game audio forums and be a fly on the wall or put up a website and hope that strangers will check it out. You need to dive in headfirst and really interact with people, start conversations with them and allow them to know who you are. Don't try to get a job, try to make friends instead. People want to work with people they like.

As a fun example, at the G.A.N.G. website, they had a section with many playable classic arcade games, and the games registered the users' high scores. Things became competitive and we began to talk a little trash and rib each other, just having fun. This became a great icebreaker and led to several great friendships, most of which remain to this day.

I went to GDC for the first time in 2009, and I already knew many of the other attendees there through my interaction with them on game audio forums. It quickly became a chain reaction with the added benefit of face-to-face conversation, which is rare in a group of individuals who live in different countries. Soon, I started collaborating with some of them, and eventually passed around work that I was too busy to handle myself.

Good networking is a commitment, just as important as the actual audio work that I do. And it should be fun, too!

accomplishment even when it comes from a competitor. Keep the industry a healthy, supportive, thriving environment for all comers. What goes around will eventually come around, and usually in multiples.

GATHERING

At this point in the hunting process, the composer will have located a game to work on, a developer to work for and a peer to work with. It is an exciting moment in the hunt, as the composer has a viable prospect. Armed with information about the prospect's track record, personality traits and contact details, it is time to engage in the gathering process.

First Contact

The first step is often just an email or phone call expressing interest in the new game. Keeping this communication relatively brief is generally appreciated. Here is an example.

Hello John,

My name is New Composer. I'm a HUGE fan of your past work on SuperSpace 3D. I just read on Twitter that you are developing a new sci-fi shooter set in the Centauri system. Congratulations, that's exciting news!

Do you have a composer attached to the project yet? If not, I would love to learn more about your vision for the game's music. May I call you in the next week to discuss?

Cheers!

New Composer

(Phone number, website, YouTube channel, LinkedIn profile, etc.)

Please note what is included in this email and what is not. The composer does not ask for an opportunity to demo for the game, nor even cite qualifying experience. Those things can and should come later. The primary purpose of first contact is to "shake hands" with the prospect—to make them aware of the composer's interest, learn if there is an opening, and highlight the composer's client-focused orientation. Future steps will provide the composer with opportunities to pitch qualifications and services. First contact should be a more subtle affair.

The composer can actually provide vast amounts of additional information unobtrusively by including links in the signature file, such as to the composer's website, YouTube channel, etc. In fact, leaving a little bit of a vacuum in the correspondence may open room for the prospect's own curiosity to find expression. Including relevant links at the bottom of the email is a subtle invitation to learn more.

It is important in making this initial contact to use proper grammar and spelling. Bad grammar and spelling errors always cast aspersions, even if only subtly. No composer can afford careless negatives in any professional communication, especially during a first contact. Enlist a friend or other member of the support community as a proofreader, if needed.

While first contact may seem intimidating for some, a change in perspective can show this to be an invigorating and much anticipated experience. First contact is the opening of potential's doorway, the courting of unimagined possibilities. Composers who have prepared themselves with relevant knowledge about their prospect can look toward this step with eagerness and positive anticipation. They can approach it with the Great Yes!

THE GREAT YES

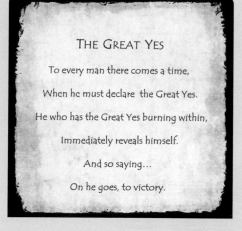

THE GREAT YES

To every man there comes a time,

When he must declare the Great Yes.

He who has the Great Yes burning within,

Immediately reveals himself.

And so saying...

On he goes, to victory.

Original Greek poem by Constantine P. Cavafy;[6] English recasting by Chance Thomas.

GUEST LECTURE
PERSISTENCE

Bob Rice, Retired Music Agent

During the 70s, I was the vice president of marketing for GRT Corporation. My regional sales manager in Los Angeles called me to tell me that Leon Hartstone, the President and Founder of Wherehouse Records, would not meet with him. My salesman had made numerous attempts to talk to Leon but Leon refused. I told my salesman that Wherehouse Records was very important to our record company and that I would get a meeting with Leon. I called and left messages for Leon over and over again and Leon never returned any of my calls.

So I went to Los Angeles to Leon's office with a pillow, a couple of books, a cup of coffee and a bag of doughnuts. I went into his building and told the receptionist that I was there to visit Leon. She asked me if I had an appointment and I said, "No, but I'll just sit here on the couch and wait for him." She said, "I don't know if he will be able to see you today." I said, "That's okay. I am prepared to sit here for several days until Leon has five minutes to see me. I don't care if it takes a week, I will sit here until I can see him." I told her that I was sorry to make her feel uncomfortable and that if she needed to she could call the police to have me removed.

Next Steps

Response to a first contact may come quickly—*"Thanks for writing, we have hired Michael Salvatori to do our next score."* In such a case, a brief and gracious response from the composer will leave a classy impression and keep the composer's foot in the door for future inquiries. Careers are long, the industry is relatively small, and it is generally better to build a positive relationship than it is to force an opening where none exists. There may be exceptions now and then, but the general rule is to retreat with grace and wait for other opportunities. Meanwhile, continue to nurture the relationship with persistence and graciousness.

On the other hand, the composer may not get any response at all. Developers are extremely busy, sometimes harried, and may not address a need until it becomes urgent. Not to worry, successful composers in the video game business are both patient and persistent. Wait a few days, then send a brief follow-up. If no answer is forthcoming, try calling. Visiting the studio is another option—whatever it takes to make a connection. On the other hand, the composer may also consider setting that contact on the shelf for a time, circling back a few months later to enhance the relationship, then reaching out again with the next project. There are always other games in the sea.

Now consider a best case scenario. The prospect writes back—*"We haven't found a composer yet, but were impressed with the music samples on your website. Would you be available for an exploratory call next Tuesday to discuss?"* Yes, this does really happen. And it is undoubtedly a great moment, one worth celebrating. The answer, by the way, is always, *"Yes, I would be delighted to. Is morning or afternoon better for you?"*

Cheers. The gathering process has begun.

Exploratory Call

From the perspective of the developer, the purpose of an exploratory call is to find out, at a very precursory level, if the composer might be a good fit for the project. To that end, there will usually be some small talk to gauge personality, creative and technical questions to measure knowledge base and skillset, and some discussion about schedule and deliverables. If the composer is prepared, there is no need to feel overly anxious about the exploratory call. Relax, show genuine interest in the project, be articulate and natural. Don't be afraid to speak about the game's music in terms of the conventional purposes of music scoring—setting the mood, heightening the emotion, propelling the action, providing contextual clues, enhancing the aesthetic and contributing to structural unity.

As an alternate approach to the phone call, ambitious composers may offer an onsite meeting instead. This gives the composer a more in-depth opportunity to interface with the prospect, learn about the game and make a compelling pitch for the project. Onsite meetings can be kept in focus by honing a two-part mindset. The first part of the visit is all about them. This is where the composer asks as many questions as possible. What are the developer's hopes and ambitions for the title and its music? What are the priority needs? Who are the key stakeholders in the decision? What matters most to each of them? Only with this information is the composer in a position to tailor a pitch to meet each concern.

The second part of the visit is *also* all about them. But this time the frame of reference shifts to how the composer can best *serve* the needs discovered in the first part of the visit. How can the composer most successfully fulfill the prospect's ambitions, meet their priority needs and address the issues that matter most to each of the key stakeholders?

About five hours later Leon came downstairs, came over to me and said, "Come on upstairs, let's meet." I met with him and it was very successful relative to establishing an excellent relationship between our company and his company. He said to me, "I wish my employees had as much dedication to doing their job as you have to doing your job. Henceforth, any time you want to have breakfast, lunch or dinner with me or any time you want to meet with me, please call me. I love your style." Our company went on to enjoy a spectacular relationship with Wherehouse Records and they became one of the most important accounts in our entire company.

PITCHING WITH THE CONVENTIONAL PURPOSES OF MUSIC SCORING

Composition student Or Kribos struck gold with a client by utilizing the conventional purposes of music in his music pitch. These purposes gave Or a framework within which to discuss the client's vision and demonstrate how music could successfully fulfill that vision. He got the gig.

GUEST LECTURE
COMMUNICATING VALUE

Joel Klebanoff (*BYTE-ing Satire*); adapted for composers

Composers can get so caught up in the "gee whiz" of their own work that they forget to ask, "How can potential clients benefit from my expertise and how can I best inform prospects about those benefits?" Consequently, many composers with outstanding skills are left wondering, "Why isn't the industry beating a path to my door?"

Value means different things to different people. For example, should you promote your high production standards, your emotionally stirring melodies or your expertise with middleware? The engineering team might be more interested in how elegantly your middleware integrates with their game code and whether it adheres to the conventional wisdom as to state-of-the-art. Ease of integration and code stability may be their primary concerns. However, management may be less concerned about the mechanics under the hood. They may want to know, for example, if you have a track record of delivering on time and within your allotted budget.

This is where many composers go astray. They think it's all about the composer and the music. But it's not. It is always, always, always and forevermore amen about the client. The client! THE CLIENT! The video game composer is part-artist and part-servant. Composers bring their artistry to bear in the service of the developer, not of themselves. Never forget that.

The Demo

If everything has progressed positively up to this point, it is very likely that the developer will ask for a custom demo. Most will expect the composer to do this for free, but some may offer a nominal payment. It is highly probable that other composers will also be asked to submit demos. Surprised? While one composer is trying to understand the developer's needs and ambitions on Tuesday, another composer is arriving on Thursday to do the same thing. Due to a continuing oversupply of composers in the marketplace, developers have lots of options at their fingertips.

Not to worry. Now is the time to shine. All those years of studying music, all of that investment in a solid core of production equipment, all of the composer's passion for the art and language of music scoring is about to have a meaningful outlet. This part of the process, finally, is all about the music.

Composers should never approach a demo with complacency, arrogance or casualness. Every demo submission should absolutely be the composer's finest work, sparing no effort. Game scoring is a business, a highly competitive business. Hundreds of talented, eager and energetic hopefuls flood into the marketplace every year. They are creative, intelligent and saturated in the language of music scoring. They all want to be successful. They all want the next gig. They tend to be better educated and more tech-savvy than any previous generation. Among so many creatives, how does one stand out from the crowd? The composer must either do something unexpected and original, or do something traditional better than most. Everything else is just noise.

Waiting

Said the maître d' to the long column of people in the buffet line, "Take your time. Hurry up." Composers may feel the same way toward a developer as they await the verdict on their submission. The period of time between sending a demo and receiving word from the developer can seem like an eternity. Especially for young composers, this no-man's land of uncertainty can create an uncomfortable level of anxiety. It probably goes without saying, but sinking in a sea of anxiety is not healthy and does nothing to enhance the composer's chances of being selected.

One positive suggestion is to move on immediately to another business activity to keep the mind occupied, such as throwing energy into updating the website, balancing the books or making travel plans to visit other developers in a neighboring city. Another suggestion is to cultivate a sense of dispositional optimism, which is "the tendency to assume things will work out well in the end".[8]

The waiting is unavoidable. With any demo submission, there is a marinating period where the developers weigh and appraise their options. The composer must be cautious with additional contacts during this phase. A relevant follow-up

Many hiring decisions require a consensus. The audio director may offer input based on musical suitability, while a producer may focus on cost and schedule. It is important to address all parties' concerns. Be aware that because different disciplines speak different languages and fixate on different issues, trying to address everyone with the same message usually satisfies no one.

You must communicate the relevant benefits to each of the key participants in the hiring process. This means finding out who has a voice in the decision and what their hot buttons are. Your messaging must address each on their own terms, in their language, highlighting the benefits that matter most to each individual. Keep in mind that what matters to a dev team may not be the same thing that impresses your music friends. All other things being equal, if multiple composers offer equal value in the developer's eyes, the winner will be the one who most effectively communicates the relevant benefits of their services to each of the key stakeholders.

You must also make it easy for developers to hire you. That might mean a number of things depending on the developer, the market they compete in and your own pool of competitors. It may mean relocating or traveling to visit dev teams. It may mean competing on price or additional deliverables. It might include simplifying your contract or giving up certain rights in the deal. All other things being equal, the easier you make it for a developer to hire you, the more likely they will.[7]

GUEST LECTURE
DELIVERING A KNOCKOUT DEMO

Rod Abernethy
(*Dead Space, Rage, The Hobbit*)

I think most composers have a love/hate relationship with creating video game music demos. I actually love doing demos. Demos give composers the chance to compete for gigs. There's no way around them if you want to compete in the marketplace.

The Hobbit is a perfect example. When Dave Adams and I were asked to demo for Midway's *The Hobbit,* it was our first chance at a AAA title. We jumped into the ring with our boxing gloves on, eager to create a demo that would convince Midway that we were the right guys for the job.

After receiving the pitch docs and guide tracks, we ate, drank and slept in the Tolkien universe. Day in and day out, we listened to nothing but Celtic music, from traditional artists like Kevin Burke to more contemporary groups like Clannad. I bought Celtic instruments, including a mandolin, a bouzouki and a bodhran. I even bought a new Taylor 12-string guitar just for the demo. I studied books on how to play traditional Irish, Scottish and Celtic melodies and chord progressions. We experimented with all kinds of Celtic melodies and arrangements. We also beefed up our orchestral sample libraries.

or value-added communication can be useful. But pestering is not helpful. No one likes a pest. Things can be very precarious during the marinating phase. If two composers are seen as more or less equal, pesky composers can take themselves right out of consideration. A confident composer will have gathered all the important information, tailored their demo to meet those needs and will respect the developer's space, having patience for the dev team's deliberations. Some developers take great pride in their ability to judge and select the best possible choice for a gig. They don't need to be convinced again and again. Give them space to decide. Be patient with the process.

Now for a caveat. None of the foregoing is perfect science, nor will it always apply in every circumstance. As Captain Barbossa famously quipped in the film *Pirates of the Caribbean*, "The code is more what you'd call *guidelines* than actual *rules*." So it is with this discussion. The text has outlined some reliable guidelines and solid principles on which to base a gathering strategy. But they may not always apply at all times to all developers. There may be some circumstances where it is acceptable to check in with a developer and ask if they have any additional direction after hearing the composer's demo. Indicating a willingness to submit further demo work based on supplemental direction may be seen as proactive and enthusiastic. But others may view it as intrusive and desperate instead. It is difficult to predict how people will react without knowing them incredibly well. Sometimes a composer just has to roll the dice and go with their instincts.

Payoff

If the hunting and gathering has been effective, and the demo submission hits the right target, the composer will receive the exciting news that they have been selected to score the game. Yes, the gig is theirs. Congratulations are in order. This is a hard-earned victory, worthy of celebration. Next up is sorting out the terms of the deal. That is where the next chapter will come into play.

SUMMARY

What Red Motley said about businesses in the 1940s is as true today as it was back then, "Nothing happens until somebody sells something." For a successful video game composer, sales is about identifying games, developers and peers that need original music, understanding their range of needs, designing services that meet those needs, and communicating in a way that leaves the client believing that the composer's services will be superior to those of any other competitor.

The process of finding clients and winning their business is divided into two broad categories, *hunting* and *gathering*. Hunting activities include searching for upcoming games, researching compatible development studios and finding peers with whom the composer can effectively collaborate. Gathering activities include initiating first contact, meetings, demos and nurturing the relationship.

All hunting and gathering activities of the composer must be undertaken with a positive, service-oriented mindset of opening and building a relationship. This approach has been proven effective at finding clients and winning their trust.

After many revisions, Dave came up with the melody for the *Hobbit* main theme and I filled in the blanks with Celtic-style guitar, mandolin, and percussion. Dave played the main melody with a sampled penny whistle, and we hired a live fiddle player to add more emotion and authenticity. We added orchestral elements wherever it felt right. Our goal for the demo was to give it an intimate and epic Celtic feel with modern and earthy orchestral elements.

All of this came out of our own pockets. I think the emotion and love for the genre that we put into the demo won the gig for us. Many times after you've finished a demo, you hit the "send" button, and as your demo is making its final journey through the internet, you find yourself wondering what you could have done better. Questioning yourself about the mix, the melody, the brass line … whatever. All of those things that you could angst about forever that you wish you had done. But with the *Hobbit* demo, I felt that it was as good as it could be when I hit "send". Some demos are like that; you know that you've done your very best. Those are the ones that usually get the job.

PERSONAL SPACE

Paul Simon famously sang that there are "Fifty Ways to Leave Your Lover". Likewise, there are myriad ways to sour a composer's relationship with a developer. Composers, because they spend so much time alone at their craft, may have a powerful need for connection and communication. They may want lots of interaction with a developer. But most developers don't have that same level of need. They may be swamped with emails, meetings, reviews, training, crowded offices and their own list of production tasks. The developer may only want as much communication as absolutely necessary for the composer to understand their needs and hit their targets. When building relationships with developers, remember: you're courting, not stalking!

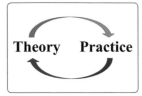

APPLIED LEARNING

1. Making use of IGN's database of upcoming games, select one game in a genre and on a platform you would like to score. List the game, its developer and publisher.

2. For the game selected in #1 above, visit the developer's website and list five important facts you learned about the developer. Locate the developer using GameDevMap and GameIndustryMap. List the developer's physical address, phone number and email contact.

3. For the game selected in #1 above, find the name of the audio director at the game's development studio. Utilize the company's website, MobyGames and/or LinkedIn to assist in your search. List the audio director's name and contact information.

4. For the audio director selected in #3 above, create a brief profile about the person. Include past games worked on, notable skills, personality traits, tastes in popular culture, work history, educational background, etc. Utilize all tools at your disposal including Facebook, LinkedIn, Google search, etc.

5. Write an introductory email to the audio director using the first contact principles outlined in the chapter.

6. Imagine that you've been invited to have a meeting with the audio director and the development team. Write down a list of questions that will help you determine the needs, ambitions and priorities of the audio team, the engineering team, the art team and the producer. Role-play the meeting with a friend.

7. Create a two-minute demo for the game selected in #1. Pull out all the stops. Make it amazing, A+ material. Or rather, AAA material.

8. If you have the courage and the ambition to do so, step out of simulation mode and into career launch mode. Make first contact with the developer you've selected and see where it leads. After all, you have researched your prospect, prepared for a meeting and even have a demo waiting in the wings. Good luck!

REFERENCES

1. http://www.fripp.com/blog/10-sell-yourself-strategies-for-speakers/.

2. http://www.nytimes.com/1984/05/31/obituaries/arthur-h-motley-dies-at-83-parade-magazine-publisher.html.

3. http://www.barrypopik.com/index.php/new_york_city/entry/nothing_happens_until_somebody_sells_something.

4. http://www.klebanoff.com/mousetrap.html.

5. Kurt Bestor, in personal conversation with the author, circa 1993.

6. http://poemsetc.blogspot.com/2008/11/che-fece-il-gran-rifiuto.html.

7. http://www.klebanoff.com/mousetrap.html.

8. http://www.psychologytoday.com/blog/ulterior-motives/201407/the-waiting-is-the-hardest-part-you-can-make-it-easier.

CHAPTER 11
MONEY MATTERS

You don't get what you deserve, you get what you negotiate.[1]

Some composers have peculiar ideas about money. There was once an afternoon panel at a regional Comic Con which featured four composers. Three of the four composers stated that money was not a motivating factor in their work: "It's not about the money, man. It's about the art, the purity of expression, being true to yourself." "I never think about the money. I just think about the music." "If you're in it for the money, you might as well hang it up now." And so the dialogue went. But the fourth composer disagreed. The fourth composer posited that music scoring is a business. Although the business delivers a highly artistic service, it is nevertheless a business. He said that only with sufficient money is a composer empowered to devote full time to composing. Full-time devotion leads to higher quality work because, in general, the more time a person devotes to a particular pursuit, the more proficient they become. Additionally, a robust cash flow provides money to upgrade capital assets, engage in professional education and employ outside experts who can make artistically elevating contributions to the composer's work. All of these positive actions flow from a prosperous business, allowing the composer to deliver music scores of increasingly enhanced artistry and excellence.

It is interesting to note that the fourth composer had worked on dozens of well-known, award-winning music scores, while the other three composers were struggling in relative obscurity.

This chapter presupposes readers who share the fourth composer's perspective, that money matters and that an understanding of best practices in business will benefit the composer both financially *and* artistically. The text will offer *perspectives* about working with corporate video game clients, outline *composer rates, production costs* and *contract negotiations*. Case studies and anecdotes (both successful and disastrous) will be sprinkled throughout.

PERSPECTIVES

Author Darren J. Perkins penned a book with the provocative title *Business is War*.[2] It is an interesting idea to ponder, that business can be viewed from the perspective of warfare. Warfare conjures up visions of opposing forces determined to conquer or perish. In his famous treatise *The Art of War*, Sun Tzu tells his followers that, in warfare, it is imperative to know the enemy.[3] He continues, however, revealing a precocious harmony with modern business thought, by defining his enemies as "a great source of resources, not an opponent to be destroyed".[4] If business is war, and if an enemy is a great source of resources, and if warriors need to know their enemies, then from this perspective it seems prudent for aspiring composers to know something about the video game corporations they would hope to do battle/ business with one day.

Microsoft Sega
Activision Blizzard
Electronic Arts
UBISOFT TenCent
Nintendo SONY

Tencent. Electronic Arts. Sony. Microsoft. Nintendo. Ubisoft. Activision Blizzard. Sega. These are some of the highest grossing video game companies on planet Earth. Between these eight companies, more than twelve billion dollars in video games were sold in 2013.[5] These global companies and their corporate peers possess tremendous leverage. They control IP (intellectual property rights), means of production, channels of distribution and infrastructure for collecting, tracking and distributing money. They are formidable enterprises. As commercial entities, their guiding purpose is to maximize profits and grow their shareholders' equity. This can translate into reaching for as much as possible while giving up as little as possible in return.

Going into negotiations with one of these companies may feel a little bit like a pedestrian facing a column of tanks.

Composers who are unprepared for such a confrontation can emerge bruised if not battered. But looking beyond the bulwarks, one finds that every one of these mega companies is also a consortium of individuals, each of whom has needs, desires and motivations to fulfill. By understanding the needs and drives of individuals with decision-making power, a composer may gain insight into a successful business negotiation. Composers who are thus equipped, who are informed, courteous and gutsy, can survive and even thrive in such negotiations, having long and prosperous careers.

A war analogy is one perspective, but not the only perspective with merit. Perhaps it is not even the best perspective. Another vantage point, championed in an article published by *Elite Daily Magazine*, instead compares business to marriage.[6] Two parties are drawn to each other, choose to join together for shared interests, common goals and a partnering approach to achieving mutually beneficial ends. This is often how the best video game collaborations come together.

From this perspective, a negotiation with corporate behemoths is seen more as an exercise in finding common ground, collective benefits and shared rewards. Helping managers and attorneys on the other side of the table to court the composer's favor and perceive the composer's interests as inextricably aligned with their own needs—this is a healthy perspective from which to negotiate. No one wants to argue against their own self-interest. Helping the dev team see that what benefits the composer also benefits the game is the ultimate perspective from which to negotiate.

At the most fundamental level, composers are doing business with people, not with buildings, bank accounts or other assets. Understanding these people, figuring out how to meet their needs in a way which also addresses the composer's need to thrive as a business, can be an incredibly effective and productive perspective from which to engage in conversations about money.

COMPOSER RATES

Some readers will enjoy and appreciate the foregoing discussion of perspective. Such perspective can serve as a guiding outlook to frame and inform all future interactions with clients and business associates. Other readers may have little use for such philosophical exploration. They prefer to cut right to the chase: "How much should I charge?"

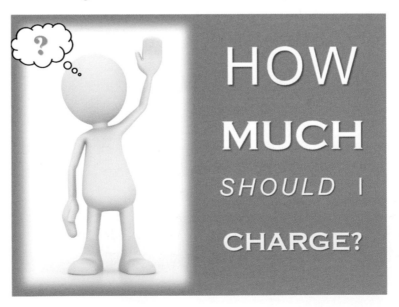

The bad news for such readers is that video game composer rates are all over the map. The good news is that at least there is a map. There are some standards in place, depending on such factors as a game's predicted commercial viability, a composer's track record and reputation, music production approach, asset types and complexity, deliverable variables, degree of implementation involvement and range of services offered. Composers can approach a negotiation with a reasonable expectation of fair business practices and generally accepted rates for comparable circumstances.

For decades, a benchmark rate for composers of original music has been $1,000 per finished minute. This is not a beginner's rate, nor is it a rate charged by top composers in the business. But for the broad middle ground of reasonably experienced composers and a mainstream swath of commercially viable video games, this rate frequently applies. At the very least, every composer should know that this rate is a long-established middle ground for professional music scoring services. This is a creative fee and does not include budget for third-party production costs. It is also a buy-out fee, generally paid when a publishing company takes ownership of the copyright in each composition, commonly referred to as a work-for-hire arrangement.

On the bottom end, rates can start as low as $250 per minute for novices, low-budget indie games or composer sweatshops. Negotiating for even this low rate as a beginner is far better than working for free. Giving away music services for free degrades the profession, cheapens composers' view of themselves and creates distorted perceptions about music in the marketplace. According to business writer Paul Petrone, " If you're not getting paid, you are either being taken advantage of, or you're doing work that has no real value to the organization."[7] Either reason is reason enough to avoid this implosive practice. Stepping up to the next level, many mobile games and apps with modest development budgets can offer composers scoring rates in the range of $500–$750 per finished minute.

On the higher end, composers with a strong track record and excellent reputation regularly charge in the neighborhood of $1,500 per finished minute. Rates can range higher, up to $2,500 per finished minute for composers working on the very top AAA games, especially if providing assets for sophisticated adaptive music designs such as mapped layers or middleware solutions. For celebrity composers who can add perceived marketing value to a title, rates can range into several thousand dollars per minute.

PEEK BEHIND THE CURTAIN

Pricing A Score With Music Assets Of Varied Costs

It's not uncommon for me to create a video game score which requires different asset classes of music, each of which may need to be billed at a different rate to accurately reflect its respective value in the music score and the amount of work needed to produce it. For a real-world look at how this breaks down, here is the pricing itemization for a recent score I completed for a small video game from a major publisher.

Because this game is relatively small, the amount of music is limited. But because the game is from a major publisher with broad commercial reach, music charges are toward the higher end of non-celebrity composer rates. Note that three different rates were applied in pricing this music score. Linear music tracks and looping tracks were all billed at $1,500 per finished minute. Layered tracks were billed at $2,500 per finished minute. Stingers and tags were billed at $500 each. Breaking down a music score bid into relevant components like this is a recommended best practice. Such a bid brings transparency to pricing discussions and clarity to contract negotiations.

As a side note, this practice of billing by the finished minute is a holdover from film and television scoring, where all music is composed along a linear time line. Determining the number of finished minutes in a game score is simple. If all of the fully mixed music tracks in a score are lined up end to end, with no silence between them, then the length of time it takes to play through the score from beginning to end equals the total number of finished minutes. In video games, a per minute approach to scoring rates works well when calculating pricing for music loops, cinematic scores and other kinds of music tracks that have a linear or near-linear structure.

Special Cases Affecting Rates

Intros, stingers, tags and transitions are scoring cue cases that deserve special attention. These functionally powerful music segments may lack the length of music loops, yet may require nearly as much creative work, energy and composer time as a full minute of looping music. Many a composer has been burned when charging by the finished minute only to have the client fill their deliverable list with stingers, intros and tags lasting ten to twenty seconds each. Adding up the combined durations of these shorter music bits does not account for their relative value to the score, nor their cost (creativity, energy, time) to produce.

For these types of special cases, it makes more sense to charge by the asset. A good middle ground rate for such music blocks is $400–$500 each. This would be in the right ballpark for a score where the composer is charging $1,000 per finished minute for longer tracks. This $400–$500 rate takes into account the shorter duration of intros, stingers, tags and transitions when compared to longer music loops, while also making provision for the value they add to the game score and the effort required to produce each one. For scores with higher or lower finished minute rates, these special case rates can be adjusted proportionally.

Other Variables Affecting Rates

In addition to the foregoing discussion, there are at least a dozen other common factors that can influence a composer's rate. These are loosely divided into four broader categories—*production approach*, *asset type and complexity*, *deliverable variables* and *range of included services*.

Production Approach

Composing an all-synth ambient score with lots of long drones may not require as much work as composing a live orchestral action score. While all music adds value to the game, pricing should reflect a difference in the amount of manpower required. For example, an experienced composer may justifiably charge $1,200 per minute for an ambient score, while also charging $1,500 per minute for a live orchestral score. Both rates reflect the value of the experienced composer's judgment, musical creativity and production skills, while providing additional compensation for the live score's added workload.

DELIVERABLE ASSETS:

Loops & Linear Tracks	Layered Tracks	Music Blocks—Stingers & Tags
Menu_01.wav 2.00	Strategy01_layer01.wav 1:40	Defeat.wav 0:08
Menu_02.wav 1:40	Strategy01_layer02.wav 1:40	Fight_01_end.wav 0:10
CharSelect..wav 1:00	Strategy01_layer03.wav 1:40	Fight_02_end.wav 0:10
Start.wav 2:30	Strategy02_layer01.wav 1:40	Fight_03_end.wav 0:10
TimeOut.wav 2.00	Strategy02_layer02.wav 1:40	SurpriseSting_01.wav 0:06
Fight_01.wav ~0:40	Strategy02_layer03.wav 1:40	SurpriseSting_02.wav 0:06
Fight_02.wav ~0:40	Strategy03_layer01.wav 1:40	SurpriseSting_03.wav 0:06
Fight_03.wav ~0:40	Strategy03_layer01.wav 1:40	Boss_end.wav 0:05
Boss.wav 0:45	Strategy03_layer01.wav 1:40	Stealth_Tag_Timed.wav 0:08
Stealth.wav 0:45		Stealth_Tag_Buy.wav 0:10
		Respawn.wav 0:10
		Purchase_Sting.mp3 0:05
		VictorySting_A.mp3 0:15
		VictorySting_B.mp3 0:15
		DefeatSting_A.mp3 0:15
		DefeatSting_B.mp3 0:15
10 Loops & Linear Tracks	3 Triple Layered Tracks	
12 min 40 sec	5 minutes	16 Music Blocks

PRICE BREAKDOWN:

Loops & Linear Tracks;
    12 min 40 sec @ $1500/min = **$18,990.00**

Triple Layered Tracks;
    5 min @ $2500/min = **$12,500.00**

Music Blocks; 16 assets @ $500 = **$8,000.00**

Total Creative Fees = **$39,490.00**

Asset Type

Some composers bill at a slightly higher rate for cinematics than they do for a looping music track. The justification given is that cinematic music requires tight integration with the timing of a particular movie file, which can sometimes generate extra work for a game composer. Ironically, some composers bill at a *lower* rate for cinematics because they find it simpler to cut music to an existing timeline than to create a music loop that meets all the requirements outlined in Chapter 4. A recommended best practice is to bill at the same finished minute rate, whether for cinematics or for other linear or looping music tracks in the score. Incidentally, it may be useful to establish a minimum charge for any cinematic regardless of length. This is prudent for the same reason as charging a per asset rate for music blocks like tags and stingers. Some cinematics can be very short, yet require nearly as much creativity and effort to set up as a longer piece of music.

Asset Complexity

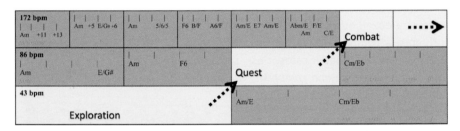

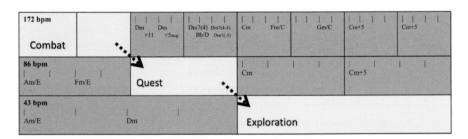

As mentioned earlier, rates are higher for music composition that involves complex adaptive music design techniques, such as layered music tracks. Recalling the mapped layers of Chapter 5, a three-layer composition is significantly more work than a single linear or looping piece of music. Composers should charge at a commensurately higher rate for these kinds of compositions. Pricing upwards of $2,000 per minute for such tracks is not unreasonable. Other kinds of complex music designs such as ambient sets or generative music also merit premium prices because of the value they add to the game and the amount of work required to create them.

Deliverable Variables

Traditionally, video game composers have been expected to deliver stereo mixes of all music tracks in a high quality music format, such as 48 kHz, 24 bit wav files. But sometimes a client may request differing categories of deliverables in additional files and formats. For example, a PS4 game developer may require a surround mix of all files at 96 kHz, 24 bit resolution. An MMO developer may ask for stems of all music files in addition to the stereo mix. An iPhone developer may want all the music delivered as AAC files or packaged in a Fabric project. Composers need to keep in mind that time is money and their time is valuable. If it takes more time to create a 7.1 surround mix than it does to create a stereo mix, then the pricing should reflect this difference. Composers who need to bounce out stems of every mixed track should have some provision in the budget for this additional work as well. Billing additional work at an hourly studio rate is one effective approach for appropriate scaling. Another method is to include such services in the original composition fee, but negotiate for other benefits such as cross-promotion or other kinds of PR. The principle here is to not give away additional services without commensurate compensation. Everything the composer delivers which adds value to the game deserves remuneration.

Range of Services

A composer may create an FMOD project or an integration package in Unity as part of their

GUEST LECTURE
TECHNICAL SERVICES AS COMPETITIVE ADVANTAGE

Brian Schmidt
(*Madden NFL, NBA Live, Zynga Bingo*)

Unless a job is predominantly technical, I tend to consider my technical work on a game as more of a perk to the client for selecting me, rather than as a separate billable item. If my tech work is primarily to make the game sound better, I generally don't charge at all. In my view, my fee is to make the game sound great, and if that means a bit of programming—or more often the case, helping educate the dev's own programming team, perhaps by providing a bit of code as a kick start—then that service is included.

On the other hand, if I'm asked to make a significant change or addition to the audio engine, such as adding a new feature that might have a life beyond the current game, then I will generally bill for that. Such programming work is billed as an hourly line item alongside my music/sfx fees.

services. This adds value to the game and saves the developer money by performing tasks that would otherwise be assigned to expensive software engineers. Rates for these kinds of implementation services can vary greatly. Some composers even include these services in their music offerings as a competitive advantage.

PRODUCTION COSTS

Closely aligned to composers' questions about what they should charge for their own services are those questions that relate to what they should pay for contracted production services. As with composer rates, production service providers charge a wide diversity of rates and fees. This section will examine a range of rates for *studio musicians and singers, orchestrators, engineers, mixing artists, music editors* and *studios*.

Studio Musicians

Musician rates are influenced by three primary factors. The first factor is whether the musician is charging union rates or not. Second, what geographic region are they working in? Third, is there a high demand for a particular musician for reasons of exceptional artistry, versatility or marketing value? All of these factors can affect rates.

The Musicians' Union can be a touchy subject for those working in the game industry. Especially in Los Angeles, the American Federation of Musicians has a somewhat checkered past with video games. In one infamous instance, the union actually shut down a large orchestral scoring session for a Sony game on the very cusp of downbeat. Los Angeles is known as a union town, since most of the top players there belong to the union and abide by union standards. Dark dates still occur, but for the most part the union musicians in LA play by the book. Though union rates are generally higher than non-union rates, many scores are still recorded in LA because of the exceptional caliber of its recording musicians and studios. San Francisco and London are also considered strong union towns.

So what do union musicians charge for a video game score? In 2014, the American Federation of Musicians ratified a new video game recording contract, developed in extensive consultation with Microsoft. Since it is expected that other major game publishers may ratify this agreement or negotiate comparable agreements of their own, union musician rates quoted here are from that agreement. Base rates for each musician range between $100 per hour and $230 per hour, depending on the number of musicians booked and whether the musicians' performances are stacked. *Stacking* refers to the process of recording additional passes of a score on top of a completed take using the same musicians. Pension and health insurance payments must also be made for each musician in the session. Sessions are usually booked in three-hour blocks, up to two sessions per day. Section leaders are paid double scale. Any musician who plays more than one instrument (doubling) is paid at one and a half times scale. Cartage charges apply for harp, double bass, tuba, various percussion instruments and a variety of the larger woodwind and brass instruments. Detailed information for all amounts charged during a union recording session can be found online on the AFM's website: http://www.afm.org/uploads/file/VGSummaryJune2014.pdf.

For orchestral and choral recording sessions, composers will typically hire a musician contractor to book the best available musicians whose talents are most appropriate for a particular score. These contractors have their fingers on the pulse of an ever-changing musician landscape. They know how to reach the right people and how to handle unexpected last minute changes in a musician's availability. Most contractors also offer bookkeeping services, handling musician payments, W9s and other necessary accounting tasks. For these services, most contractors charge a fee equaling 10 percent of the total musician cost for a given project (excluding cartage), plus an additional percentage for payment services. Union contractors' rates are the same as a section leader participating in the session, double scale for the length of the session.

The UK Musicians Union oversees rates for recording in London. Basic union musician rates in London start at £56 (pounds sterling) per hour, with a minimum three-hour call. In 2014 dollars that equals $270 per musician. Contractors charge an additional 12–13 percent of the total musician package price for their services.

For a rough estimate of total costs, consider two days of recording with a seventy-piece AFM orchestra, with two sessions per day of three hours each, and no stacking. Not counting cartage, composers will spend in the neighborhood of $120,000 for the union musicians on this session. Depending on many factors, such as score complexity, sheet music accuracy/clarity and level of perfectionism pursued, composers should expect to record anywhere from four to eight minutes of music per session hour. This equates to recording anywhere from forty-eight to ninety-six minutes of music.

In spite of the exceptional quality of their recording musicians, the high costs of recording in Los Angeles, San Francisco and London have forced composers to consider other options. As a result, several excellent non-union recording orchestras have sprung up around the world. Here are four non-union recording orchestras that have a good recording history with the video game industry. Each includes the base rate for recording musicians in the area, plus three video game credits for reference. More detailed information for each locale including studio rates, contractor rates and other important financial data is available on the website for this textbook.

Prague	$21 per musician per hour	*Heavenly Sword, Kameo, Banjo Kazooie*
Salt Lake City	$50 per musician per hour	*DOTA 2, Might & Magic, Lord of the Rings Online*
Seattle	$60 per musician per hour	*Halo, Gears of War, World of Warcraft*
Nashville	$75 per musician per hour	*Last of Us, Rachet & Clank, Resistance*

Studio Singers

As with studio musicians, singers' rates are also varied. A singer's union affiliation, regional location and/or exceptional value all impact the cost of their services. Soloists charge more than choral singers. Composers can expect to pay anywhere from $200 to $1,500 per track for a solo vocalist. Choral singer rates typically mirror the price of studio musicians for the locale in which they work.

Orchestration and Music Prep

As Chapter 1 describes, orchestration is the clothing and coloring of a score's components across all the available timbres of a selected palette. Many composers handle this task themselves. Others call on the specialized services of score orchestrators to translate their MIDI ideas into performable scores. Orchestration services are often coupled with music prep services. As explained in Chapter 7, music preparation involves making legible transcriptions of any component of the recorded score that will be performed live. In the United States, the AFM prescribes a staggering array of rates for orchestration and music prep. Their guidance is compiled into a six-page chart, which can be viewed online at this link: http://www.afm.org/uploads/image/MP_chart_no_bar(4).pdf.

Outside of the AFM, service providers tend to fall into one of three camps. The first group charges by the hour for their services. Prices for this group range from $40 to $60 per hour. One advantage of charging an hourly rate is its scalability. Simpler scores with broad lines and lots of whole notes will move through the process quickly, resulting in significant cost savings. The primary disadvantage is not knowing up front how much the service will cost. The second group charges by the page. Pricing for this group ranges between $50 and $100 per page, depending on the complexity of the score. Many veteran orchestrators and copyists use this model, which is based on the AFM's traditional approach to billing. The third group charges by the finished minute. Their rates run between $300 and $1,050 per minute of music, depending on project budget and score complexity. One benefit of this approach is being able to identify and lock in costs up front.

ORCHESTRATION & MUSIC PREP COSTS

Very Low Budget:	Strings, Brass, Light Choir $300 - $500 per minute of score
Modest Budget:	Strings, Brass, Light Choir $400 - $700 per minute of score
Good Budget:	Full Orchestra $1,050 per minute of score

With either billing approach, the costs for printing, collating, binding and delivery are extra. Some service providers will also charge additional fees for proofing, breaking out individual parts and score supervision. Some will offer emergency services, including on-call service for on-the-spot fixes during a session. Composers are encouraged to research potential service providers thoroughly, inquiring into the range of services offered and all billable costs. Look at copies of past comparable work and ask how much it cost to produce. Be careful not to overpay for similar work.

Studios and Engineers

Although studio and engineering rates likewise vary widely, it is a rule of thumb that the higher the price for musicians in a given location, the higher the price for studios and engineers in that area as well. For example, here are representative rates from two union and four non-union cities listed in the musician section. More detailed pricing plus contact information for major studios in each city is included on the book's website (www.FocalPress.com/cw/Thomas).

Prague	€650 per session (4 hrs) for Smecky Studio; €150 per session for Pro Tools; €200 per session for engineer
Salt Lake City	$150 per hour for LA East Chapel; $250 setup; $60 per hour engineer
Seattle	$5,000 per day for Bastyr Chapel; includes engineers and equipment
Nashville	$2,500 per day for Ocean Way Chapel; $1,100 per day for engineers
London	£3,500 per day for Abbey Road Studio 1, plus setup and engineers
Los Angeles	$4,500 per session (4 hrs) for Fox Newman Stage, not including engineers.

Each acoustic venue has a distinctive character, a recognizable sonic flavor. Composers are encouraged to listen critically to samples of scores recorded in each locale for comparison and contrast prior to making a booking decision.

CONTRACT NEGOTIATIONS

The delicate process of persuasive communication known as negotiation is a complex and fascinating art. It probably deserves its own library. In fact, myriad books and courses on negotiation are available. For the purposes of this chapter, rather than discuss the process of negotiation, the text will instead examine several common points in composer music contracts that deserve attention during a negotiation. These include *compensation, rights, deliverables, schedules, publicity, approvals/revisions, expenses, indemnification, methods of payment* and *additional compensation.*

Compensation

It may seem self-evident, but any contract for video game music services must specify how much money the composer will be paid. This includes any third-party production costs for which the composer is assuming liability. It is customary for the composer's compensation to be divided into two or more payments. Composers should ask for a deposit payment ranging from 20 percent to 50 percent to start the project. If possible, the deposit should be non-refundable in order to protect the composer's initial investment in setting up for the new score and doing all of the initial creative work. Additional payments are typically tied to specific deliverables. These are called milestones. Each milestone payment will be a percentage of the total, minus any deposit paid. Additional compensation such as royalties, bonuses, stock awards, equipment, product, etc., should be detailed in the contract. Composers should send an invoice for each payment due. Typical turnaround time is net thirty days. An agreement may also include a clause that adds interest and/or penalties for payments that are more than thirty days late.

Rights

The de facto position of video game publishers is to acquire ownership of the music. This means that a composer relinquishes the copyright in their compositions. However, this does not always have to be the case. For example, if a developer is low on cash, composers may negotiate to create their score under a licensing agreement, rather than selling

PACKAGE DEAL VS. CREATIVE FEE DEAL

When a video game score is to be produced with outside musicians, studios, etc., composers may have a choice of whether to structure the pricing to include third-party costs or whether to have subcontractors invoice the game company directly. There are advantages and disadvantages to each approach. Consider a hypothetical case study.

A composer is asked to score a game set in the 1940s. The developer decides on sixty minutes of music in a big band style. The composer agrees to creative fees totaling $72,000 for the project. They all agree that a live band will bring the score to life and add justifiable richness to the game experience. Let's assume that a non-union band, music prep, venue and engineers will cost in the neighborhood of $40,000.

In the scoring agreement, the composer may choose to package all of these costs together, charging $115,000 for a turnkey music solution. This offers certain advantages to the game company. For example, all costs for the game's music are nailed down up front. There won't be any surprises to the budget later on.

Also, the game company has a single point of interface for all music issues, rather than dealing with half a dozen or more different people, personalities and businesses. Busy developers and publishers like to streamline their operations when they can. A package deal provides them with this benefit.

For composers who know their team and are able to efficiently manage their production pipeline, a package deal makes sense for them too. For starters, it allows the composer to offer an attractive benefit to the client, which may be a competitive advantage. Furthermore, since composers should be compensated for all aspects of their work, they can justifiably include a small fee for their own contracting and payroll services, or any other parts of the production process which they assume themselves. Such services may include producing recording sessions, editing audio tracks, mixing and mastering. Thus, for a composer who can manage production and has developed a range of billable skills, offering a package deal can increase the composer's profitability on a project.

On the other hand, a composer without such skills may be better off negotiating a deal for creative fees only. An inefficiently managed score production can quickly balloon out of control, eroding profits while putting deliverables and deadlines at risk. In such cases, the composer should concentrate on composing the score and allow the developer to oversee third-party contractors, including paying for production expenses directly and managing their costs.

the copyright. Retaining the copyright frees the composer to seek alternative outlets for the music, potentially generating additional sources of revenue for the composer. Composers can grant a broad license to the developer, such as an unlimited, non-exclusive use, worldwide license, with no date of termination. This allows the publisher the freedom to utilize the game's music in other franchise releases, promotional materials, and so on. Or a music license could be defined more narrowly, such as for a specific video game title only, or for a specified span of time. In general, the more rights the developer acquires in the music, the more they should pay. When the composer gives up ownership of the music, certain rights for the composer can still be negotiated, including ancillary income rights. For example, if a soundtrack is released or if music from the game is used in a movie trailer, provision can be made for a percentage of those proceeds to be paid to the composer.

Deliverables

The contract should clearly spell out all required deliverables in the deal. This may include assets such as a music design document, music files and implementation notes. Deliverables may specify services such as music design, composition, studio production and middleware integration. Many agreements will also specify asset formats, such as specific file types or resolution format for master music mixes.

Schedules

The composer's contract should include a list of dates by which deliverable assets are due. For example, due dates may be listed for music design documentation, initial music drafts, approved compositions, finished masters, and so on. The contract should also list a payment schedule so all parties know when each amount is due and payable to the composer. In most cases, payments are tied to deliverable milestones.

Publicity

In the video game industry, developers and publishers treat their confidential information like industrial trade secrets. Developers and publishers do not want composers talking about the games they are working on, especially prior to a game's commercial release. They will insist that the composer sign a non-disclosure agreement before entering into any serious discussions about the project, prohibiting the composer from talking about the project or even about their involvement in the project to anyone. However, composers operate in a highly competitive business climate. Publicizing the composer's attachment to current projects is critical to maintaining a competitive edge in the marketplace. Therefore, the composer should seek a provision that will allow customary notices announcing the composer's connection to the game. This can be softened by including a clause requiring the game company's permission for a press release, website posting, etc. Composers should also ask for their name and role to be credited in any screen or print credits of the game, such as "Music by (insert name)".

Approvals and Revisions

A good agreement will include provisions for managing the approvals process. Most developers are reasonable, but some with inexperience can cause nightmares. The worst problems occur when a developer starts changing the parameters of a score mid-stream and moving the target. For these instances

FOUR NEGOTIATING TIPS FOR NEWBIES

1. Be very clear about what you want. Before diving into a negotiation, think through a range of available options and possible outcomes, then narrow those down to the core ingredients that you must have in order to be successful. Entrepreneur Peter Guber describes this principle in vivid and instructive terms: "You must describe it, write the script, and say it out loud so it's clear to anyone on a foggy night at sixty miles an hour, or don't go in the room."[8]

2. Don't make the mistake of saying no for the other side. If there is a benefit you need in the deal or a concession you want to ask for, put it out there. Don't fall into the trap of thinking, "Oh, they will never go for that." Allow the game developer or publisher to make that decision. Don't make a unilateral decision for them. If you have a fair and reasonable request, go ahead and bring it to the table. They can certainly make their own minds up about it. Often you will be surprised to discover an open mind on the other side of the negotiation. You don't have to do the deciding for both parties.

3. Don't be too hungry. Unless you are an indentured servant, you don't have to accept any offer that doesn't meet your needs. Tim Rushlow, former lead vocalist for country band Little Texas, described it this way: "You gotta have walk-away willpower in a negotiation." In telling the story of his first record deal, something he had dreamed of all his life, Tim said that the record label president initially made him a good offer.

But it didn't have everything Tim and his band needed from the deal. So he rose up from the president's big desk, shook his hand, and turned and headed toward the door. Just as he was about to exit, the president called to him and said, "Wait a minute." He then made Tim the offer he had hoped for.[9]

4. Invest in and study reputable books on negotiation. Negotiating skills can have an enormous impact on a composer's income. Here are three good books that come highly recommended. There are probably dozens more. *You Can Get Anything You Want: But You Have to Do More Than Ask*, by Roger Dawson; *Getting to YES: Negotiating Agreement Without Giving In,* by Roger Fisher, William Ury and Bruce Patton; *In Business as in Life, You Don't Get What You Deserve, You Get What You Negotiate*, by Chester L. Karass.[10]

and others, it is wise to define such details as how many cycles of revisions are included in the price, how long the developer has to respond after each submission, what constitutes an approval and how to handle irreconcilable differences. Particularly when working with a less experienced developer, it is wise to include a specific provision that ensures composers will be paid for any reworking of music requested after an approval has been granted.

It may also occur that partway through a project, there is a leadership change at the studio. Or perhaps focus group feedback suggests an about face on some aspect of the game's vision or design. Previously approved assets may be rejected and new material enjoined. In such cases as these, and many more, having an approvals clause in the composer agreement will allow the composer to rework the music as needed without having to deliver inordinate amounts of new, uncompensated work.

Expenses

Often a composer will incur miscellaneous expenses on behalf of a client. For example, a composer may need to make an onsite visit to a developer in another state. Defining what kinds of expenses are reimbursable, and how the reimbursement process works will help the composer avoid absorbing these costs by default.

Indemnification

This is a potentially devastating clause which comes standard in most video game music agreements. The boilerplate version of this clause often states, in effect, that the composer will assume all financial liability for any legal claim levied against the publisher relating in any way to the game's music. This can include frivolous lawsuits and other kinds of legal action which may have no actual basis in composer impropriety whatsoever. The justifiable legal basis for an indemnity clause is to protect the publisher from potentially

fraudulent acts of a composer, such as plagiarism. But the template version often used by publishers is so broad in its wording and so far reaching in its implications as to be almost comical. To think that a single composer, who will be lucky to break six figures in a given year, is going to stand as a financial shield and bulwark in front of a multi-billion dollar corporation is absurd. Composers should insist on wording that limits their liability specifically to damages from an actual breach (such as plagiarism), as proven in a court of legal jurisdiction.

Methods of Payment

Because exchange rates are unpredictable, composers should generally negotiate for payment in the currency of their own residency. Payment can be made by check, wire or electronic funds transfer. There are pros and cons to each method. For example, banks may put a hold on large checks, meaning that the funds are not available to the composer for several days, even after the check has been deposited. Checks from foreign publishing companies can be especially cumbersome, taking up to two weeks to clear. A wire deposit offers the advantage of fast transfer from the client and instantly available funds from the bank, but service charges can be hefty on both ends. Electronic Funds Transfers (EFT) and Automated Clearing House (ACH) transfers are other payment processes

REVISION HELL
(COMPOSER NAME WITHHELD BY REQUEST)

We just wrapped up a project with revision number … *58!!!* Seems like every single person in upper management wanted to have their say in the music, and in the most minutely frustrating way possible. Of all the revision notes we received from the team, my particular favorite was from the company's CEO, which came after putting one of our tracks on loop while he was jogging. He generated a list of specific mix critiques, requiring changes at specific moments in the track, all derived from his morning jog "critical listening" session. Priceless!

PEEK BEHIND THE CURTAIN

A Case Study In Negotiation

About a week after I sent in my music demo for the *Avatar* video game, my agent Noemie Dupuy called with some good news. "Congratulations! They loved your demo and have selected you to work on the game." I was thrilled. Then she told me the rest of the story. They had also selected another composer for the game. We would split the score roughly in half between the two of us.

Normally I am a generous person and a total team player. But I was currently employed full time as a Studio Audio Director for EA. If I was going to leave EA and return to composing full time, I would need the whole *Avatar* gig. Otherwise, it wasn't worth making the jump back into freelancing. I mentioned this to Noemie. She told me that the dev team had two big concerns with hiring me for the score without an additional composer. First of all, the timeline was incredibly tight and it was a massive music score. They were worried that there simply wouldn't be enough time to complete the project with one composer. Second, they wanted two very distinct styles of game music for the alien Na'vi and the human RDA. They doubted that a single composer would be able to deliver this diversity.

which make funds available when deposited. They generally take two to four days to process but rarely incur a fee. Composers should investigate the details of these options at their bank before negotiating a music scoring agreement. This will help the composer understand which method of payment would be best for a given circumstance.

Additional Compensation

Sometimes a game team can catch lightning in a bottle. A game can become a classic, resonating with millions in a way that few could have predicted. When this occurs, it is both fair and smart to share the bounty with all contributors. Members of the development team have such perks built into their employment agreements, such as stock options and bonuses. But outside service providers like composers need to negotiate for these kinds of benefits.

With small game companies, composers might ask for bonuses at certain sales milestones. Aaron Marks describes one potential bonus structure in his excellent reference book, *The Complete Guide to Game Audio*:

"Bonuses are usually more palatable for a game company. For example, if their break-even point on a game is 60,000 units, a bonus after 100,000 units sold is a comfortable margin and the game company shouldn't have any problem sending additional money your way. [Bonuses] can be set up in various stages, say a $10,000 bonus after 100,000 units, a $25,000 bonus after 250,000 units, and so on. It's completely up to you and the company during contract negotiations. Bonuses are easy to calculate and audit because they are based solely on the number of units sold." [11]

Composers may also negotiate for stock. This is especially viable with new companies. Newer companies may be short on cash, and trading some percentage of the composer's fee for stock may be one way to please all parties. If a game is successful, then the composer shares in the increased value that a hit game brings to the company's worth. If the game is unsuccessful, however, then the composer is out whatever discount was traded for stock potential. As an aside, the vast majority of small game companies do not turn out blockbusters. It is extremely rare for a composer to make more money from a stock deal than they would have made by charging their normal rate. Although the occasional gusher does occur, composers are encouraged to engage in ample due diligence about the game and company, applying their best judgment before agreeing to trade cash fees for stock potential.

There are still other items of value that composers can negotiate for in a music agreement. Game companies buy computer equipment in bulk and frequently turn over their gear more frequently than composers do. Computing towers, monitors, laptops and A/V equipment may be acquired in a music deal as barter for some of the composer's services and at a reduced cost compared to a marketplace purchase. Composers can also negotiate for copies of the game, posters or other promotional swag to augment their pay.

I weighed and appraised the situation carefully. Then summoning all of the courage and wisdom within my grasp, I penned the following letter to the team:

"Regarding the tight schedule and large amount of music: We are more likely to rise to great achievement in the face of great challenge. We are more likely to find profound inspiration in the face of profound difficulty. By our very human natures, we are more naturally rallied to our finest efforts by a daunting task. The simple, the easy, the ordinary—these lack the power to reach the deepest part of our natures, therefore failing to draw out the superlative that lies within us. Only by extending our grasp to the very apex can we reach and deliver the otherwise unreachable.

A case in point is James Horner's experience in scoring the final climactic scene of *Aliens* for James Cameron. In the insanity of all the reshooting and re-editing that took place because of Cameron's intense focus on details (another hallmark of greatness), Horner had only three weeks to create the entire score. I've never forgotten the interview where Horner describes pushing himself to all extremes, detailing a thirty-six-hour straight composing session where he scores the final scene. Not surprisingly, it's the music from that very scene that producer Gale Ann Hurd says is 'the signature cue from the film' and has found a resonance far beyond the film, being used in countless action film trailers to this very day.

My team and I thrive on intensity. I once scored thirteen commercials for an international client in sixteen hours. The haunting and award-winning game theme from *King Kong* was created during a single intense all-nighter, with the Montpellier team waiting across the ocean. The Oscar-winning *ChubbChubbs* score was composed in a week. We do amazing things under a deadline.

Regarding the two very different styles of music required to underscore the Na'vi and the RDA: Great veteran composers, like great veteran actors, possess tremendous range. Consider the actress Meryl Streep, and her performances in two recent films, *Doubt* and *Mamma Mia!* They couldn't have been more diverse roles. Neither could she have delivered more perfectly for each film. Great veteran composers also do this. Consider James Newton Howard. His scores for *The Sixth Sense*, *Dinosaur* and *Snow Falling on Cedars* couldn't have been more dissimilar, yet each is perfectly on target. Likewise, my own range of voices is expertly diverse. Consider the scores from *Lord of the Rings Online*, *King Kong*, *The ChubbChubbs*, *Left Behind*, *Quest for Glory* and *Inspire: The Chicago Spire Art Film*. A more diverse collection of music may be difficult to find! But each delivers the right musical voice, and each delivered award-winning scores in every case.

The Montreal team faces an important and exciting decision. I hope these thoughts will offer encouragement to the team, and build their confidence in entrusting the *Avatar* score to my veteran experience. There's nothing I would like more than to dive deeply with them— and deliver an *Avatar* game score that surpasses everyone's hope and ambitions. I look forward to the team's decision."

That letter hit the bull's-eye. It fired up the team and gave them confidence in me. After some deliberations, they decided to award me the entire score. I made good on my word, delivering nearly four and a half hours of music tracks in just under three months. The Na'vi music is tribal, atmospheric and other-worldly. The RDA music is militant, earthy and action-oriented. The score was honored as a Music of the Year Finalist in the G.A.N.G. Awards and won critical acclaim and recognition from media outlets and industry awards around the globe. I learned so much about negotiation from that experience.

Performing Rights

ASCAP SESAC BMI

Composers are encouraged to affiliate with one of the three major performing rights groups, ASCAP, BMI or SESAC. Performing rights organizations track public performances of music, such as broadcast television, background music in restaurants and live concerts. Based on how many times a piece of music plays, what function the music plays and what venue or media stream the music plays in, composers will be paid a derivative performing rights royalty. If not handled by the game publisher, composers should register each piece of music in their catalogue with a performing rights org to ensure proper tracking and payment.

Since most games are played in private, music scores for games rarely qualify for public performance royalties. However, if players are posting a composer's music on YouTube, performing rights groups can track this. For registered pieces of music, this can generate a small stream of extra income for the composer. If a composer's game music is licensed for a commercial which plays on network television, the performing rights income can increase substantially. Even live concerts such as Video Games Live and PLAY can generate performance royalties under certain conditions.

Agents

The story is told of a young woman who dreamed of becoming a champion swimmer. She read books and magazines about swimming. She went to local swim meets and watched Olympic swimming on television. She bought bathing suits and goggles and swimming caps. She had a membership at the local recreation center. Her bedroom walls were decorated with posters of Rebecca Soni, Camille Muffat and Ranomi Kromowidjojo. All she ever talked about was how she was going to become a champion swimmer. But each time she got into the water, her only thought was getting out as quickly as possible. The water made her wet, cold and uncomfortable.

Thousands of composers want to be financially successful in their profession. But jumping into the deep end of a business negotiation makes them feel uncomfortable. They can't wait to get out. For such composers, finding a good agent to represent their business interests during contract negotiations may be advisable.

Composer agents specialize in music contract negotiation. The best agents do a fair amount of business with a wide variety of composers, developers and publishers. As a result, they should be savvy to the latest rates, trends, rights and other facets of a negotiation. But contrary to popular myth, a music agent does not go out and beat the bushes trying to find the composer work. Generally, the composer finds their own work and asks the agent to negotiate the terms of the deal.

Agents can be a mixed asset. Agents make their money by building relationships with and closing deals with developers and publishers. Thus, their motivation may be skewed toward serving the

GUEST LECTURE
ANCILLARY USAGE AND PERFORMING RIGHTS

Marty O'Donnell (*Destiny, Halo, Myth*)

Most of us end up composing music for reasons other than for the "sake of music" itself. Our compositions are meant to enhance a collaborative work such as a film, game, TV show or commercial and are usually made under a work-for-hire agreement. This doesn't mean that our music is without intrinsic value (value apart from its original context). Music is unique and malleable and can often stand on its own as a fully realized independent listening experience. However, when our music is separated from its original use and repurposed in a new and different way, this is referred to as an ancillary use of the music. Because this can happen, a connection between composer and composition needs to be maintained, since music has ancillary value that must be accounted for and protected. I believe that, at a minimum, all original music should be registered with a performing rights organization such as ASCAP, BMI or SESAC. In addition, the work-for-hire contract should specify how the composer will be compensated if the music is monetized in the future outside the intent of the original context. Soundtrack products, music libraries, live performances, sync uses with completely different projects, and other possibilities should be covered in the initial contract between the buyer and the seller (the composer). Often it is hard for a composer, especially one just starting out, to grasp the idea that underlying compositions have intrinsic value and exploitable potential apart from the original video game context. Sometimes the true value is discovered much later and in unanticipated ways. Protect yourself and your compositions. Even after you sell them, you are always the composer of that music—music that has intrinsic value.

needs and interests of video game companies, rather than building the careers of their composers. They may not be willing to push very hard for terms the composer feels strongly about. Also, most agents need to represent many composers in order to make enough money to qualify as a successful business. Thus, a composer may feel lost amid a metaphoric cast of thousands. In return for their services, music agents charge between 10 and 15 percent of the total amount they negotiate for the composer.

Attorneys

Unless composers have legal training and experience, it is advisable to enlist the help of a lawyer when entering into significant contractual agreements. Attorneys who specialize in video game music contracts can look over a proposed agreement, point out potential trouble spots and steer the composer away from potentially troublesome language and costly mistakes. They may be able to help the composer negotiate more favorable terms and even uncover hidden opportunities.

To a cash-strapped young composer, an attorney may seem like an extravagant luxury. But if something goes disastrously south in the business relationship, having had an attorney build an iron-clad contract will be worth its weight in gold. In this sense, attorneys are like insurance. They might seem expensive ... until something goes wrong.

Post Script Caveat

It is noteworthy that the composer rates, production costs and contract principles outlined in this chapter have remained relatively stable for many years. Notwithstanding a long period of stability, things can change at any time. Printed content that may be relevant and impeccably accurate today could become outmoded tomorrow. As often stated in mutual fund brochures, likewise with the numbers and best practices outlined in this chapter: "Past performance is no guarantee of future results."

SUMMARY

This chapter is written for composers who want to earn a living writing music for video games. For such composers, money is an important asset to understand and pursue through informed negotiation. Composers can approach a business negotiation from the perspective of warfare. They may also approach it from the perspective of marriage. In either case, understanding the people on the other side of the negotiation and their needs is critically important.

Most video game composers charge by the finished minute for original linear, looping and near-linear music tracks. These rates range from $250 per minute for novices working on low budget games up to $2500 per minute for the top composers working on major titles. Special case music blocks like intros, tags, stingers and transitions are more equitably billed by the asset. A good mid-range rate for such music blocks is between $400 and $500 each. Composer rates are additionally varied based on score complexity, types of assets being delivered and the range of services offered.

Production costs vary widely. Union options exist for recording video game scores in cities such as Los Angeles, San Francisco and London beginning between $270 and $300 per musician per session. The exceptional quality of musicianship and studios in these union towns continues to draw projects. Lower cost centers have developed in other cities with recording orchestras, such as Prague, Salt Lake City, Seattle and Nashville. These rates range between $21 and $75 per musician per hour. Orchestration and music prep services are likewise available from both union and non-union service providers, ranging from $40 per hour for services to $1,050 per finished minute of score. Studios and engineers can come as a packaged deal or bill independently. In general, the higher the cost of musicians in a particular locale, the higher will be the cost of recording studios and engineers as well.

Contract negotiation is a complex undertaking. Negotiating skills will pay dividends on the composer's bottom line in any number of ways. Composers are encouraged to make a serious study of negotiating techniques through reputable books and/or courses on the topic. Several points of importance to composers were suggested for consideration when engaging in contract negotiations, including compensation, rights, deliverables, schedules, publicity, approvals and revisions, expenses, indemnity, methods of payment and additional compensation. The roles of performing rights organizations and music agents were also touched on.

It's all about value. Music services and assets add value to the game. The composer's time, creativity, expertise and energy need to be compensated fairly. The data, terms and best practices learned in this chapter can empower composers to understand what to look for, what to watch out for, and how to succeed in negotiations with powerful video game companies, make a good living and thrive in an incredibly competitive professional environment.

APPLIED LEARNING

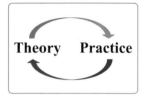

1. Write down your philosphy toward money as it applies to your career as a composer. Consider providing answers to the following questions: Is your primary goal to maximize profitability, or to deliver an artistically impressive piece of work? Is money a natural result which will spontaneously flow in proportion to your career progression and talents? Or is money something that stands apart, independent? How motivated are you by money in your work? Which factor do you think plays a bigger role in obtaining higher pay, your artistic excellence or your knowledge in business?

2. Using the music design you created for Chapter 3 and the Bid Sheet template contained on the book's website, prepare a competitive bid using the composer rates learned in this chapter.

3. Prepare three optional production budgets for recording twenty minutes of music with a sixty-piece orchestra and thirty-voice choir in Los Angeles, Salt Lake City and Nashville. Assume you will be able to record five minutes of finished music per hour in each location.

4. Find at least three different recordings of video game scores recorded in Prague, Salt Lake City, Seattle, Nashville, London, San Francisco and Los Angeles. After listening critically and comparing each recording, write a summary of the characteristic pros and cons of each locale, from a sound and performance quality perspective.

5. Imagine that the music bid you prepared for #1 is accepted by a client. Select the city from #4 above that you feel is the best choice for this approved score bid, and prepare a contract that covers all of the issues addressed in the section on Contract Negotiation. Use the Music Services Contract Template included in the book's website resources.

6. Research music agents and performing rights organizations. Select an agent and performing rights group you would most like to work with and describe the reasons why. Also list the reasons why other options are less desirable.

REFERENCES

1. http://www.amazon.com/Business-Life-Dont-Deserve-Negotiate/dp/0965227499.

2. Darren Perkins, *Business is War—The Unfinished Business of Black America* (Atlanta: Mind Altering Publishing, 2010).

3. Sun Tzu, *The Art of War*, Ch. III.

4. http://scienceofstrategy.org/main/content/basics-sun-tzus-playbook.

5. http://www.newzoo.com/free/rankings/top-25-companies-by-game-revenues/.

6. http://elitedaily.com/money/entrepreneurship/having-a-business-is-like-having-a-marriage/.

7. https://www.linkedin.com/pulse/article/20141022174039-283620963-what-mark-cuban-and-donatella-versace-get-wrong-about-hiring?trk=tod-home-art-list-large_0.

8. https://www.linkedin.com/today/post/article/20130411174413-101213441-the-magic-and-mystery-of-negotiating-winning-deals.

9. Personal conversation with the author, *Caribe* cruise ship, 1989.

10. Roger Dawson, *You Can Get Anything You Want: But You Have to Do More than Ask* (New York: Regency Books, 1985); Roger Fisher, William Ury and Bruce Patton, *Getting to YES: Negotiating Agreement Without Giving In* (London: Penguin, updated revised edition 2011); Chester L. Karass, *In Business as in Life, You Don't Get What You Deserve, You Get What You Negotiate* (Beverly Hills, CA: Stanford Street Press, 1995).

11. Aaron Marks, *The Complete Guide to Game Audio* (Lawrence, KS: CMP Media, 2001), 6.1.8.

Creativity. The heart of a video game composer's business is creativity—reliable, productive creativity across decades of music scoring. This kind of creativity requires a brain continually percolating with ideas—an active, healthy brain, chugging along at sustained energy levels for hours, weeks and even months at a time. Maintaining vibrant physical, mental, emotional and spiritual health is critically important for composers who aspire to work in the industry for more than just a few years.

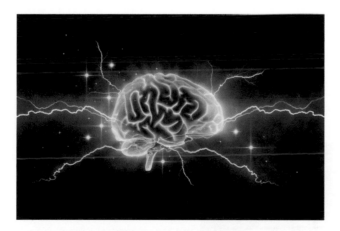

Original, resonant and captivating musical ideas all flow from the inspired human imagination. The brain is the very workshop of imagination. It is the single most important piece of technology any composer will ever use. It is without question the composer's most prized and precious asset. In fact, the value of the brain is so stunningly preeminent among all other components of a composer's business that it deserves a lifetime of research, investment and care to keep it robust, active and strong.

Sports teams go to great lengths to protect and cultivate their franchise players. Research facilities spare no expense to develop and guard their trade secrets. Exotic car owners lavish disproportionate amounts of time and money to keep their dream machines in tip-top condition. Likewise, composers who aspire to long and thriving careers should invest generously in the health and maintenance of their mind and body, thus preserving their ability to create at an extraordinary level.

This chapter will explore a number of principles and practices that have been helpful to many video game composers in keeping their energy level and creative productivity high. Topics will be organized under broad headings of physical, mental, emotional and spiritual health. Guest Lecture sidebars in this chapter are from video game composers who have remained at the top of the game since the 1990s and, as of this writing, are still among the best in the business. Composers are encouraged to use this chapter as a springboard to lifelong learning and committed engagement in a healthy lifestyle. A healthy composer is not only good for business, but good for life.

PHYSICAL HEALTH

This chapter offers no pretense of being a medical text. However, common sense, easy access to published research and years of shared experience have borne a few gems of collective wisdom. Topics covered in this section will include *water intake, exercise, good nutrition, adequate sleep, hearing* and *avoiding damaging substances.*

Water

From the Mayo Clinic's *Healthy Living* website: "Water is your body's principal chemical component and makes up about 60 percent of your body weight. Every system in your body depends on water. For example, water flushes toxins out of vital organs, carries nutrients to your cells, and provides a moist environment for ear, nose and throat tissues."[2] Doctors, nutritionists, personal trainers and mothers have all preached the general health benefits of ample water intake for years. But recent research published in the journal *Frontiers in Human Neuroscience* has shown that water consumption can specifically and measurably increase the brain's performance. Scientists in the UK, from the universities of Westminster and East London, found that under certain conditions, "drinking three cups of water before completing a task can increase the brain's reaction time by 14 per cent."[3]

On the other hand, lest composers rush to affix their mouths to a faucet, extreme water intake in a short period of time can lead to a dangerous and sometimes deadly condition known as water intoxication.

When a person drinks too much water in a short period of time, the kidneys cannot flush it out fast enough and the blood becomes waterlogged. Drawn to regions where the concentration of salt and other dissolved substances is higher, excess water leaves the blood and ultimately enters the cells, which swell like balloons to accommodate it.[4]

So how much water does a composer need? The Institute of Medicine, an appendage of the National Academy of Sciences, issued a report in 2004 outlining recommended daily water intake for healthy, active adults. For women, the average requirement is 2.7 liters (91 ounces) daily. For men, the daily average is 3.7 liters (125 ounces). The report estimated that only 20 percent of a person's required daily liquids comes from their food.[5] So drink up! Just not to ridiculous extremes. Keeping water near a workstation may be a good idea.

PEEK BEHIND THE CURTAIN

Water, the Magic Elixir

My current writing studio is downstairs, inside my home. Like many middle-class Americans, I have a refrigerator which dispenses local municipal water through a filter. The filtered water tastes pretty good. But the refrigerator is upstairs.

For years I have engaged in a practice of keeping a large mug of water on my desk, which I sip from regularly while composing. This has many benefits. For starters, it keeps my brain and body hydrated, which seems to increase my energy level, mental sharpness and sense of physical well-being. As another benefit, I have to get up out of my chair periodically to walk upstairs for a refill. It feels good to move up and down the stairs. Finally, ingesting all of that water gets me out of the chair again for *another* reason, one that helps keep my system flushed. These are all good consequences that flow from drinking water throughout my work day.

GUEST LECTURE
WALK THIS WAY

Nobuo Uematsu (*Final Fantasy*)

Video game composer Nobuo Uematsu (*Final Fantasy*) once told a room filled with nearly 500 game developers that he finds it beneficial to get up and go for walks. He says it breaks up his work day and refreshes his mind.[8] Uematsu continued, "Walking the dog and pacing a room is somehow helpful. When I'm walking, I find that I can solve problems and find inspiration … I walk to my car, then I realize: Oh! That's how!"[9]

The positive effects of walking regularly are well publicized. According to the American Heart Association, even thirty minutes of daily walking can reduce the risk of heart disease and certain cancers. It can also lower blood pressure and improve mental well-being.[10]

Exercise

Video game composers do an inordinate amount of sitting. They sit while they work. They sit while they look for work. They sit while they promote their work. They sit, sit, sit, sit. Myriad studies have shown that long periods of daily sitting can add up to serious health problems over time.[6] This growing body of evidence suggests that remaining sedentary is not a good thing for the body. Happily, composers need only rise and move about periodically during their day, even for just a couple of minutes at a stretch, to minimize the negative effects of prolonged sitting.[7] Get up every hour or two. Refill the water jug, visit the bathroom, grab a snack, check email or phone messages standing up. It is important to move, to get out of the chair regularly throughout the day.

Another easy practice which can help keep the body moving is to bounce a leg up and down, or drum otherwise inactive fingers while working. Especially for composers with a strong intrinsic sense of rhythm, this can be a natural and continuous outlet for minor muscle movement.

Walking is good for the body and good for the mind. Composers can add steps to their day by making small adjustments, such as taking stairs instead of elevators or escalators, parking further away from entrances, gently pacing instead of standing in line, walking into restaurants instead of using the drive-through, taking a break during the day to walk outside, and so on. Composers who get moving in even these simple ways are more likely to keep their creative engines running longer and better than those who don't.

Of course, some composers also engage in more rigorous forms of exercise. Many run, swim, lift, spin, play basketball, soccer, racquetball, ski, bike or hike. The physical benefits of exercise are widely published and well known. Keep in mind that most activities that benefit the body also benefit the brain. A healthy composer is a composer who can work. And a working composer is good for business.

Nutrition

The music business is not exactly known for its healthy eating habits. Ask music students how to ensure they are getting all four food groups in their daily diet and they may answer, "Pizza". Nevertheless, if the brain is a composer's most precious commodity, it stands to reason that healthy eating is an important investment in the brain's performance and longevity.

An internet search for "brain foods" returns nearly one hundred million results. A conscientious browsing through several pages of articles and lists reveals a whole smorgasbord of ideas. Dig deeper into the research and a number of recurring foods emerge. The most ubiquitous entry by far, showing up in nearly every article and nearly every list of top brain foods, is avocado. Benefits from avocado are significant and numerous. Many articles mention such things as protecting astrocyte nerve cells, keeping the brain's membrane flexible, and improving blood flow in the brain. Other frequently mentioned brain foods include eggs, blueberries, salmon and kale/spinach/broccoli. Walnuts and curry make a good showing, with honorable mentions for beans, lentils, oatmeal and grass-fed beef. Unfortunately for many music students, there is one item that is noticeably absent from all articles on foods that benefit the brain—pizza.

On the flip side, processed sugars came up on nearly every list and article as having a negative impact on brain function. A few articles even compared its negative impact to that of cocaine. Processed sugar can impair natural metabolism, cause cognitive deficits and trigger inflammation and damage to cells in the brain. It can spur constant hunger and unhealthy cravings. None of that is good for a composer's creativity. The list goes on and on. There is such a unanimity of voices condemning high intake of processed sugars, and from such a broad diversity of disciplines, as to leave very little doubt of its undesirable impact. Sweeteners like corn syrup fall into this same category.

Nutrition is a big topic. This is a small chapter, in a business section, in a textbook about writing music for video games. Composers are thus encouraged to seek their own nutrition research from a variety of sources and make committed decisions that will provide the best possible care and protection for their brains and bodies for years to come.

GUEST LECTURE
HOW TO NOT BURN OUT

Neal Acree (*World of Warcraft, Starcraft II, Diablo III*)

The most important thing for me to stay creative is knowing when to take a break. Sometimes you need to push through an uninspired patch and sometimes you need to take a break and recharge. Even with a looming deadline you need to be careful not to keep the pedal to the metal non-stop or you'll burn out and lose more time than you would have had you taken a nap here and there or gone to bed early that one time when you were just completely blocked. Creativity is not unlike a well. If you keep drawing from it without replenishing it you will come up dry. And how do you replenish? By filling the well with experiences and art that stimulates your senses. Know what moves you and make time to experience it when you're feeling creatively taxed. For me it's watching movies, listening to music or creating something completely unrelated to music. Fill the well and you will never come up dry.

The mind and body are a delicate but resilient machine and it's extremely important to know how yours works and what kinds of things affect it positively and negatively. Here are a few tips I've learned along the way. Eat slow burning foods that are low on the glycemic index to avoid crashing and burning.

Sleep

Because of tight deadlines and sprawling music designs, many composers may find themselves doing all-nighters periodically throughout their careers. At the very least, they may often have to burn the candle at both ends. In a perfect world, game developers would plan better and bring composers onboard early in a project. Composers would avoid procrastination, diving in early and leaving plenty of time to compose, revise and produce their music. But this is not a perfect world and all-nighters are an unfortunate but all too common custom in the industry.

Going without sleep can have a surprisingly negative impact on the composer's ability to create. The United States Government's Center for Disease Control and Prevention states that adults need seven or eight hours of sleep each day.[11] This is not exactly a startling news flash. But what may come as news to some readers are the ways in which a lack of sleep can negatively affect the brain's performance. In a frequently cited study published in 1996 by professors Pilcher and Huffcut from Bradley University, participants who slept less than five hours in a night took a measurable hit to their mental functionality, as evidenced by a level two standard deviation underperformance on a diversity of cognitive tasks and motor skill functions.[12] In 2009, the Harvard Medical School went even further, warning that sleep deprivation "wreaks havoc in the brain", negatively "affects levels of neurotransmitters and stress hormones" and "impairs thinking and emotional regulation."[13] The following year, the National Center for Biomedical Technology Information summarized their findings on sleep deprivation by adding that not only are basic cognitive skills impaired, but also the higher brain functions of creativity, innovation and divergent thinking are degraded.[14] None of this is good for composers. In today's hyper-competitive music scoring marketplace, no one can afford to have the creative capacity of their brain degraded. No one can afford to have their cognitive skills impaired.

These implications are thought provoking. How does a composer handle an overflowing bucket of tasks under a tight deadline, without working beyond exhaustion? Composers want to impress, they want to deliver, they want to be seen as indispensable in order to win the loyalty of their clients. These attitudes are generally good for business. Composers will be asked to work under unreasonable deadlines again and again throughout their careers, which is an ugly reality of the video game scoring business. And so, careful consideration must be given to weighing and appraising what a composer is willing to sacrifice in order to win a client's loyalty. Ironically, because of the volatile nature of the game industry and high rates of turnover, a composer may win a loyal client at a major publisher today, only to find the same person working for a phone carrier or insurance company tomorrow. Thus the costs of sleep deprivation are known, while the benefits to a composer's business are not always clear or permanent.

Caffeine can be a tool for some of us to stay focused and provide artificial energy but know your limits and stay hydrated as it can also burn you out after a long day. Try to inject a little physical activity throughout the day even if it's a quick stretch or a walk. Physical activity is not only good to counter the negative health effects of sitting for long periods of time, it also helps stimulate the brain which helps stimulate creativity. Motion is another great creative stimulator. Peter Gabriel swears by writing on the train but I've found a short drive will do wonders.

It's important to realize that there is an ebb and a flow to creativity and inspiration and while we can help nurture it, ultimately we have less control over it than we might think. The best I can hope to do is to create a conducive environment for inspiration and try to maintain it as long as possible.

PEEK BEHIND THE CURTAIN

MIXING *DOTA 2*

One of the strangest and most disturbing experiences I ever had in a studio happened while I was mixing my music score for *DOTA 2*. I had booked a top mixing studio for a week. But due to the complex nature of the score and the sheer quantity of music that needed mixing, I found myself going at it pretty much around the clock. When exhaustion completely overcame me, I would pull three chairs together and lie across them to sleep. I would set my phone alarm for two or three hours, then get up and go at it again.

Toward the end of the week, probably Thursday afternoon, I became frustrated. I was trying to create a blend of the live strings and sampled strings, but everything I did sounded distorted. No matter what I dialed back—EQ, FX, levels, etc.—nothing removed the distortion. I rebooted the system, checked amplifier and speaker thresholds, soloed tracks, everything I could think of to troubleshoot. No good. I knew those tracks were clean because I had listened to them critically during the sessions and afterwards while editing. Still the distortion persisted.

Simply stated, the brain needs seven or eight hours of sleep daily in order to perform at its best. Composers need to understand that cutting corners from that norm, whether occasional or chronic, will always incur some cost. Sleep on that.

Hearing

Second only to the brain in its importance to a composer are the delicate and complex organs that comprise the middle and inner ear. One way composers inadvertently damage these organs is through prolonged exposure to high decibel sound levels. There is no denying the thrill that many composers feel when listening to one of their own creations played back loudly on high fidelity studio monitors. No argument here, it is an emotional and physiological rush. But please be wise. Don't crank the volume up too much or too often. The impact of intense sound waves on the delicate nerve and cell hairs of the cochlea can be irreversible.[15] Once the ability to hear at certain frequencies is gone, it doesn't come back.

Hearing loss can affect a composer's judgment at every stage of the process, from composition through tracking, editing and mixing. An inability to clearly discern the interplay and blend of frequencies in a piece of music can have obvious negative effects. In addition to partial or total hearing loss, there are other unfortunate conditions that can follow years of listening too loudly. Tinnitus, which is a continuous ringing sound in the ears common in musicians, recording engineers and composers, can be annoying at best and debilitating at worst. Hyperacusis, which causes an increased sensitivity or intolerance to certain common or low level sounds, can make background walla grating, excessively loud and even painful. Composers need to fearlessly protect and preserve their hearing. It is their second most important business asset.

Damaging Substances

Cocaine, crystal meth, heroine, krokodil, ecstasy … these are dangerous, incapacitating drugs that destroy both the brain and the body. For a sobering look at the impact that these poisonous substances can have on the human body, try performing an internet image search using the phrase, "drug use before and after". The external damage visible in these photos, even after just a few short years, is both stunning and frightening.

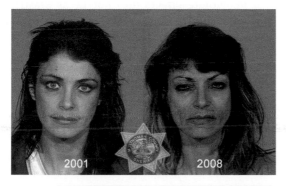

2001   2008

The internal damage is even more significant. Of the ten major organ systems in the human body—skeletal, muscular, circulatory, nervous, respiratory, digestive, excretory, endocrine, reproductive and lymphatic—all ten are injured by drug abuse. Fragile bones, muscle fiber breakdown, kidney damage, anemia, liver cirrhosis, brain cell destruction, sepsis, erectile dysfunction, cancer and a compromised immune system are but a few known effects of drug abuse on the body.[16] This cross-section brain model shows an example of the kind of damage that can be caused by cocaine use. It is a sobering image.

Then something truly alarming happened. I accidentally knocked something on the floor, and it sounded distorted. I stopped in my tracks and paused to try to make sense of what my ears had just told me. Then I snapped my fingers. Distorted. I clapped my hands. Distorted. I made several other noises in the room on various surfaces. All fuzzy and distorted. I called my wife. Her voice sounded fuzzy and distorted. By now I started focusing on a feeling within my ear canals. They felt swollen on the inside. Somehow I had bludgeoned my hearing so relentlessly for those four days and nights of mixing that every sound coming through the mechanism was distorting. At that point I decided it would be a good idea to go home and get a full night of sleep. *Silent* sleep. The next day, there was enough improvement to return and finish the mix. I have never experienced that before nor since. I hope to never experience it again!

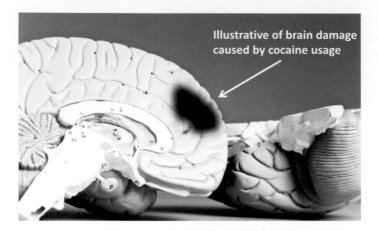

Illustrative of brain damage caused by cocaine usage

Other less overtly toxic substances can be also be detrimental to the composer's mind and body, including alcohol, marijuana, tobacco, caffeine and misuse of prescription drugs. Although their immediate effects may not be as drastic, nevertheless these too can be abused, leading to impaired brain function or damage, chronic illness and disease. Alcohol in particular, especially considering its popularity at business gatherings and social settings, poses a risk. Short-term impacts of alcohol consumption are widely known and sometimes winked at, including slurred speech, impaired motor function, compromised judgment, vomiting, diarrhea and blacking out. Long-term effects include high blood pressure, alcohol poisoning, liver disease, nerve damage and permanent brain damage.[17] Drinking while pregnant is an especially egregious act. Fetal alcohol syndrome destroys capacity in the unborn, debilitating a completely innocent person for a lifetime.

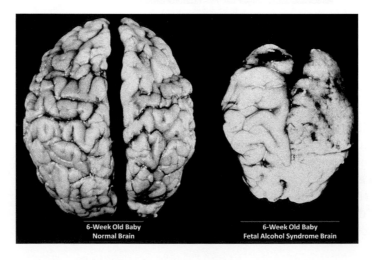

6-Week Old Baby
Normal Brain

6-Week Old Baby
Fetal Alcohol Syndrome Brain

Drug abuse has taken a high toll in the entertainment industry. Shining stars like Whitney Houston, Phillip Seymour Hoffman, Michael Jackson, Chris Kelly, Heath Ledger, Chet Baker, John Belushi, Jimi Hendrix, Janis Joplin and too many others have been snuffed out prematurely because of drug abuse.[18] What masterpieces they may have yet showered upon the world, had they been able to better care for their bodies and minds! What sadness and suffering they may have avoided for themselves and those who loved them! It is a tragedy from every possible angle.

While the perspective of this chapter is focused on keeping the brain healthy and vibrant for the sake of the composer's work, there are a thousand other important reasons to stay away from these addictive and corrosive substances. Do not get involved. Do not indulge. Better to never dabble or experiment, not even once, than to risk the well-documented ruin that so many of these substances bring in their wake. Live healthy, take care of the brain and body for a good quality of life and a long and prosperous career in music.

MENTAL FITNESS

The human brain conducts its creative activities through billions of microscopic processors called neurons. The adult brain likely contains over 200 billion neurons, divided into approximately 10,000 different categories. These tiny micro-processors are all connected to one another by web-like tendrils called synapses. These hair-like nerve fibers pass electrical and chemical impulses from one neuron to the next.[19] Imagine an infinitesimally small, biological version of the entire world wide web encased in a single human skull. This is the delicately robust apparatus within which all musical ideas are born, develop and flow from concept to completion.

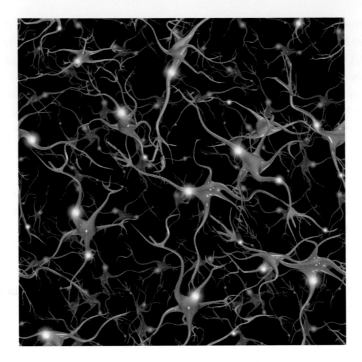

Growing this network of fibers and keeping them well lubricated and tuned up for optimum chemical and electrical performance is a top priority for any serious composer. The positive benefits to the brain from water intake, good nutrition and exercise have already been discussed in previous sections. But please consider this one additional plug for keeping fit. In 2008, Stanford University hosted a gathering of top neuroscientists from around the world. Their mission was to pool their expertise and find areas of accord in the field of mental fitness. The results of the summit were published as a manifesto entitled, "Expert Consensus on Brain Health".[20] They concluded that peer-reviewed research demonstrates unequivocally that physical exercise spurs the growth of new neural connections and adds a wealth of mental side-benefits, including enhanced reasoning abilities, better focus and improved memory. Composers are encouraged to get up, get out of the chair and get moving!

OK, now sit back down and read some more. Physical exercise alone does not build all the neurons and synapses needed for creative and productive thinking. The Stanford conclave also agreed, not surprisingly, that *education* also builds and strengthens the brain. Stimulating learning is certainly not limited to a classroom. The aforementioned manifesto also makes this point by mentioning a wide range of representative learning activities, such as trying a new recipe, playing with children, exploring nature, getting involved in the community and pursuing formal education activities. All of these can lead to neural growth and mental fitness.

It is fascinating to observe what happens to the physical structure of the brain when learning occurs. New ideas trigger the outgrowth of new synapses and connections, while repetitive learning adds bandwidth and speed to existing connections. BCU professor of neuroanatomy Tara Gaertner boils it down with a musical example:

"Every thought is encoded by the firing of a specific group of neurons, all connected in a circuit. So a particular circuit fires when we think of the note, middle C, for example. And there's another circuit that fires when we picture a note on the first ledger line below the treble clef staff. When we learn that this position on the staff corresponds to middle C, both of these circuits fire at the same time. And when neurons fire at the same time, the connections between the neurons get stronger. The synapses get stronger, and/or new synapses form. This means that the next time we fire the circuit that means "note on the first ledger line below the staff", the circuit that corresponds to middle C is more likely to fire. Neuroscientists have a saying for this: 'Neurons that fire together wire together.' From a learning standpoint, it means that we have learned to connect those two ideas by physically altering the way the neurons in our brain are connected."[21]

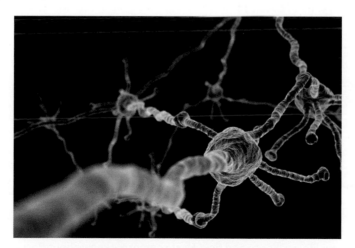

Now, what is the practical application for a video game composer? For one thing, the more a composer exercises and expands the skill of writing music, the more those neural pathways will be stimulated, grow and get stronger. Thus, composers should be writing music consistently. Also, the more a composer's mind is exposed to new music, new thoughts and new skills, the more neural pathways will form and develop, making new thought processes and ideas available to the composer. It is critical to keep learning, to continue exposing the mind to new ideas and to exercise existing knowledge skills. The mind stays fit when the mind is used. It grows when it is pushed. New neural pathways can form and older bundles can become stronger.

In practical terms, this can include listening to great works of music, both historical and contemporary. Embrace it. Composers should never be afraid to provoke the mind with a continuous and evolving supply of listening materials. Read the thoughts of great thinkers. Jesus, Plato, Einstein, Gandhi, Emerson, Kant, Jefferson and Confucius, among others, are sure to challenge and inspire. Keep a journal and practice good writing skills. Engage in debates on complex issues. Teach others a skill or principle. It is an axiom that we learn more by teaching a topic than by merely studying it. Even good entertainment can stimulate the brain. Play games with smart friends. Watch a great movie. Follow a favorite TV series. Just beware of entertainment oversaturation to the point of inertia (vegging). The key is to continue practicing important skills and to keep learning, working out various parts of the brain so that the organ stays fit and strong.

EMOTIONAL HEALTH

In 2009, the Harvard Medical School published a book entitled *Positive Psychology*. This text links positive emotions to a slew of desirable benefits, including better health, longer life, resilience and flow. Most composers know about flow, a condition where hours pass like minutes, concentration is spontaneous and continual, and work seems effortless and fulfilling. Most would agree that achieving flow is a highly desirable professional benefit. One surprising insight from the book is that people often misjudge the things that will actually make them happy, thus promoting a state of flow. Researchers discovered that gratitude, meaningful service, savoring pleasure and maintaining supportive relationships proved to actually be among the most reliable sources of positive emotions.[22]

Concerning supportive relationships, it must be said that relationships take time. Composers with a spouse or serious girlfriend/boyfriend will discover that the strength and benefit of that relationship is often proportional to their recurring investment of time and energy. William F. Harley, Jr., a clinical psychologist and marriage counselor, has advised spending about fifteen hours of undivided attention together each week to maintain a loving relationship.[23] From a business perspective, the question must be asked—is this kind of investment worth the return? News magazine *Intelligence For Life* gathered data from around the web addressing this question and found some startling answers. Among their findings about married couples: they tend to be happier than their single counterparts; they live longer; they make more money; they are less likely to get involved in drug or alcohol abuse.[24] Composers with children also need to find ways to keep those connections alive and growing, not only for their children's benefit but for their own. Many studies have demonstrated the emotional health benefits that flow to involved parents, including increased self-esteem, more laughter, renewed involvement in learning and deep feelings of loving and being loved. Composers should take a look at the high value relationships in their lives and decide how best to keep them vibrant and strong.

In spite of strong relationships, exercise, service or any number of known contributors that tend toward happiness, sometimes traumatic events can intrude

PEEK BEHIND THE CURTAIN

Date Night, Family Night and Obi Wan Kenobi

Three small practices have made a big impact on the quality of my marriage and family relationships. First, I continue to date my wife. We got married in 1985 and still go out together weekly. We may have dinner together at a restaurant, take a walk, attend a show, park in a beautiful setting, listen to music, talk, or any number of a hundred other activities. It almost doesn't matter what we do, as long as we are together for several hours, just the two of us. Second, my family and I gather together at least once each week for a family night. We may talk, laugh, sing, learn something, watch a movie, play a game, eat something delicious, discuss problems and plan our coming week. Third, I try to keep an open door policy in my studio. If my wife or kids need my attention for a moment, they can come right in and talk with me. Some composers are afraid their children will monopolize their time. This can certainly happen if some boundaries aren't set. But more often than not, the kids just want to touch base. Here's one example. My youngest son came bounding into the room in complete Obi Wan Kenobi apparel and said, "Dad, have you seen Darth Vader?" I replied, "Yes, I think he's hiding under the stairs." He said, "Thanks, Dad! Gotta go!" He spun around and off he went. That's all it took.

GUEST LECTURE
HOW TO MAINTAIN YOUR
MUSICAL MENTAL HEALTH

Inon Zur
(*Dragon Age, Crysis, Prince of Persia*)

As a composer for many years in the industry I have come to understand many issues that young composers will have to struggle with on a daily basis. Among them:

- Rejections. There are many times that music that you are writing to pitch on a new project will be rejected and you will end up not getting the job. It is very likely that almost any music cue you are writing for any project will meet criticism, and you will be asked several times to change it or redo it. It is also possible that after the project will be done and published you will receive some negative criticism from your audience. This is mentally hard—the music you write comes from within you and criticizing your music is like criticizing your very being.

- Politics and non-music related issues. It is likely that during the course of your career you will face some political decisions that will work against you—even though your music was right and great for the project. This is an injustice that is very hard to conceive of, yet it exists on a very large scale. And as high as you go in your career, you are likely to meet more and more of these.

- Productivity. Most composers can't maintain the same level of creativity and originality all the time. It is hard to accept, but sometimes you just write music that is less good than at other times. And yes, this can sometimes hurt you.

unexpectedly, effectively torpedoing a person's emotional health. The death of a loved one, a severe accident, bullying, sickness, unemployment— these are all high stress disturbances that can cause a person to experience serious struggle and distress. One factor that influences whether a person will recover quickly from such events, rather than becoming immobilized and stagnant, is the person's resiliency. Scientists have identified five specific traits or practices engaged in by resilient people:[25]

1. They keep a positive outlook.

2. They recognize the temporary nature of any setback. All storms eventually pass.

3. They are adaptable. Change and flexibility are part of their nature.

4. They stay healthy. Exercise, good nutrition, adequate sleep are part of their routine.

5. They have a strong support group.

Even during periods of relative normalcy, negative feelings can come with the ordinary ups and downs of life and the natural ebb and flow of human emotions. Try not to worry about this too much; everyone has down days from time to time. On the other hand, if a composer experiences severe or chronic depression in spite of healthy lifestyle management, professional counseling and/or medical help may be necessary.

SPIRITUALITY

For many creative people, nurturing the spiritual side of human nature is both personally fulfilling and professionally constructive. The sense of peace, purpose and direction that can come to a spiritually centered individual is extraordinary. The human craving for spiritual connection transcends geography, culture and time. People from all walks of life—young, old, rich, poor, intelligent, impaired, whatever—have felt drawn to something or someone greater than humankind. There is an upward or inward pull, tapping into a broader spectrum of influence, something outside the mortal shell.

Ancient mythology talks of mortals reaching for the divine muse, a voice of inspiration that brings transcendent ideas to poets, artists, musicians and so forth. Some of the greatest works of Western classical music have come from a composer's attempt to tap into, capture, celebrate or convey this sense of the spiritual. Bach, Handel, Mozart, Beethoven, Mahler, Brahms, Verdi and Mendelssohn are but a few of the familiar names whose arguably crowning works have risen from this perspective. There seems to be something about reaching toward the unfathomable that brings out the very best.

How can this possibly apply to video games? Surprisingly, some of today's top video game composers also include a spiritual striving in their musical creativity. Composer Jack Wall (*Call of Duty, Mass Effect, Lost Planet*) is one proponent of the modern muse. He says,

"There is a spiritual component for me where I meditate on something related to what I'm writing for and ask for guidance. I take myself

- Competition. In most cases there are *many* other composers that are after the same job—and they are good, and you know it. This is a very difficult situation. Not only that you are working so hard to produce your music, but you also need to compete with others.

So … what to do??? How can we maintain our well-being while maximizing our potential and ability? Here are few points that I found work quite well for me. They might not work for everyone, but at least you can try them. It's my top ten list of musical mental health behaviors.

1. Maintain a precise schedule and routines. Your body has its own daily time line and you need to recognize it and find where in the day you feel the most productive and stick to it. *Listen* to your body, don't try to force on it habits that it is not built to do.

2. Eat well and try to do it at the same hours every day.

3. Sleep well—you need it for your good musical judgment.

4. Exercise on a regular basis—you need a well-maintained stamina to do what you do and physical strength is a very important component.

5. Try to have a competitive sport you can take part in. For example, I play competitive basketball twice a week. This really helps to support and enhance my competitive edge as well as my teamwork abilities. Any sport is recommended.

6. Try *not* to take into your heart every criticism. We know that we are all very sensitive as artists so we need to develop thick skin to block many things that are being said to us and about us.

7. Don't try to mimic becoming like someone else. Know who you are, learn to love and accept it and try to write your real self rather than trying to mimic what you perceive as successful or current or trendy.

8. Know how to learn from others and accept your need to learn no matter how old you are. I'm trying to learn from *any* composer I listen to—because what they have to say can enrich my musical thoughts.

9. Use failures as a spring to make you jump back and rise even higher. Say to yourself that every setback is an opportunity; every door that is closing can lead to an opening of another one. It is not your failure that defines you but rather how you respond to it.

10. Learn to love and accept who you are—with the good and bad. The less you struggle with yourself, the more productive you will be.

GUEST LECTURE
NATURAL IMMERSION

Tim Larkin
(*Counter Strike, DOTA 2, Uru*)

So composing music isn't always about composing music. Sometimes it's about finding the energy and spark to create, and sometimes it's about staying away from the studio in order to come back to it feeling motivated enough to create from a fresh perspective. I've always been a strong proponent of a healthy work/life balance feeling, and that weighting any one place or situation for too long can inhibit creativity.

out of it as much as I can and that can often yield extraordinary results. When that happens, it's not about me anymore, but rather, about tapping into a deeper idea. It's like I'm channeling music that's already there, just waiting to be discovered."

Likewise, composer Sam Cardon (*Overwatch, World of Warcraft*) says,

"I'm pretty confident that anyone involved in the creative process is tapping into something very powerful from the cosmos, far greater than our human condition. I feel lucky to be in a profession where I have to find a way to tap into that regularly. Certainly my finest work happens when I've done that successfully. I don't have a strict regimen as it relates to my creative work but I do have a regular and consistent belief, and that gives me hope when I am in my moments of creative desperation. I'm grateful for that every day."

Quieting the soul and opening up to the infinite may lead a composer to new creative vistas that might otherwise be inaccessible to them.

Some video game composers nurture their spiritual connection while immersed in nature. Standing on top of a mountain peak, diving to the bottom of a coral reef or gazing thoughtfully into a star-filled sky can fill the soul with wonder, awe and resonance with the irresistible aesthetics of the natural world. Get out in nature, breathe in its vastness and majesty!

Composers can struggle with doubts, fears and ambiguity about the future. A strong faith and spiritual grounding can help composers move forward, trusting that things in their life and career will work out. This quiet underpinning of conviction can keep them progressing in spite of uncertainty.

As Steve Jobs, the founder of Apple Inc., once said,

"You can't connect the dots looking forward; you can only connect them looking backwards. So you have to trust that the dots will somehow connect in your future. You have to trust in something—your gut, destiny, life, karma, whatever. This approach has never let me down, and it has made all the difference in my life." [26]

SUMMARY

There are many influences at work that shape the human brain and impact a composer's access to its treasures. Composers should care for their brain as their most prized creative asset. It is the one asset that is uniquely and inescapably irreplaceable. Lifelong research and continual commitment to positive action can add firepower and vitality to the brain, delivering better music across a longer career span of creative productivity.

There are many brain-friendly principles and practices which composers can engage in for enhanced physical health, mental fitness, emotional health and spirituality. Applying these positive principles and practices toward lifestyle management is a smart investment in the composer's business and a good move for life.

For me, I feel that spending as much free time as possible doing activities such as hiking, fly-fishing, skiing or just being outdoors soaking in the sights and smells of open spaces often pulls me away from the stress and focus of being behind a keyboard trying to knock out the next theme while my ADD brain is sending me signals that the hatch is on and I should be casting to the nearest rise in the river.

There's energy in these places that we harness unknowingly. Whether it's just our pupils being exercised by the contrasting sun and shadows in the surroundings or ions that are charged from incoming surf, I almost always come away with a relaxed and recharged feeling I don't get elsewhere. Just as I often strive to create tension and release in the music I write, I feel that our natural rhythms need that parallel to balance out. And while I generally try not to actually think about composing melodies or what orchestrations might be on the menu for the current composition, I have been known to pull out a small portable recorder that I carry with me to capture some of the ambience of the moment. Often I end up using that recording in a project down the line, but even if I don't, I can pull it up and listen when I'm stuck at my desk and remember for a short time that the hatch was perfect that day.

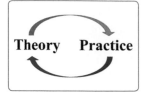

APPLIED LEARNING

1. Devise a plan for regular water intake that meets the US Government's daily recommended amount for you. Execute your plan for at least one week. Write down any positive results you observe.

2. Make a simple chart for each day of the week. Mark a notation for each time you get up and walk around. Increase your total each day as the week goes by.

3. If your current diet lacks some of the brain-beneficial foods listed in this chapter, make a plan which rectifies that. Eat consistently healthier, including many brain-healthy foods in your diet, for at least one week. Write down any positive results you observe.

4. For one week, test the benefits of sleeping a full seven or eight hours each night. Write down any positive results you observe.

5. Complete an internet search for the effects of drug and alcohol abuse on the body and the brain. Describe at least ten ways in which these substances can destroy your prospects for a long and prosperous creative career in video game scoring.

6. Ask five friends whose musical tastes you trust to recommend a soundtrack they think you should listen to. Pick at least one you have never heard, find it and listen to it all the way through. Write down your impressions.

7. Make a list of at least fifty things in your life for which you feel genuine gratitude. When an item on your list involves someone else, take the time to express your gratitude to them.

8. If you are in a committed relationship, schedule a date night out together for several hours. Do it this week.

9. Consider your own approach to the spiritual side of human life. Write down the experiences you have had that fill the emptiness of the soul, bring you peace and/or help you feel connected to the infinite. Describe any experiences you've had where you felt inspired in your music.

REFERENCES

1. Steven R. Covey, Jr., *The Seven Habits of Highly Effective People* (New York: Free Press, 2004), Table of Contents.

2. http://www.mayoclinic.org/healthy-living/nutrition-and-healthy-eating/in-depth/water/art-20044256.

3. http://www.medicalnewstoday.com/articles/263648.php.

4. http://www.scientificamerican.com/article/strange-but-true-drinking-too-much-water-can-kill/.

5. http://www.iom.edu/reports/2004/dietary-reference-intakes-water-potassium-sodium-chloride-and-sulfate.aspx.

6. http://www.nytimes.com/2011/04/17/magazine/mag-17sitting-t.html.

7. http://www.nytimes.com/2012/04/29/sunday-review/stand-up-for-fitness.html?_r=0.

8. http://www.gdcvault.com/play/1020258/Interview-with-the-Maestro-Nobuo.

9. http://www.nobuouematsu.com/nobgama.html.

10. http://www.startwalkingnow.org/whystart_benefits_walking.jsp.

11. http://www.cdc.gov/sleep/about_sleep/how_much_sleep.htm.

12. http://www.journalsleep.org/Articles/281110.pdf.

13. http://www.health.harvard.edu/newsletters/Harvard_Mental_Health_Letter/2009/July/Sleep-and-mental-health.

14. http://www.ncbi.nlm.nih.gov/pubmed/21075236.

15. http://www.jneurosci.org/content/29/45/14077.full.

16. https://bradfordhealth.com/damaged-organs-i-drug-alcohol/.

17. http://www.drugfreeworld.org/drugfacts/alcohol/short-term-long-term-effects.html.

18. http://www.drugs.com/celebrity_deaths.html.

19. http://www.mind.ilstu.edu/curriculum/neurons_intro/neurons_intro.php.

20. http://longevity3.stanford.edu/brain-health/expert-consensus-on-brain-health/.

21. http://trainingthemusicalbrain.blogspot.com/2012/04/cellular-mechanisms-of-learning.html.

22. http://www.health.harvard.edu/special_health_reports/positive-psychology-harnessing-the-power-of-happiness-personal-strength-and-mindfulness.

23. Willard F. Harley, Jr., *His Needs, Her Needs for Parents* (Grand Rapids, MI: Baker Book House, 2003), p. 57.

24. http://www.tesh.com/topics/love-and-relationships-category/are-married-people-more-successful-than-singles/cc/13/id/573.

25. https://www.anxiety.org/blog/traits-of-resilient-people.

26. http://news.stanford.edu/news/2005/june15/jobs-061505.html.

EVOLUTION

CHAPTER 13
DISRUPTIVE INNOVATION

Innovate or die.[1]

C layton M. Christensen is a distinguished professor of business at Harvard University. In 1997, he published a landmark work entitled, *The Innovator's Dilemma: When New Technologies Cause Great Firms to Fail.* The book describes a business phenomenon which Professor Christensen labels *disruptive innovation.* In a nutshell, **disruptive innovation** occurs when leading companies in an established industry, through the process of refining products to meet the needs and demands of their most profitable customers, eventually bypass the needs and means of their least profitable customers, creating a vacuum at the bottom of the market. New companies come in with innovative basic products which meet underserved needs and means at the bottom. The new products and companies evolve and grow as the bottom grows in market share, eventually upending the existing economic model and driving the old guard out of business.

One example of this comes from the early computer industry. There was a time when mainframes and mini-computers ruled the world of business and academic computing. When serious processing was needed, expensive mini-computers were purchased, or time was leased on a mainframe to do the job. Working with these machines required specialized training, time-consuming processes and significant capital investment. For many years, there simply was no other choice. Personal computers at the time were little more than toys or curiosities. And while established companies like Digital Equipment Corporation continued to position their computers to meet the demands of top clients (leaving their bottom-tier customers farther and farther behind), personal computer manufacturers like Apple began to innovate to meet basic business and academic needs. Though they were clunky and inelegant compared to their high end counterparts, personal computers began to gain a small foothold at the bottom of the market.

Meanwhile, the best mini-computer companies were busy evaluating how to continue improving their products to meet needs at the top of the market where their most profitable and demanding customers were. There was no foreseeable business reason to abandon this strategy. Why change their focus from providing excellent, award-winning, high-margin products for their best customers and switch to producing cheap, low-quality, slim-margin products in a race to the bottom to acquire this new fringe customer? And so they continued to make better and better products at high profit margins to keep their best customers and shareholders happy.

But the bottom continued to grow. As a result, more resources began to pour into these new startups, allowing them to continue innovating and improving their products to serve new customers, growing a burgeoning market for personal computers. As the new machines grew more powerful, more intuitive and affordably accessible to the masses, their market share swelled, diverting yet more resources back to their manufacturers, enabling continued innovation and improvement.[2]

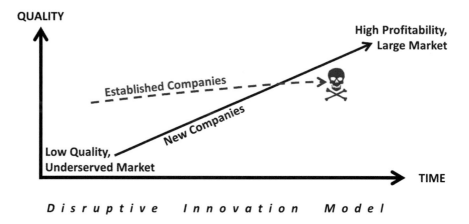

Disruptive Innovation Model

To be short in writing, the new market for personal computers eventually overtook the demand for mini-computers completely, making the older machines obsolete and driving their manufacturers out of the market. What irony! In attempting to serve the needs of their best customers, the mini-computer manufacturers put themselves right out of business. Professor Christensen summarized it in this way, "It is actually the principles of good management which we teach at the Harvard Business School that sow the seeds of every company's ultimate failure."[3]

None of this should be lost on those who have observed the video game business for any length of time. The history of the game industry is filled with disruptive innovations of one kind or another. Circuit board games, cartridge games, CD-ROM games, online games, motion sensing games, mobile games, new virtual reality … and what next? No one really knows for sure.

Why include this discussion in a textbook about writing music for games? Because there are vital lessons here for video game composers up and down the food chain, from newbie music school graduates to the gnarliest old veterans in the business. This chapter is intended to serve as a three-alarm call to awareness for video game composers in all phases of their careers. Make note: disruptive innovation is coming, again and again. It cannot be stopped. It will not be stopped. The following pages will explore what implications this brings for video game composers at the beginning of their careers, in mid-career and at later stages of a career.

New Composers

Disruptive innovation is a recurring fixture in the game industry, continually churning the market and repeatedly opening up new opportunities for young composers to enter the business. This is great news for music students at the start of their careers. There will always be opportunities again and again at the bottom of the market. Entry barriers are low, colleagues are young, energy is high and openings are everywhere. As new game ideas ripple through the industry, hungry young composers willing to work hard and cheap can find gigs at the bottom where most of the unexpected innovation is often occurring.

One of the exciting things for young composers is that every once in a great while, one of these innovations will hit the market with the right product at the right time, and it will take off like a rocket. This is a lucky break for the entire team, including any composer attached to the project. Such successes usually translate to another round of funding for the company, often giving the team greater resources with which to make their next game. For the composer, this dramatically improves the likelihood of a second gig with the developer. This is no small feat in and of itself.

But most startup developers die quickly and ignominiously. Composers who work for the bulk of these game makers work hard and cheap … and once. Then they have to start the process over. So working on a hit game and getting a shot at doing a second game with a better budget is like winning the career lottery for a young composer. There is something exponential that happens when composers are attached to a hit. In addition to rising with their original team, a hit gives a composer the first modicum of credibility within the broader industry. This kind of credibility is essential to start climbing out of the primordial ooze of no-budget/garage/college/indie development and start pitching for bigger budget projects.

On the flip side of the coin, all of these opportunities for young composers can breed peril as well. Work is hard and pay is low at the bottom, so composers can burn out and lose faith trying to hit the jackpot again and again as they work for one indie developer and then another. It is a hard racket to break out of. It certainly can be done and it has been done. But it can be very tough at the bottom. In addition, sometimes young composers will catch a ride on a hit game out of pure luck, then find themselves woefully unequipped to handle the demands of higher profile development. These demands may include:

- Higher production values
- Shorter time constraints
- More complex music designs
- Varying stylistic requirements
- More cooks in the kitchen to answer to.

The learning curve can be very steep.

Therefore, one possible success route for young composers is to dive into the bottom of the market with both feet. Research and meet indie developers. Contact and interface with development teams at colleges and universities. Look at their game designs. Play their prototypes. Pick some games that appear to have a shot in the marketplace. Using the principles learned earlier in this book, offer your services, negotiate the best possible deal and do the best work you possibly can. Then do it again with another game. And another. Remember, because of the principle of disruptive innovation, the bottom of the market is where many of the great game-makers of tomorrow will undoubtedly arise. This is where, to borrow the phrase introduced by Josh Aker in Chapter 10, many composers will find their "sacred pair". But even if that ship never comes in, so to speak, many young composers will eventually pick up enough skills, contacts and credibility to move up to the next level of game-scoring opportunities. On the other hand, some composers will simply run out of interest, stamina or money, and move out of the business altogether.

Mid-Career Composers

The mid-career stage for a video game composer can be a complex, fascinating, perplexing and exciting place to be. For purposes of discussion here, mid-career is considered from five to fifteen years working in the industry. Composers in this stage will likely see at least one completely transformative change in the nature of the game business, maybe more. They may feel pulled in many different directions as they try to keep their low budget client base happy while expanding into higher paying gigs. They may wonder how best to grow their skillset. For example, should they study more about orchestration or devote their attention to middleware implementation? And of course, there is the constant clamor of competition. New composers flood the marketplace every year. Ladders to more lucrative projects are crowded with other mid-career composers, ambitious newcomers and cagey veterans alike. Mid-career can be incredibly perplexing to navigate.

Having said that, there are three sequential objectives which every mid-career composer may want to consider. The *first goal* would be to improve upon existing core competencies that have immediate commercial application. An honest self-evaluation will generally yield a reliable view of where a composer's strengths have been emerging and which of those have been resonating with the marketplace. One reliable measuring stick for such self-evaluation is the collective content of this textbook. For instance, if a composer has developed a knack for certain advanced music design techniques, such as interior pathing, and has gained positive response from clients, players and the press, that skill should be targeted for continued enhancement. This may include developing more sophisticated mapping techniques or more efficient processes. It may also mean devoting more of the composer's website to promoting this growing skill and trumpeting the market's positive response.

Second, mid-career composers should start developing new areas of expertise. They can look both up market and down market to find new skills to develop. For example, looking up towards the skills needed to obtain higher paying or more consistent contracts can offer the composer one set of choices. Paying attention to new trends and innovations percolating at the ground level can offer the composer another list of skills to choose from. When selecting a new area of expertise to develop, composers may consider such questions as:

- What are some needs I've encountered from potential clients, that I can't currently meet?
- Which new skills would allow me to better serve a wider range of clients?
- Which new skills will meet the needs of higher paying clients?
- What resources do I have available to invest in my own career development?

- Where do I go to find/learn/acquire/develop these new skills?
- Do I have any show-stopping weaknesses that must be shored up now?

Third, mid-career composers should consider diversifying their portfolio. In this sense, a composer's portfolio consists of those clients, market niches and musical styles in which they currently operate. The reasons for diversification are many. Game developers come and go. Fads rise and fall. People enter and leave the business or change companies in a constant stream. Today's hit becomes tomorrow's parody.

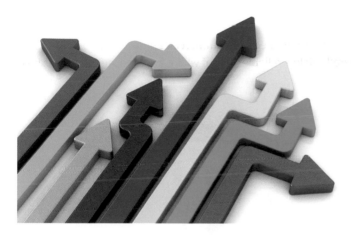

There are a few rare composers who have managed to ride a single client or single style for most of their careers. But for every other composer in the entire industry, disruptive innovation and industry volatility make such a myopic strategy untenable.

Mid-career composers may also consider the merits of expanding their work beyond the game industry. Traditional media can help fill the coffers and teach a few things about music scoring that may not be as easily learned from a constant diet of video games. For example, composers can pick up valuable insights about dramatic flow from

MID-CAREER BOOM AND BUST

For years a composer may struggle in anonymity. Then, all of a sudden, they have a big hit—and boom! Everybody knows them. Here come the press with endless requests for interviews, quotes, high res photos and music samples. Here come the accolades, as awards and nominations start to pile up. Friend requests swell the composer's Twitter and Facebook accounts. Invitations for speaking engagements trickle in. There may even be an uptick in demo requests and general inquiries from potential clients. This is all good.

But then, just as quickly as this tsunami of attention came to overflow the composer's life, it can recede and disappear completely. The phone doesn't ring, text notifications and emails drop off, work dries up … and the composer is left scratching his head and wondering, "What just happened?" One year a composer is everybody's darling, the next year she can't get arrested. Just as the composer thinks he has finally arrived, the momentum can dissipate, dropping the composer back into the fray of hustling hunters and gatherers. The stark contrast of this dynamic can be difficult to absorb. Those who take the flash of success too seriously can swell with arrogance or entitlement. Those who mourn its loss too deeply can sink into discouragement or depression. The lesson here is to not be caught off guard when it occurs. Or, as Rudyard Kipling wisely suggested, "Meet with triumph or disaster and treat those two imposters just the same …"[4] Like the dynamic waveform of a great music track, most careers tend to cut a jagged path through the middle years. Highs and lows. Peaks and valleys. Fertile fields and barren deserts. Don't be surprised when it happens to you. It is a common trajectory experienced by many mid-career composers.

film directors. They may gain new insight into human psychology working with advertisers. Writing for a television series may add more efficiency to a composer's workflow. And so on. All of these improvements can subsequently be brought to bear to improve the composer's work in video games. Video game composers thus engaged become transmedia composers, evolving not only their skillset and client base, but their perception in the marketplace as well. As another side-benefit, sometimes a composer will gain a significant measure of cachet within the game industry for noteworthy work done outside the industry. All of this helps.

Veteran Composers

Ironically, for video game composers who have built long and successful careers lasting more than fifteen years, big changes can be imminent and unavoidable. Veteran composers are at a high risk of becoming irrelevant due to the arc of most life-cycle curves in this business. Recall the skull and crossbones on the graph at the beginning of the chapter? By this stage in a composer's career, games will have changed radically from the time they first entered the business. There may be more urgency than ever before for the composer to evolve.

For veteran composers, the time may have arrived for reinvention. In considering their own reinvention, composers should analyze carefully whether to make a radical break from their past or gradually ease into new roles. Each has its benefits and drawbacks. When Marty O'Donnell broke from Bungie, it was big news because of his iconic, long-term connection to their brand. Big news like this can capture people's attention for a time, delivering marketing value to the composer and opening doors while such awareness remains top-of-mind. Imagine if Russell Brower left Blizzard and launched a company designing 3D music for virtual reality games. That kind of bold, reinventive contrast would generate widespread interest. This combination of juxtaposing something old and familiar with something new and unexpected, together with the inherent risk involved in making such a drastic change, is what draws the attention. The question that must be asked and answered is whether a composer can capitalize on that kind of splash, manage the risk and generate a sustainable new business. If yes, then a radical transformation may be the best way to go. If not, then perhaps a gradual path to reinvention is preferable.

A gradual path to reinvention has many benefits. Veteran composers can maintain current clients and associated income while making small forays into new territory. They can dip their toes in and test the waters in multiple areas, evaluating possible interests and aptitudes, without risking total commitment to unproven paths. This approach is wise for veterans with busy composing schedules who want to keep riding the old train as long as possible while laying away for an airplane ticket to the future.

The gradual path can take on many forms. It may include working with student dev teams twice a year to get a handle on the next wave of game making. It might involve lending their name and clout to upstart music tech or virtual instrument companies in exchange for access to new scoring tools or methodologies. Some veteran composers pursue speaking engagements at universities and colleges or try out a modest teaching schedule. Some seek cross-pollination with fresh collaborators—young composers brimming with new ideas, mixing artists and engineers from another industry sector, or musicians in a different recording locale. This brings to mind an important point to consider. While having a loyal group of familiar collaborators is important for reliability and efficiency during mid-career growth, breaking out of the old mold and getting in touch with new influences may be more important for veterans.

Fortunately, by this stage of a career, most veteran composers will have acquired a formidable arsenal of skills, broad networks of associates and plenty of professional savvy. This puts veterans in an excellent position to evolve. Among other things they will have learned how to learn. They will know who knows what and where to find them. Reinvention is certainly easier than building a brand new career from scratch.

In whatever form it takes, the overriding goal of the foregoing discussion is to help composers prepare for the inevitable. And change is the one thing that is inevitable. Unforeseeable innovations are coming. Disruptive events and trends are coming. Change ripples continually through the industry. Change runs through people's personal and professional lives. And change comes with age. Activities and achievements that felt thrilling and meaningful to someone in their twenties may ring hollow to someone in their forties. Whatever passions a composer may have once had, these may have run their course. This is completely normal in a person's personal and professional trajectory. Successful composers will evolve and grow through all phases of their careers. It is an exciting prospect to look forward to.

SUMMARY

Disruptive innovation occurs when new products enter the bottom of the market to address underserved basic needs, while established leaders keep evolving existing products to meet the most sophisticated needs at the top of the market. As the distance between the two customer types increases, new companies gain space to grow, gathering market share and resources from the ground up. Growth of new product innovation can evolve to make the old product obsolete, driving the former market leaders out of business.

The video game industry is rife with disruptive innovation. New technologies and methodologies percolate up continually, wreaking havoc among existing business models, making kings and paupers in a continuous round of change. Video game composers must not be blind to this fact. They must prepare to evolve and reinvent as appropriate during each stage of their career.

Because of this phenomenon, new composers have a seemingly endless supply of opportunity within the constant churn of indie-scene developers and academia's annual game-making programs. The work is hard and the pay is low here, but inventiveness and energy abound. Occasionally a new composer will get lucky and score a hit game, launching a career with a burst of attention. But most new composers will use this early time in their careers to score games with limited commercial success, acquiring essential knowledge, skills and contacts along the way. This slow and steady preparation empowers new composers to begin moving up the ladder to better opportunities.

Composers in the middle of their careers can expect to face some turbulence. Industry volatility makes change inevitable. Mid-career composers can more successfully navigate these times by keeping a level head and concentrating on three important developmental goals. First, they can improve on any of their existing core competencies that have immediate commercial application. Second, they can expand into new areas of expertise. Third, they can diversify their portfolio within the game industry and outside into traditional media. Such a strategy can keep the composer both steady and growing through the challenging mid-career years.

One of the trials facing many veteran composers is the challenge of reinvention, in order to avoid the risk of obsolescence. This can be tackled head-on with an abrupt and radical reinventive change, or it can be approached gradually. There are potential advantages to either approach. Most veterans have acquired the expertise necessary to pilot these changes with poise.

Change is inevitable. Disruptive innovation is a fact of industry life. Video game composers must evolve with the changes to stay engaged in the business.

APPLIED LEARNING

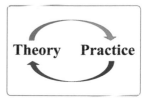

1. Identify and describe three disruptive innovations you have seen in your lifetime.

2. If you are a new video game composer, research and make contact with at least one academic game development program and two indie game developers. Select at least one game from among them that looks promising. Utilizing the principles learned in this textbook, obtain a scoring contract and deliver a knockout music score.

3. If you are a video game composer in mid-career (five to fifteen years in the business), conduct the self-examination suggested in this chapter. Make a list of your core competencies with the highest potential market value. Next, look up market and down market and identify those areas of expertise that you most need to develop. Finally, identify at least three ways you can expand your current portfolio. Make and execute a plan to build your strengths, add new expertise and expand your portfolio.

4. If you are a veteran composer, describe whether an abrupt or gradual reinvention program is best for you. Explain why.

5. Again, for veterans, identify three possible ways to reinvent yourself. Create a plan to learn more about each path. Make a summary report listing pros and cons of each. Continue exploring or dive into your own career reinvention based on your findings.

REFERENCES

1. http://tompeters.com/blogs/freestuff/uploads/Innov_tactics121_Appends011309.pdf.

2. Vinson Carter. "Disruptive Innovation in Technology and Engineering Education: A Review of the Three Works by Clayton Christensen and Colleagues, A Comprehensive Review", *Journal of Technology Education* 24(2, Spring, 2013): http://scholar.lib.vt.edu/ejournals/JTE/v24n2/pdf/carter.pdf.

3. Video clip: http://www.youtube.com/watch?v=WxwR_TTuKdc#t=46.

4. Rudyard Kipling, "If": http://www.poetryfoundation.org/poem/175772.

CHAPTER 14
CONTEMPORARY VANGUARDS

Lead, follow or get out of the way.[1]

A *vanguard* is a person on the forefront of a new movement or field. Vanguards are agents of change behind the disruptive innovations described in the previous chapter. These are the people who will build tomorrow's hit games, grow new markets and provide exciting opportunities for video game composers in the years to come. Those who cultivate the ability to successfully identify such vanguards can reap exciting opportunities for artistic creativity in their careers and profit substantially.

IDENTIFYING VANGUARDS

Imagine possessing the intuition to identify the next Gabe Newell, Shigeru Miyamoto, Kellee Santiago or Will Wright. Short of looking into a crystal ball, are there attributes which can be observed in such individuals before they rise to success—attributes which could give composers a hint of good things to come? What makes the difference between a Carl Freer, father of the doomed Gizmondo game controller, and a Jack McCauley, inventor of *Guitar Hero*, when they both had possession of the same guitar-riffing game code?[2] If composers had some metric, some methodology for separating high probability prospects from a bad bet, they could fine tune the focus of their hunting and gathering activities for maximum potential.

Predicting the future is a tricky business, and there are no claims here for a fool-proof system of finding tomorrow's hit makers. But according to emerging scholarly research, there are a few identifiable traits that run through vanguard personalities.

Dr. Tomas Chamorro-Premuzic, an expert in personality profiling and a professor at London's University College, cites over a hundred scientific studies showing that "some people are disproportionately more likely to come up with novel and useful ideas, and ... tend to display a recurrent set of psychological characteristics and behaviors."[3] Those characteristics and behaviors are summarized in an article published in the *Harvard Business Review* in May of 2013:

1. *An opportunistic mindset* that helps them identify gaps in the market. Opportunities are at the heart of entrepreneurship and innovation, and some people are much more alert to them than others. In addition, opportunists are genetically pre-wired for novelty: they crave new and complex experiences and seek variety in all aspects of life. This is consistent with the higher rates of attention deficit hyperactivity disorder among business founders.

2. *Formal education or training,* which are essential for noticing new opportunities or interpreting events as promising opportunities. Contrary to popular belief, most successful innovators are not dropout geniuses, but well-trained experts in their field. Without expertise, it is hard to distinguish between relevant and irrelevant information; between noise and signals. This is consistent with research showing that entrepreneurship training does pay off.

3. *Proactivity and a high degree of persistence,* which enable them to exploit the opportunities they identify. Above all, effective innovators are more driven, resilient, and energetic than their counterparts.

4. *A healthy dose of prudence.* Contrary to what many people think, successful innovators are more organized, cautious, and risk-averse than the general population. (Although higher risk-taking is linked to business formation, it is not actually linked to business success.)

5. *Social capital*, which they rely on throughout the entrepreneurial process. Serial innovators tend to use their connections and networks to mobilize resources and build strong alliances, both internally and externally. Popular accounts of entrepreneurship tend to glorify innovators as independent spirits and individualistic geniuses, but innovation is always the product of teams. In line, entrepreneurial people tend to have higher EQ, which enables them to sell their ideas and strategy to others, and communicate the core mission to the team.[4]

Filtering the Data

The personality traits listed above deserve further exploration. What makes for an opportunistic mindset? How is it possible to spot a person who can recognize holes in the marketplace and envision how to fill them, even when no one else can? How could Thomas Edison have recognized that his one-time employee, Henry Ford, was constructing the next big thing in his off hours, thus possibly promoting him within the Edison empire instead of letting him go? After all, Ford himself stated that if people were asked what they wanted before the automobile's invention, they would have simply said, "A faster horse."[5]

Ford's life may provide a few clues. He left home at sixteen to apprentice as a machinist. He repaired steam engines, worked in factories and operated a saw mill. There was a relentless restlessness about this young man as he went about gathering education and experiences. In his twenties, he obtained employment with Edison, where he quickly rose to the position of chief engineer in just two years. Somewhere in the midst of this whirlwind, Ford envisioned his idea of a four-wheeled carriage run by a gasoline powered engine. He sold his prototype, founded a new company, then another, always striving for improvement in all areas of design, production, labor and distribution.[6] Thus, a restless drive toward understanding how things work, toward experimentation, building and betterment seems to be evident.

Vanguards crave novelty and complexity in their life experiences. So look and see who is out in the world, drinking in life with big gulps, constantly trying new things. Nolan Bushnell, the founder of Atari, comes to mind. *Pong*, Chuck E. Cheese, "Made in the USA", BrainRush … these are but a few of Bushnell's well-publicized novel and diverse ventures. Or consider Mike Morhaime, president and co-founder of Blizzard. According to the *Los Angeles Times*, a young Morhaime took a Bally gaming console apart and figured out how to program new games on it. He was in sixth grade. He went on to study engineering at UCLA, worked in Silicon Valley and founded his first game company in 1991, Silicon & Synapse.[7] Morhaime is also a world-class poker player, an avid gamer and the bass player in a heavy metal band.

What other factors from Harvard's list deserve additional examination? Formal education may sound like an unexpected filter point. But its focusing influence on developing a person's judgment cannot be ignored. Judgment is what allows a person to understand intuitively between a good idea and a non-starter. Judgment connects an individual's personal vantage point—how they process their observations of the world—to broad trends in good taste and style. Education helps in that regard. The video game industry has a rich history of well-educated leaders. BioWare founder Ray Muzyka graduated as a doctor from medical school. Sims creator Will Wright studied architecture, economics, mechanical engineering and military history at universities in Louisiana before graduating from the Manhattan New School in New York.[8] Oculus Rift founder Palmer Luckey was home schooled, taking his first college courses at fourteen or fifteen years of age.[9] Unreal Engine's software architect Tim Sweeney studied mechanical engineering at the University of Maryland.[10] Rockstar Games co-founder and lead writer Dan Houser graduated from none other than Oxford University. Education runs deeply through those who rise in the video game industry.

Tomorrow's vanguards will be finishers. Persistence tops many lists of success attributes, and for good reason. Pulling something off, building anything of value, takes a tremendous amount of hard work. Undertakings of significance are always cumbered with road blocks, unforeseen forks in the road and myriad other challenges which only relentless energy and determination can overcome. Remember that all puzzles yield to persistent, intelligent effort. Persistence requires strength, health and vitality of body and purpose. Look for those who rise again and again, see their projects through to completion, and have the wherewithal to keep going when other peers relent.

Reckless abandon, contrary to popular opinion, is not a characteristic of tomorrow's leaders. Calculated risk-taking is. According to data collected from over 7,000 test takers by corporate consulting organization PsychTests, "Calculated risk-taking involves a careful balance of sensation seeking, harm avoidance, conscientiousness, locus of control, comfort with ambiguity and reward orientation."[11] Which is not the same thing as abandoning risk. Risk is a necessary part of moving forward. As James Conant, the United States' first Ambassador to West Germany, famously said, "Behold the turtle. He makes progress only when he sticks his neck out."[12] Consistent winners have learned to sort out and analyze relevant factors and mitigate risk with good judgment. Andrew Wilson, the EA veteran who took over as CEO in 2013, made a calculated risk in pushing *Battlefield Hardline* out of the 2014 holiday lineup in order to deliver a more polished gameplay experience

GUEST LECTURE
SOCIAL CAPITAL

Penka Kouneva
(*Prince of Persia, Transformers, Gears of War*)

Social capital is very important, especially for young composers who think networking is going to functions and handing out their business card, unsolicited, after exchanging two words with someone—before they have learned to make eye contact or properly shake hands, before they have even mastered basic social graces. Some composers try to dominate a social conversation with their insecurity and narcissism and never stop talking about themselves, without asking the other person a single question about them. These composers must embrace the notion that entertainment is built on give-and-take, that they have to first contribute something, before expecting some return. I think it's good to just keep hammering into the heads of young composers how this career is *so not* about them, or about their music. Acquiring social capital with savvy and grace are the absolute foundations of innovation and success for composers. As American poet Maya Angelou pointed out, "I've learned that people will forget what you said, people will forget what you did, but people will never forget how you made them feel."

Here are some pointers for enhancing your own social capital:

- Learn to make deep eye contact.
- Shake hands properly, firm but not overbearing.
- Talk less and listen more.
- Ask questions of people about their passions, about their hopes, something outside of career and jobs.
- Cultivate many *and* meaningful relationships outside of your musician buddies.

to the players.[13] He weighed the short-term benefits of a holiday cash-in against the longer-term benefits of impressing players with a higher quality standard from his company. Battling a reputation of "America's Worst Company"[14] for the shoddy releases of the past, Wilson is using judgment to inform his decisions. As Will Rogers said, "Good judgment comes from experience, and a lot of that comes from bad judgment."[15] It's a circular kind of feedback loop, where people learn from decisions of the past (their own and others') to enable better decisions in the future. Tomorrow's winners will demonstrate that ability. Look for it.

The final point in the *HBR* list is social capital, otherwise known as networking. People need other people to go places in this world. A quick search for any successful game maker on LinkedIn will show they consistently have more than 500 professional connections. Facebook accounts and Twitter followers show a similar level of high connectivity among those who are moving and shaking in the industry. Lone wolves tend not to rise to the top.

Success and innovation most often sprout from a richly cultivated ecosystem of creative collaborators, advocates, mentors, peers and friends. Individual success stories rise most frequently on the collective shoulders of a vibrant community. Like crowd surfing over a mosh pit, successful composers are most often lifted to glory by the crowd of friends they are most engaged with.

None of these traits on their own yield a successful vanguard. Neither does their combination guarantee a commercial winner in the game industry. But they can certainly provide useful intel to young composers wondering which basket to put their eggs in. In searching for contemporary vanguards, this combination of traits could be considered a very good place to start.

GAME MUSIC VANGUARDS

As important as it is for composers to identify tomorrow's innovators in game design, development and distribution, there are some video game composers who will become vanguards in their own right. These composers will shape game music for future generations. It follows that some of the same characteristics which apply to innovative and successful game makers would also apply to innovative music making.

A study of history often reveals insightful details which can be applied toward the future. In that spirit, consideration should be given to those composers who have shaped the current video game music landscape. In preparation for writing this chapter, the membership of G.A.N.G. was surveyed for their thoughts on the most influential innovators in video game music history. The resulting list was long and insightful. In fact, because innovative types tend to be drawn toward technology industries like gaming, an entire book could probably be written on the topic of game music innovators. But as the purpose of this section is to provide a few stimulating examples to spur inspiration, only a handful will be highlighted here. In browsing these brief cameos, readers are encouraged to look for the qualities and circumstances that allowed or enabled each individual to become a contemporary vanguard in video game music. How did they demonstrate an opportunistic mindset? Did a formal education empower them in their craft? In what ways are persistence and prudence evidenced in their careers? Did they cultivate and exercise social capital to achieve success?

Finally, consider how those qualities might be nurtured in one's own professional development.

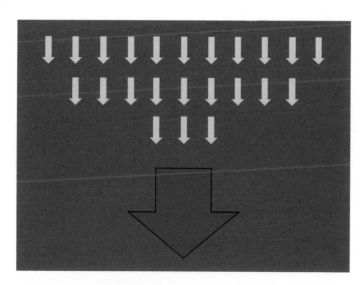

Koji Kondo
(*Super Mario Brothers, Legend of Zelda*)

Koji Kondo came to work for Nintendo in 1984 as the company's first music employee. He passed much of his first year tinkering in sound design and writing code for music playback, then exploding onto the world's stage and permanent collective consciousness with his themes for *Super Mario Brothers* in 1985. In approaching this scoring assignment, Kondo made a decision emblematic of musical vanguards throughout the ages. As he told *Wired* magazine, "I wanted to create something that had never been heard before."[16] And that he did. He played the game extensively, composing, rewriting, iterating, striving to find a way to make the music become as much a part of the game experience as the gameplay itself. Eventually, he crafted a stylistic amalgam of Latin influences, ragtime and jazz, voiced with square waves and accompanied by a noise channel swing beat. Kondo's *Mario* themes came to define the sound of games for a generation. Flowing as much from the limitations of the medium as from his decision to match the mood, movement and playfulness of the game's characters, *Mario*'s score emerged from a perfect storm of determination, innovation, intelligent problem solving and artistic expression. These traits continue to define the best video game composers today.

Kondo's career blossomed to encompass dozens of titles, including the widely beloved scores for the *Legend of Zelda* series. Over subsequent years, Kondo's role at Nintendo became more managerial, as he built a world class audio department, helping to guide younger composers and sound designers in populating the company's expanding portfolio with outstanding quality audio. As of today's writing, Kondo remains active in a supervisory role, continuing to lead Nintendo's sound creators in a quest to accentuate each game in well-crafted, creative and relevant ways.[17]

George Sanger
(*Wing Commander, Seventh Guest*)

George Alistair Sanger is one of game music's most flamboyant showmen. Known widely by his nickname, "The Fat Man", Sanger rose quickly to prominence in the mid-1980s, partially on the strength of his larger-than-life persona. Wearing a ten-gallon hat and a Nudie Cohn-made, hand-stitched suit, with a cigar in his teeth the size of a railroad spike, The Fat Man struck an indelible image. But there was more behind that grin than a penchant for showmanship.

Sanger exhibited an entrepreneurial instinct that often took him to the forefront of new ideas. As the market for home computer-based entertainment was just heating up in America, George went to work for Intellivision, producing audio for their 1983 game, *Thin Ice*. For the next ten years he pushed technical and creative boundaries in game music, pioneering live-to-MIDI recordings of musicians, adding songs and music videos to his projects, developing FM tones for sound cards and ultimately delivering the first General MIDI soundtrack for a game with *Seventh Guest*. His impressive score for *Wing Commander* was marketed as a key selling feature of the game, a rare feat even in today's market.

Sanger's path through the industry is a monument to the opportunistic mindset characteristic of vanguards. As the International Game Developers Association was being organized, he jumped onboard. As *Game Developer* magazine rose in circulation, he began authoring a monthly audio column. As conventions for game developers spawned, George started hosting music demo derbies. He co-founded the Interactive Audio Special Interest Group (IASIG) and helped establish the Video Game Archive at the University of Texas. He joined the Recording Academy as its first member qualified through game credits, and with the author was instrumental in the push for Grammy recognition of game music.

The burgeoning field of video game audio has provided myriad outlets for Sanger's restless intellect. From 1996 until 2010, he hosted a think tank dubbed Project Bar-B-Q, where game industry luminaries gathered to confront the limitations of current game audio technology, culture and technique. He launched a certification company which tests General MIDI software and hardware compatibility. He has ventured into slot machines, released an autobiography, served on advisory boards and judging committees, written debut columns for new publications and hosted a popular webcast. And where can George Sanger be found today? Not surprisingly, as the Audio Director of a new startup on the front edge of gaming, a half-billion-dollar company called Magic Leap, which aims to make holographic gaming a visual reality.[18]

Nobuo Uematsu
(*Final Fantasy*)

Nobuo Uematsu exudes the aura of a happy man. And why not? The popularity of his music has eclipsed that of many rock stars. When interviewed by the author for a keynote session at the 2005 Game Developers Conference, Uematsu's broad smile and twinkling eyes cut through cultural boundaries effortlessly. A self-deprecating sense of humor permeated the conversation and it soon felt like everyone in the room was a personal friend. And yet, as his story unfolded, it became clear there was more to this man than a cheerful disposition. Here was a man who was driven by a desire to connect to the world through music, and to find or make his own destiny in the music business.

Nobuo graduated from Kanagawa University in Yokohama, Japan, with an art degree in 1981. He was a self-taught musician, picking up piano and guitar while in his youth. After college, he obtained a job at a music store where a friend told him about an opportunity at a new game company called Square. He pursued the opening and soon found himself collaborating with Square's Director of Development Hironobu Sakaguchi. A string of games followed, but none would achieve commercial success or critical appeal. It was a discouraging time. Sakaguchi decided to make one final effort at a new fantasy game before throwing in the towel. It was to be, ironically, his final fantasy game.

As fate would have it, *Final Fantasy* became a runaway hit, launching a franchise that has spawned over a dozen games, a feature film, blockbuster soundtracks and a series of symphonic concerts. Central to the rise and popularity of the game has been its iconic music. From the very beginning, Uematsu emphasized memorable themes and captivating harmonies. Though working within the early constraints of three-note polyphony, he created a delightful score for the various areas and functions in the game. During the GDC interview, Uematsu related how this hardware-imposed limitation was both confining and liberating to his compositional process. Though confined to a narrow range of compositional possibilities, he felt freed to focus his time and energy on crafting unforgettable melodies, truly interesting harmonic progressions and compelling rhythmic constructs.

With every advancement in hardware capabilities, Uematsu pushed himself to create ever more complex and dazzling scores. With a growing worldwide audience, he began to arrange and record soundtrack albums of his music, and to provide orchestrations for live concert performances of his works. The first live orchestral game music concert in Japan (1991) featured three of Uematsu's themes from *Final Fantasy IV*. Other concerts in Japan followed, including an exclusive *Music from Final Fantasy* concert tour in 2002. The *Symphonic Game Music Concerts* in Leipzig, Germany, which began in 2003, also featured his works from the *Final Fantasy* series. The following year, *Dear Friends—Music from Final Fantasy* came to North America. Today, popular video game music touring shows such as *Video Games Live* and *PLAY! A Video Game Symphony* continue to perform Uematsu's works as standard repertoire.

Uematsu eventually moved on from the *Final Fantasy* series to compose and produce music for a wide diversity of video game, studio album and concert performance projects. His track record and discography, which continue to grow with each passing year, would be the envy of composers in any era.[19]

Troels Folmann
(8dio, *Tomb Raider, Transformers*)

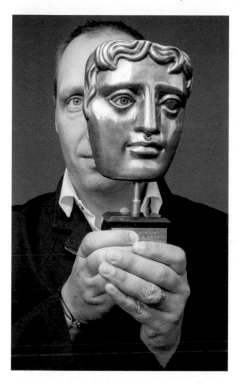

Unlike many of his peers in game music, Troels Folmann's instrument of choice has always been the computer. For Troels, the computer opened up a wider range of expression than any other single instrument he had encountered. He could find his way around a piano keyboard easily enough. But something about the ever-expanding possibilities of technology beckoned to him. After obtaining an art degree from the Copenhagen Art Academy, his fascination with computers led him to pursue additional degrees in information technology (BA) and artificial intelligence (MSc) at the Royal School of Information Science. Eventually, Troels would became a PhD scholar in adaptive music at Copenhagen's IT University.

Running parallel to this long-term courtship of technology was an equally ardent attraction to video games. Dating back to the Commodore 64 and the subsequent generation of evolving devices, Troels could always be found in the embrace of a good game. Games seemed a perfect antidote for his craving for intellectual stimulation coupled with serious fun. He immersed himself in MOD communities, finding a network of brilliant and creative friends who would later make their way into powerful positions in game development. These relationships, and Troel's reputation for doing "a whole lot of freaky and funny things", opened up music scoring opportunities for major franchises like *Tomb Raider* and *Transformers*.

In spite of the fun, while in the midst of these computer-centric adventures Troels Foelmann experienced a gnawing frustration. The sonic palettes available to composers and the tools that accompanied them were woefully dissatisfying. To remedy that, in 2005 Troels and a group of friends embarked on recording their own, fairly ambitious custom samples. They sampled a symphony orchestra and full choir together. The results were promising. They made more recordings, sampling a wider and wider range of instruments, eventually deciding "it could be fun to make some of the libraries commercially available." As an outgrowth of this "fun" would emerge three juggernauts of the sample library industry, Tonehammer and its successors 8dio Productions and SoundIron. To say that thousands upon thousands of music tracks have come to life with the sounds of these libraries would not be an exaggeration.

Never one to rest on either his laurels or his laureates, Troels continues to push boundaries today. Yet, in spite of his inclusion in the vanguard section of this textbook, he refuses to see himself as a forerunner.

"I don't think it's healthy to pass judgement on myself in regards to innovation. I will let others be the judge—and this is actually an important point! The worst thing you can do as an aspiring composer is to get high on your own stuff. I spend the majority of my time thinking about how I suck and how I can get better. The day I start thinking of myself as an innovator will be the day my career ends."

Innovative thinking, indeed! [20]

Simon Ashby
(Wwise, *Myst III*, *Myst IV*)

While Simon Ashby was pursuing a bachelor's degree in Music Education at the University of Quebec in Montreal, he found his attention continually drawn away into all manner of electronic music experiments with sequencers, synths and samplers. Thus it was not terribly surprising that after graduation, instead of going to work as a music teacher, he found himself working for Ubisoft Montreal as one of the first fifty employees of the company. Those first fifty employees were all learning on the job, jumping into the guts of creating games with tools that were barely usable at the time. At least, they were barely usable for sound artists like Ashby. It was during this time, when he was fighting through painful constraints to accomplish even the simplest tasks—like fading sounds in and out without having to write code—that a lightbulb came on in Ashby's mind. Why not create an audio tool that would simplify and streamline this process? Why couldn't there be an audio tool made by audio artists, for audio artists?

It took about three years of evening and weekend work before he and his partners finally got everything in place. Audiokinetic opened its doors in June 2003 with a mission to create Wwise, a sound engine that would empower audio creators to enhance the whole game experience by contributing engaging soundscapes on any platform and under any technical constraint.

Enabling an audio artist's unencumbered creative flow in the highly technical and challenging environment of game development was the pillar of Ashby's vision. The guiding star was to abstract as much of the technical complexity as possible from the process, without removing control, so that users could think in terms of emotion, focus and finesse instead of buffer size, voice count and other technical constraints imposed by each platform.

Surprisingly, there was considerable resistance in the beginning from the development community. As Ashby quipped, "Convincing smart people that built their own sound engine to abandon their tech and switch to Wwise—when you're mostly unknown and unproven—has been a journey in itself!" It took several years to get traction and persuade leaders in the industry to realize that Audiokinetic was a serious software developer with meticulous engineering and serious support.

Looking back on the whole experience from his current perspective, Ashby says,

"Twelve years after we moved into our first office, I'm still deeply passionate and enthusiastic about game audio. When I take a step back on this little idea we had fifteen years ago that is now helping thousands of audio artists and programmers in realizing their visions, I recognize that leaving Ubisoft to start this project for the greater good of the community was the best decision I could have taken back then."[21]

Guy Whitmore
(*Peggle 2, Gears of War, Fable*)

Guy Whitmore studied music composition and guitar performance at Northwestern University and Southern Methodist University, where he received graduate degrees in music. While at SMU he came under the tutelage of a remarkable theatrical director from whom he learned principles and practices that ultimately transferred well to games. For example, theater production, like game development, is a multidiscipline art form, which includes music composition, lighting design, set design, costume design, sound design, etc. Theatrical composers have to learn to be successful collaborators and team players. These university experiences led to professional work with regional theaters including the Dallas Theater Center, the Dallas Children's Theater, and the Attic Theater in Los Angeles. Here Whitmore learned the hard realities of immovable deadlines and tight schedules. Come what may, the show must go on. Theater sound also drove home the idea that context is everything, another principle naturally transferrable to game audio.

In an interview for this book Whitmore said, "These theatrical experiences may well have started my obsession with game audio integration and adaptability. Because game elements are dynamic by definition, our music needs to be dynamic in order to better support the game." As he learned in theater, the principle that "context is everything" became a kind of mantra in Guy's approach to game audio.

His entree to gaming came at Sierra Online, where he first got his feet wet with *Mixed Up Mother Goose*, then moved to Monolith where his quest to create contextually driven music started to pick up steam. One early innovation was creating a music system that included a "transition matrix". The transition matrix was a lookup table of transition segments to move the score seamlessly (on transition boundaries) from one music cue to any other. Having six major music intensities or "mood cues" resulted in a matrix of thirty-six transitions. On games such as *Shogo*, *No One Lives Forever* and *Tron 2.0*, scores flowed easily between game states with seamless musical transitions. These transition matrices were built using a technology called DirectMusic from Microsoft, a program based on sophisticated MIDI transitions which could be programmed to respond in real-time to changes in game states.

In 1999 Whitmore set out as an independent freelancer, expanding his range and style of games but still always pushing for contextually driven, seamless music scores. He took a chance with startup Bootleg TV, founded by Robert Fripp of the band King Crimson. There he explored the possibilities of non-linear music as a standalone format, which is a concept he still plays with in his spare time today. After a second freelance stint, he joined Microsoft Game Studios where he built the central audio team and became Director of Audio. There, Whitmore and his team assisted in the audio production of several major Xbox franchises including *Fable*, *Gears of War*, *Project Gotham Racing, Crackdown* and *Halo*. The primary mandate of his role was innovation, including technical advances, creative exploration and improved production practices. One such innovation was creating instrument level variations for *Butterflies* and *X-Girls* to convey a subtle sense of non-repeating music which could sustain a given emotional node until the next game state change. This method can turn a linear twelve-bar phrase into an undulating non-repeating cue with hundreds or thousands of possible versions. For example, five instruments with five variations each equals 3,125 possible combinations!

As the Microsoft years passed with ever-increasing management duties, Whitmore felt the urge to get back to his roots of creating music and sound. He took a position at PopCap Games as Studio Audio Director, overseeing audio for classic franchises such as *Bejeweled*, *Plants vs. Zombies* and *Peggle*. With a goal to bring AAA audio practices and highly adaptive music to casual and mobile games, his successes have been recognized with several G.A.N.G. Awards and nominations. The score for *Peggle 2* merged the rich quality of live orchestral recording with innovative music integration, demonstrating that an extremely dynamic score can also have high production values. Today Guy enjoys speaking and writing about his audio experiences and about adaptive music scores, which aims to promote the evolution of game audio and its community.[22]

Jonathan Mayer
(*Infamous, Uncharted, God of War*)

Jonathan Mayer joined the Playstation Music Group in 2005. He came to the team with a professional background focused heavily on production and engineering, primarily in the music industry. That background, coupled with an intense love of all things video games, led Jonathan to arrive in the gaming industry with many strong and even unusual ideas about music composition and production. One of his core beliefs that carried over from the recording industry was to find an approach to scoring that would ensure each score had unique character and sonic identity.

Splitting his time with Playstation as a composer, re-mixer, engineer and producer, Jonathan has contributed to a number of successful franchises including *Syphon Filter, Uncharted, God of War, Infamous* and *The Last of Us*. With each project he likes to push everyone involved to find ways to make the score stand out both compositionally and sonically in a way that best supports the overall creative direction of the product. Through this process Jonathan has learned to identify barriers to production and creativity in this realm and focuses his energy on finding ways to remove those barriers while keeping all of the stakeholders thoroughly engaged. This is a process that can be challenging and unintuitive, often generating something of a creative "mess" prior to finding the bull's-eye.

Composers are chosen for projects primarily based on their established sound and it is a delicate and occasionally difficult task for collaborators to come together and find a way to innovate. Jonathan believes it is this type of collaboration that is essential to success. He thinks that too often there is a concern in the industry to brand a music score as the work of an individual, while the best scores often come together through a team effort. Regardless of the scope or budget, Jonathan feels a composer should always look for a production team that will provide support and perspective. He also believes that composers should look for ways in which to disrupt their own comfort when approaching a new project. In this area he has pointed out that simple things can go a long way such as limiting and manipulating the project's instrumentation in sometimes extreme ways, writing for instruments that are new or unusual for the composer, swapping out processed live instruments for sounds that are typically synthesized, and so on. Additionally, Jonathan applies this perspective to recording and production by placing mics in unusual places and asking orchestral players to set up on a stage in nonconventional patterns. With his background as a percussionist he also believes strongly in leveraging just about anything he finds as an instrument.

Jonathan has utilized this approach on several projects during his tenure with Playstation. In 2007, Jonathan was tasked with creating a sonic palate for the first game in the *inFAMOUS* series. The style guide from the director was mostly traditional, cinematic percussion with tribal rhythms. Because the game was set in a dystopian city that had suffered much devastation, Jonathan elected to replace traditional percussion with found objects and non-percussion instruments used as percussion. This collection of objects was heavily sampled and the resulting grooves and sounds were shared with composers Jim Dooley and Amon Tobin to be used as their sonic basis from which to create the sound of the game.

A similar approach was suggested for the sequel, *inFAMOUS 2*; however, this game was to be set in a fictitious version of New Orleans. To further identify the score with the surroundings, Jonathan took the sonic baseline established for *inFAMOUS* and incorporated musicians from New Orleans, eventually commissioning the band Galactic to contribute original composition to the score. The band was encouraged to create music in the sonic style of the first *inFAMOUS* but with their deep understanding of the city's musical DNA incorporated into each cue. The score was given further identity when Jonathan tasked the project's orchestrator, Tim Davies, with embellishing Galactic's cues with a jazz string quintet (two violas, two celli and a bass).

More recently, for the Playstation exclusive title *The Last of Us*, Jonathan sought out the opportunity to work with multi Grammy and Oscar winning composer Gustavo Santaolalla on the score. The direction for the music was right in Gustavo's sweet spot but he and Jonathan were tasked by the director with adding some sonic "tweaks" to make the score unique to the game. Jonathan went once again to collaborator Tim Davies and together they designed a very strange orchestral ensemble comprised of only very low woodwinds and strings to provide the underpinnings of Gustavo's typically guitar and ronroco driven cues. Tim and Jonathan took this even further and recorded many gestures and elements with the ensemble intended to be programmed into a sampler as a replacement for synthesizer pads, thus achieving a completely organic and unusual sound for all of the project's underlying beds and tension pieces.

According to Jonathan, none of this type of innovation can happen without strong relationships and an immense amount of trust. Creating music can be very difficult and creating music to order can often feel overwhelming. However, Jonathan likes to quote the old adage that, "inspiration is for amateurs" when it comes to creating and performing under pressure. Instead, he has come to depend on the support and goodwill of the vast number of brilliant creative contributors that are available in the video game industry of today. [23]

SUMMARY

Vanguards lead people and industries from where they are to where they've never been. Successful vanguards in business can open up new markets, creating opportunities for themselves and others where nothing existed previously. Composers who learn to identify and attach themselves to future vanguards in the video game industry can improve their chances for creative and lucrative career opportunities.

Historically, vanguards tend to display an observable collection of traits in common. These include an opportunistic mindset, formal education, proactivity, persistence, prudence and an active professional network of friends. Several examples of game industry vanguards were cited evidencing each of these traits. While no claim is made for predicting the future, composers are advised to look for as many of these characteristics as possible when considering and selecting potential clients.

Composers can be vanguards in their own right. Today's video game music world has been shaped by the innovations of the past. Several composers who have led growth in the industry in significant ways were highlighted. In studying the life of each composer, readers are encouraged to draw inspiration for their own innovative tendencies and development. From today's game music students will come tomorrow's game music vanguards, shaping the future of video game music for generations to come.

APPLIED LEARNING

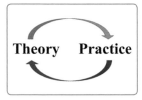

1. Not including the persons profiles in this chapter, write down the names of three people who you consider to be vanguards of the video game industry. What qualities have you noticed that contribute to their success?

2. Recall the new contacts you were assigned to make at the end of Chapter 13. Using a chart referencing the *Harvard Business Review*'s list of vanguard personality traits, rate each new contact on a scale from 1 to 10 for each trait. Summarizing your findings, explain which of these contacts (if any) appears to offer the most potential.

3. If one or more of the contacts listed above shows a high level of promise (for example, an aggregate score between 45 and 50), draft a plan outlining the productive steps you would take to build a strong relationship of trust with that contact. Implement your plan.

4. Select three composers from among the composers profiled in this chapter, or select three of your own choosing. Write a paragraph which offers your assessment of what makes each composer a contemporary vanguard (or not) in video game music. Add your opinion about how those qualities have contributed to their career success (or lack thereof).

5. Again referencing the *Harvard Business Review* list of vanguard personality traits, rate yourself on a scale of 1 to 10 for each trait. Now ask a fellow student, friend or peer to rate you on those same qualities. Compare any differences. Select one trait with a lower score and draft a plan to improve. Go to work on your plan.

REFERENCES

1. Attributed to Thomas Paine, no original reference found.

2. http://venturebeat.com/community/2014/07/23/the-thin-line-between-video-game-success-and-failure/.

3. http://www.enterrasolutions.com/2014/07/innovators-thinkers.html.

4. https://hbr.org/2013/10/the-five-characteristics-of-successful-innovators/.

5. http://onproductmanagement.net/2010/06/29/why-i-hate-that-henry-ford-quote/.

6. http://www.history.com/topics/henry-ford.

7. http://articles.latimes.com/2010/aug/08/business/la-fi-himi-morhaime-20100808.

8. http://en.wikipedia.org/wiki/Will_Wright_%28game_designer%29.

9. http://www.businessinsider.com/oculus-rift-inventor-talks-about-journey-2013-7.

10. http://www.gamasutra.com/view/feature/4035/from_the_past_to_the_future_tim_.php?print=1.

11. http://corporate.psychtests.com/pdf/risk_taking_behavior_study.pdf.

12. http://www.nextlevelsalesconsulting.com/sales-insights/sales-library/inspirational-quotes/james-bryant-conant-behold-the-turtle/.

13. http://www.fastcompany.com/3038121/innovation-agents/electronic-arts-ceo-on-transforming-the-worst-company-in-the-us.

14. http://consumerist.com/2013/04/09/ea-makes-worst-company-in-america-history-wins-title-for-second-year-in-a-row/.

15. http://www.cmgww.com/historic/rogers/about/miscellaneous.html.

16. http://www.wired.com/2007/03/vgl_koji_kondo_/.

17. http://www.vgmonline.net/kojikondo/; http://mentalfloss.com/article/20079/koji-kondo-our-beethoven;

18. http://www.mfiles.co.uk/ragtime-music.htm; http://www.zeldainformer.com/news/interview-with-composer-koji-kondo-the-compositional-process#.VORJLObF-So; http://www.wired.com/2007/03/vgl_koji_kondo_/.

19. Bio and photo courtesy of George Sanger. Also: http://fatman.com/stories.htm#s1; http://www.technologyreview.com/featuredstory/534971/magic-leap/.

20. http://www.vgmonline.net/nobuouematsu/; http://www.pixcelation.com/?p=5768;

21. http://info-biography.blogspot.com/2010/03/biography-hironobu-sakaguchi-final.html;

22. http://www.ign.com/articles/2009/06/18/ign-presents-the-history-of-final-fantasy; http://en.wikipedia.org/wiki/Final_Fantasy_concerts.

23. Personal interview with the author, used with permission.

24. Personal interview with the author, used with permission.

25. Personal interview with the author, used with permission.

26. Personal interview with the author, used with permission.

CHAPTER 15
CAREER PHILANTHROPY

Pay it forward.[1]

In 2001, Tommy Tallarico delivered the audio keynote address at the Game Developers Conference in San Jose, California. The room was packed with game audio professionals and hopefuls alike, eager to hear from one of the industry's most charismatic stars. Tallarico had risen from the ashes of homelessness to blaze a fiery trail of success straight to the top of the business. He had dozens of contracts providing music and sound services to game developers. He was co-host with Victor Lucas of the popular television program *Electric Playground*. His annual income was rumored to top seven figures. To the surprise of most people in the audience, Tallarico openly discussed how much he charged, how he structured his contracts, how he maximized profits and frankly opened up about a number of points that most businesses would consider proprietary information.

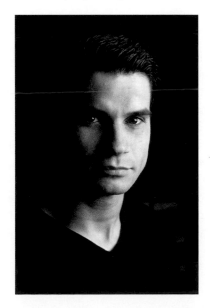

The following year, on March 21, 2002, Tallarico led a small group of pioneers in forming the Game Audio Network Guild, the industry's first organized guild for audio professionals. Among its purposes was that of honoring the top video game composers, sound designers and audio directors each year with an annual awards program. The G.A.N.G. Awards have arguably become the most prestigious game audio awards in the business, with dozens handed out annually, typically to business rivals in direct competition with Tommy's own music and sound company.

Three years following the founding of G.A.N.G., Tommy and partner Jack Wall launched Video Games Live!, a symphonic concert extravaganza which has exposed millions of people around the world to the original game music of dozens of modern video game composers. Each and every one of these actions has had a direct, positive impact on Tallarico's competitors.

Why would he do this? Why would a businessman deliberately assist, honor and promote his competition? Going back to his GDC keynote talk in 2001, Tallarico said that he didn't mind giving away his secrets because, as John F. Kennedy had famously stated, "A rising tide lifts all boats."[2] Tommy smiled and wryly added, "Including mine!" And then he went one step further and said something that demonstrated a deeper motive behind his actions: "Besides, I like to help others. I want to give back to the industry that has given so much to me."

GIVING BACK

The final chapter in this textbook, the culmination of all the learning that has preceded it, is about giving back. It is about cultivating a sense of philanthropy throughout the breadth of a composer's career—finding ways to lift others, to encourage and empower fellow travelers on the road, even those who may be direct competitors. As discussed in Chapter 9, the video game music community has a strong tradition of vibrant mutual support, even within its necessarily hyper-competitive environment. Composers who aspire to join this community are invited to cultivate a similarly supportive mindset. To distill this idea down to a simple phrase, "Be a builder, not a breaker."[3] The balance of this chapter will explore a few practical ways in which composers of today and tomorrow can give back to the video game music community at large.

Mentoring

There may be no more valuable gift that one composer can give to another than the gift of mentoring. The National Mentoring Partnership broadly defines a mentor as "a caring, adult friend who devotes time to a young person … All mentors have the same goal in common: to help young people achieve their potential and discover their strengths."[4] One business group in Canada views mentoring in such high regard that they have established a Mentors Hall of Fame, celebrating high impact mentoring among the world's most exceptional artists. Some of the famous musical pairings in the Hall of Fame include Nikolai Rimsky-Korsakov mentoring Maximillian Steinberg, Isaac Stern mentoring Itzhak Perlman, Charles Ives mentoring Elliott Carter, and Leonid Nikolayev mentoring Dmitri Shostakovich.[5]

There are many effective ways mentoring can be done. One experienced video game composer invites promising students and young composers to attend large-scale live orchestral and choral recording sessions. These sessions provide singular lessons about the raw collision of artistic vision, time pressure, budgetary constraints and human limitations. All of these stresses converge as clients, engineers, musicians and singers look collectively to the composer for artistic direction, problem resolution and split-second decisions. Watching veterans handle such pressures with wisdom and composure teaches volumes. This kind of mentoring experience offers lightbulb moments and nuances of insight to students and young composers which a classroom or home studio could never provide.

Another prominent video game composer subcontracts parts of his major scores to talented young composers who haven't had the experience

GUEST LECTURE
THANK YOU TO MY MENTOR

Or Kribos (Haifa, Israel)

Having the opportunity to be mentored by you has been one of the greatest experiences I've had. This isn't an exaggeration. When I compose, I sit in a room alone and create something. With you, I had the chance to gain access to so many insights about the workflow of scoring and recording music for a video game, which is one of my real passions. You might take it for granted at this stage in your career, but for me, having the opportunity to be part of a big recording session and experience you navigating between all the artists, the music, the client and the studio, was incredible and very insightful. I was able to absorb more valuable real-life professional awareness in two days than you could possibly imagine. One of the coolest things I'm taking with me as a lesson for life was the lesson you showed me, that no matter where or who great ideas are coming from, we want to make sure that we find and capture them to achieve the ultimate result. Beyond all of that, which was priceless and so expansive for me, you generously introduced me to your colleagues and opened doors for me. That has already helped to move my career forward. There are many ways to say thank you, but to encompass them all still wouldn't be enough. A WORLD of thank you for these gifts!

GUEST LECTURE
BOTH SIDES OF MENTORING

Penka Kouneva (*Prince of Persia, Transformers, Gears of War*)

I acknowledge my mentors as having most profound, life-changing and career-changing impact upon me. Duke professor Stephen Jaffe, orchestration mentor Scott Lindroth; in Hollywood: Bruce Fowler in orchestration, Patrick Williams in scoring, Chance Thomas and Victor Rodriguez in video games.

In the last ten years I've become a mentor myself, hiring young media composers on hundreds of big and small jobs in orchestration, additional composing and synth programming, training them intensely, and opening doors for them. Being able to pay it forward is a profound joy, honor and privilege. I am inspired by the energy, enthusiasm and innovation young professionals bring. I feel blessed and grateful for the mentors who have opened doors for me. To grow as an artist, one must be challenged on a real job: the real learning (and upward leaps) begin when one must prove oneself on a real job, "in the line of fire". Having a caring mentor who illuminates the way and provides feedback is how we excel in media composing and score production.

of working on a big title yet. Cues are developed in cooperation with and under the tutelage of his guiding hand, giving the young talent tremendous insight into music design, composition and craft. In addition, the contracted composers gain an enormous career boost by working on a hit game. This can open up new opportunities for these composers which may never have come otherwise.

Another veteran regularly takes in student interns from local universities. These interns learn how to build tempo maps and mark up sheet music in preparation for live sessions. They learn how to engineer and record live performances and mix large sessions. They learn these and other fundamental technical abilities which most composers need in order to progress in their careers. In addition to such technical capabilities, the interns also pick up valuable life skills and subtle lessons about business practices, work flow and interpersonal communication.

Mentoring is one of the most direct, personal and concentrated ways to pay it forward. It is an impactful and easily accessible approach to career philanthropy for any established composer. Whether it is inviting a student to help make new sounds for a scoring template or walking a young composer through their first contract negotiation, established composers can offer a leg up to the rising generation through any number of mentoring activities. For those young composers who are privileged to become successful in the years ahead, remember to mentor others who follow on the road behind. In the video game music business, to borrow a phrase from an old song, "That's just the way we roll."[6]

GDC

The Game Developers Conference offers an unprecedented brain transfer to members of the game development community every year. GDC gives successful game composers a persistent pulpit from which to share their expertise with the world. Each year the industry gathers to hear top music professionals like Nobuo Uematsu, Akira Yamaoka, Garry Schyman, Paul Lipson, Austin Wintory, Jason Graves, Brian Schmidt and many others share their technical knowledge, artistic insights and war stories in formal presentations and feedback sessions. The quantity and quality of knowledge passed on to conference attendees can be tremendous.

GDC is an effective forum for giving back to the industry. Any composer who has achieved a significant breakthrough, whether artistic, technical, logistical or otherwise, may create a talk proposal for GDC summarizing the key points of their insight or achievement. This proposal is then reviewed by GDC's audio advisory board for consideration. If approved, the composer works with a board member to flesh out the content and polish the presentation, ensuring the best possible delivery of relevant information to those in attendance. Admittedly, it is not always a perfect system. Sometimes speakers have been known to dispense more self-promotion than meaningful education. But for the most part, speaking at GDC offers accomplished video game composers the opportunity and privilege of sharing things they've learned with a large, pre-qualified, captive audience. It is a great way to give back. And as a side-benefit, GDC is a massive gathering of game industry professionals (including prospects), on a scale currently unequaled by anything else in the world. Not a bad place for networking.

G.A.N.G.

G. A. N. G.
GAME AUDIO NETWORK GUILD

The Game Audio Network Guild welcomes members into its community from among the student, apprentice and professional ranks of game audio practitioners in the United States, Canada, Europe and Japan. This includes sound designers, voice actors, educators, audio programmers and management. It is a great forum for young composers to rub shoulders with the other audio disciplines in the industry. But from the beginning, G.A.N.G. has always had an exceptionally large and active contingent of professional composers. Composers have been among the most active contributors to G.A.N.G.'s forum discussions. Composers submit the largest number of entries to the G.A.N.G. Awards each year. Composers undoubtedly devote the largest block of time to screening and voting on awards submissions each year. As a result, participating in G.A.N.G. is a great way build a large network of peers, potential mentors and friends.

Getting involved in G.A.N.G. can also provide several ways to give back to the industry. For example, G.A.N.G. sponsors critical listening and feedback sessions at a number of conferences and seminars. Accomplished composers can volunteer to take part in these sessions, listening to submissions of eager hopefuls and offering advice about what they have done well and what needs improvement. Additionally, G.A.N.G. sponsors peer gatherings in various cities to build rapport, camaraderie and a localized sense of community. Supporting these gatherings with a veteran presence can add to their draw, opening up further opportunities for mentoring and networking. Of course, the G.A.N.G. Awards themselves offer a very public way for members to get involved. These awards are most meaningful when submissions are thoroughly reviewed by the broadest and most qualified spectrum of screeners. G.A.N.G.'s Advisory Board can always use experienced and devoted critical listening ears to participate in this process. Furthermore, all video game composers can enhance the prestige of the G.A.N.G. Awards by joining the Guild and participating in the final awards voting. Members should listen carefully to each finalist, then cast a vote that reflects their expert opinion on the inherent value of the audio work represented. Don't just look at the title of the game and vote by popularity. The G.A.N.G. Awards are meant as a merit award honoring outstanding creativity and achievement within the audio arts. They are not a game popularity contest. Cash registers around the world have already awarded winners in that contest. Members should listen to every finalist, then judge and vote on the audio merits of each. Students, apprentices and professionals are all encouraged to get involved with G.A.N.G. Joining together to promote excellence in game audio has made a positive difference as the industry has grown. Today's new members can help to shape the direction game music will take in the industry for decades to come.

In addition to G.A.N.G, other outstanding professional associations may provide video game composers the opportunity to give back to the community. These include the Society of Composers and Lyricists (SCL), the Interactive Audio Special Interest Group (IASIG), the Academy of Interactive Arts and Sciences (AIAS) and the National Academy of Recording Arts and Sciences (NARAS).

Guest Lectures

Recent years have seen an increase in the number of universities and colleges which address video game scoring within their music programs. As a result, there is a growing need for experienced video game composers to share their expertise with students though guest lectures, master classes and other formal interactions. When a composer who is actively scoring successful games comes to a college campus, there are many positive results. The contemporary and popular nature of games tends to stir high interest among the students, generating a big turnout for these kinds of events. A guest lecture and master class from an active professional in the business can give students and faculty alike new insights into the current state of the art and best practices in business. Successful video game composers also convey hope to music school students who may worry about the difficulty of finding employment after graduation. As a side note, the game industry is still a rapidly growing business. *USA Today* and GeekWire published research in 2013 indicating that video game composition is one of the fastest growing professions in the United States.[7] Composers who are properly educated, assertive, hard-working and smart are well equipped to find their place and build successful careers of their own.

There are many topics around which a successful video game composer can focus a guest lecture. Traditional composition students need to understand how to apply the conventional principles of music scoring within the framework of video games. They need exposure to music design principles and techniques which distinguish video game scoring from music scoring in traditional media. Students need to learn about middleware authoring and integration, coming to understand the terms, techniques and resources which can demystify this technology for them, making it both available and accessible. They need to learn about how to find and pursue opportunities after graduation, how to build support groups and how to keep in shape. Nearly any topic in this book could provide a useful focus for a university audience.

Selecting a good topic, even one about which the lecturer has substantial expertise, does not guarantee a successful presentation. Composers will also need to acquire some skills in public speaking and apply sound pedagogical principles in the preparation and delivery of their presentation. While there are entire books written on the subject, composers can benefit from understanding and applying even a few fundamentals. Consider the following:

- After a brief introduction, ask the audience a compelling question, share a brief story or tell a good joke. This can be a comfortable way to shake hands with the audience. This helps the audience settle in, drop their guard and tune in for the balance of the lecture.
- Most presentations work best when they are divided into ten-minute blocks. Research indicates that people viewing a lecture or presentation tend to check out mentally after about ten minutes.[8] Consider changing the pacing or teaching approach for each segment. It can also be helpful to insert a new emotional trigger into the talk at the start of each new segment, such as a video clip, volunteer interaction or special guest in order to re-engage the audience.
- Take advantage of the rule of threes. The brain likes to grasp things in groups of threes: "Red, white and blue." "Good, better and best." "Life, liberty and the pursuit of happiness." Try building a presentation on three main ideas. Or, introduce three benefits the students will gain from the lecture. Decide which three things are most important for students to remember about the lecture and concentrate on those.[9]
- Use slides, visual aids, object lessons, audio, smells, etc., to enhance the experience. "Those in multi-sensory environments always do better than those in unisensory environments. They have more recall with better resolution that lasts longer, evident even twenty years later."[10] The author often passes out donuts during guest lectures, not only to underscore a key point in an important story, but also to engage the students' senses of smell, touch and taste.

EFFECTIVE PRESENTATIONS

It doesn't hurt to take counsel from great presenters. Steve Jobs was one of the very best. His business presentations became sell-out, standing-room-only events. An analysis of his presentation style reveals as much about theater and drama as it does business and education. There was always a villain to vanquish (IBM, Microsoft, the music business, the cell phone industry) or a problem to solve (too slow, too bulky, too unintuitive). Apple would come to the rescue with a new product to skewer the villain and solve the problem in an elegant way. Jobs incorporated large visual images in his presentations, projected on a screen behind him. The images were always simple, clean and iconic. If there was detailed information that the audience needed (lists, specs, etc.) this would be delivered on a handout. If there were words on his slides, they were usually short phrases that would sum up an entire idea in a few words. He let his personality come through and wasn't afraid to use fun words like "zippy" or "insanely great" in his talk. And Jobs rehearsed his presentations. He rehearsed them relentlessly, so that like a well-prepared actor, he could deliver his lines with the impression of spontaneity, as if he were having a naturally brilliant conversation with the audience.

Scholarships

For those composers who have acquired significant financial resources, the endowment of a scholarship is an especially powerful method of giving back. What better way to invest in the future than by providing opportunities for young talent to gain an education? Most scholarship endowments require the donor to contribute a specified lump sum to the selected university or college of music. The college invests the deposit in a suitable income-generating account. Each year thereafter, 5 percent of the original deposit amount can be withdrawn by the college and given to students as scholarship funds.

Scholarship endowment amounts vary widely, depending on the tuition and fees charged by each program. Consider Oklahoma City University's music composition program as a mid-tier cost example. The tuition for an undergraduate studying composition at OCU is about $27,500 each year. In order to generate that amount in an annual, full-tuition scholarship, a donor would need to make a contribution of about $550,000 ($550,000 x 5% = $27,500). An annual scholarship endowment for a composition student at Juilliard would require a donation of about $800,000 ($800,000 x 5% = $40,000). A similar endowment at the University of Michigan would cost about $1,000,000 ($1M x 5% = $50,000). Endowing a Harvard or Yale full tuition scholarship would cost about $2,000,000 ($2M x 5% = $100,000) each. Lower cost alternatives are also available, even at many fine universities. For example, donors can provide one-time or annual contributions in amounts such as $5,000 or $10,000 to fund a particular program or capital expense. Contact the music school business office at any college or university for more information on available options and amounts.

Scholarships are generally named after their donor. They may alternatively be named for someone whom the donor designates, such as a spouse, parent or admired mentor. Students receiving scholarships will often send updated reports to the donor, describing their progress in the program. Expressions of gratitude are also common, and may continue for years after the student has graduated. Scholarship endowments have benefited thousands who might have never had an opportunity to expand their talents and their horizons otherwise. The author was lucky to be the recipient of a university scholarship and it has made all the difference.

Simple Things

Giving back is certainly not limited to large-scale contributions. There are so many small and simple ways to help. Composers can answer emails, texts and other kinds of messages from young hopefuls. They can visit professional forums, posting counsel and answering questions. They may even take a phone call, have a drink or go to lunch with those who just want to "pick their brain".

When video game composers become successful, they will inevitably begin to receive a growing stream of requests asking for advice, critique and encouragement. It can be time-consuming to answer such requests, and for busy professionals time is always at a premium. But there can be ways to manage this with wisdom and planning. Perhaps the composer could set aside one day in the week, at a time when energy is too low for high priority tasks like composing, and answer these requests. Maybe an FAQ of sorts could be prepared in advance, responding to common inquiries with previously prepared answers. Composer Lenny Moore received so many inquiries asking the same basic questions that he created a blog post summarizing his viewpoints and advice. Now he simply points inquirers to a link on his blog. Penka Kouneva has packaged together a mentoring folder to send to serious inquirers, with four to five months' worth of reading in lieu of a lunch. These simple acts of sharing bring tremendous enlightenment, hope and courage to young composers.

Do busy video game composers always have the time to respond to every inquiry? Not always. Composing work for paying clients always takes priority. The idea is to find those times when the composer has some flexibility, and then plan to offer a helping hand. One side note is worth mentioning. Ambitious students and young composers may not always have the most tact and polish in their communications. But they have hopes and dreams just like everyone else. Their reaching out certainly required some research, some initiative and maybe even some courage. Consider that these kinds of inquiries may be worth vetting, validating and possibly supporting, all with good judgment and within reasonable limitations of the composer's time, energy and wisdom.

SUMMARY

Giving back is part of the heritage of video game composers. It is a hallmark of this professional community. Those entering into the business are encouraged to carry on in this tradition in a variety of ways. This kind of rising tide lifts everybody in the business.

Mentoring is one of the most direct and effective ways an established composer can help a newcomer. From taking on an intern to simply answering email inquiries, every experienced game music composer can engage in mentoring on some level.

Both GDC and G.A.N.G. offer composers hive-like collectives of association within which learning and teaching can occur. GDC excels as an annual mindshare of the industry at large. G.A.N.G. provides an ongoing through-thread of focused community engagement and support. Those with experience in both have ready-made opportunities to share their expertise and insights with the rising generation. Similar opportunities exist in other professional associations, including IASIG, SCL, AIAS and NARAS.

Universities and colleges provide opportunities for speaking, teaching and motivating students. As seats of great learning, they represent the most formalized way to train up new video game composers. Scholarship endowments in particular offer successful composers a most tangible and permanent way to give back.

Please consider joining in this tradition of career philanthropy. Do whatever is possible and do it frequently enough that it becomes a habit. Helping others is part of the culture of video game composers. It's just the way we roll.

APPLIED LEARNING

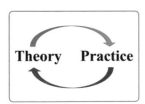

1. Identify some of the people who have given to you in ways discussed during this chapter. Write and send a note of appreciation to one of the persons you have identified.

2. List five areas of knowledge or skill which you have acquired or improved through your study of this textbook. Target an individual in need who you can share this learning with. Write up a summary plan for how you will mentor this person. Implement your plan.

3. Learn about the Game Developers Conference. Visit its website. Talk to at least two people who have attended the conference and ask them what

they gained from the experience. If you have attended GDC in the past, describe how you can get more out of the conference in the future. If you are a veteran composer, write up and submit a proposal for a GDC talk based on one of your areas of expertise.

4. Research the Game Audio Network Guild. Explore its website. Visit its forums. Ask at least three members of the Guild to share with you what they value about the organization. Write a summary of your impressions. Consider joining and getting involved.

5. Create a ten-year plan describing ways in which you will give back to the game music industry and why. Include simple things you can do starting this week, and expand to encompass your highest career ambitions and aspirations. Draw from any or all of the elements from this chapter in your plan.

REFERENCES

1. Catherine Ryan Hyde, *Pay it Forward* (New York: Pocket Books, 1999).

2. http://www.jfklibrary.org/JFK/JFK-in-History/JFK-on-the-Economy-and-Taxes.aspx.

3. http://www.tatemusicgroup.com/epk/?id=13656&page=bio.

4. http://www.mentoring.org/get_involved/for_mentors/benefits_of_mentoring.

5. http://www.mentors.ca/mp_classical.html.

6. http://www.cduniverse.com/jonas-brothers-thats-just-the-way-we-roll-lyrics-5966544.htm.

7. http://www.geekwire.com/2013/study-video-games-causing-spike-music-composer-employment/ and http://www.usatoday.com/story/money/business/2013/09/02/10-fastest-growing-jobs-in-usa/2750169/.

8. http://brainrules.blogspot.com/2009/03/10-minute-rule.html.

9. http://www.forbes.com/sites/carminegallo/2012/07/02/thomas-jefferson-steve-jobs-and-the-rule-of-3/.

10. http://www.brainrules.net/sensory-integration?scene=.

APPENDAGES

ACKNOWLEDGMENTS

There are many capable hands which made this work lighter. I would like to personally and enthusiastically thank as many as possible in this section! To begin, thank you to Sean Connelly and Caitlin Murphy from Focal Press, who first saw the potential in this idea and successfully shepherded the project from manuscript through publication. Thank you to my Taylor & Francis production team, especially Alfred Symons, Siân Cahill, Peter Wilder, Alex Lazarou and Liz Jones. Thank you to Paul Lipson, Penka Kouneva, Jonathan Mayer and Dr. Mark Parker, each of whom invested invaluable time in reviewing my manuscript and delivered incisive, expansive and actionable input. Their recommendations sharpened each chapter into a more powerful tool for future readers. Thank you to the multitude of celebrity experts who generously shared their hard-won insights so that students could start a little higher up the ladder than we all did. This includes Marty O'Donnell, Guy Whitmore, Garry Schyman, Troels Folmann, Mike Morasky, Neal Acree, Inon Zur, Jack Wall, Tim Larkin, Benedicte Ouimet, Sam Cardon, George Sanger, Tom Salta, Rod Abernethy, Simon Ashby, Stephan Schutze, Gordon Durity, Rodney Gates, Adam Gubman, Jason Hayes, Jeff Broadbent, Josh Aker, Paul Taylor, Richie Nieto, Aaron Marks, Or Kribos and Bob Rice. Also to an enriching array of fertile minds from scattered fields whose added light brought important concepts into sharp relief, I would like to say thank you to Nancy Andraesen, Clayton M. Christensen, Megan Curtis, Gustavo Constantini, Bobby Owsinski, Neal A. Maxwell, Graham Cochraine, Winifred Phillips, Aaron Marks, Simon Tatham, Joel Klebanoff and Warren Buffet. Also, thank you to the hive mind of my Facebook friends for helping to select and refine the cover for our book. A special thanks to Joe Bourrie, Shota Nakama and Beverly Scott, who actually went to the effort to take, edit and contribute photos for the cover. Thank you especially to Pamela Thomas, for lots of encouragement to keep heading up this exhausting hill, even in the face of slogging difficulty. And finally, thank you to our awesome Creator, for the gifts and talents so generously bestowed on so many!

ABOUT THE AUTHOR

Chance Thomas is an American composer, educator and entrepreneur. He is best known for scoring blockbuster video games like *DOTA 2, Lord of the Rings Online, James Cameron's Avatar, Dungeons and Dragons Online, Heroes of Might and Magic, Peter Jackson's King Kong, Quest for Glory V* and many more. His music has underscored both commercial success and artistic honors, including an Academy Award, an Emmy Award and billions of dollars in game and film sales worldwide.

Chance has held corporate leadership positions at a number of top video game companies, including Studio Audio Director for Electronic Arts, Music Director for Vivendi-Universal and Senior Music Producer for Sierra Online. He led the movement which brought game music into the Grammy Awards and previously chaired the Music and Sound Peer Committees for the Academy of Interactive Arts and Sciences. Chance helped found the Game Audio Network Guild and serves on its Board of Directors. He served for many years as an Audio Advisor to the Game Developers Conference. He is a popular guest lecturer at universities, music schools and industry events where he helps students navigate the intersection of music scoring, technology and entrepreneurship (www.ChanceThomas.com).

IMAGE CREDITS

p.145 © iStock.com/teekid.

p.146 Used with permission: Penka Kouneva.

p.148 Used with permission: Josh Aker.

p.150 Used with permission: Argosy Film Group.

p.154 © iStock.com/ IntergalacticDesignStudio.

p.158 © iStock.com/gbarm.

p.160 © iStock.com/Massimo Merlini.

p.164 Used with permission: Paul Taylor.

p.166 Used with permission. Warner Brothers Interactive Entertainment and Middle-earth Enterprises.

p.167 Lord of the Rings Online and Dungeons and Dragons Online images used courtesy of Warner Bros. Entertainment, Inc.

p.169 Used with permission; photo credit: Ronan Murphy.

p.171 © iStock.com/RaStudio.

p.173 © iStock.com/CSA-Printstock.

p.180 (top) Used with permission: Brian Schmidt.

p.180 (bottom) © iStock.com/Ever.

p.182 © iStock.com/baona.

p.183 © iStock.com/Rogotanie.

p.184 Used with permission: John Uibel.

p.192 © iStock.com/pearleye.

p.194 (top left) Used with permission: Simon Ashby.

p.194 (bottom left) Used with permission: Guy Whitmore.

p.195 Used with permission: Stephan Schütze.

p.198 (top) Used with permission: Electronic Arts.

p.198 (bottom) Used with permission: Gordon Durity.

p.199 Used with permission: Gordon Durity.

p.206 © iStock.com/BDoty.

p.207 Photo by B. J. Hines. Used with permission: Adam Gubman.

p.208 Used with permission: Rey Gutierrez.

p.209 Used with permission: Kevin Riepl and Rich Vreeland. Image

from the album, Monsters Ate My Birthday Cake; image artwork by Dom2D.

p.215 © iStock.com/alexsl.

p.217 © iStock.com/Palto.

p.220 © iStock.com/mattjeacock.

p.221 © iStock.com/Pali Rao.

p.226 © iStock.com/lukedesign.

p.230 Used with permission: David Perry.

p.231 Used with permission: David Perry.

p.232 © iStock.com/Coffee999.

p.233 (top) Used with permission: Richie Nieto.

p.233 (bottom) © iStock.com/Rawpixel Ltd.

p.235 © iStock.com/Stanislav1.

p.236 Used with permission: Bob Rice.

p.237 Used with permission: Or Kribos.

p.238 © iStock.com/alexskopje.

p.240 Used with permission: Rod Abernethy.

p.247 (bottom) © iStock.com/Kerstin Waurick.

p.248 © iStock.com/CGinspiration.

p.250 (left) © iStock.com/Sezeryadigar.

p.253 Used with permission: Brian Schmidt.

p.259 (right) © iStock.com/alexsl.

p.261 © iStock.com/Aquir.

p.263 © it.depositphotos.com/viperagp.

p.264 © iStock.com/mstay.

p.268 © iStock.com/Grafissimo.

p.273 © iStock.com/iLexx.

p.274 © iStock.com/MKucova.

p.276 Used with permission: Hiroki Ogaway; photo credit: Shinjiro Yamada.

p.278 (left) Used with permission: Neal Acree.

p.280 Used with permission: Valve Corporation.

p.281 Used with permission: Multnomah County Sherriff's Office.

p.282 (top) © iStock.com/RapidEye

p.282 (bottom) Used with permission. Photo credit: Sterling Clarren.

p.283 © iStock.com/julos.

p.284 © iStock.com/bestdesigns.

p.285 © iStock.com/gecko753.

p.286 © iStock.com/solvod.

p.288 Used with permission: Inon Zur.

p.290 Used with permission: Tim Larkin.

p.291 © iStock.com/Farmerview.

p.299 © iStock.com/ johavel.

p.300 © iStock.com/Aquir.

p.302 © iStock.com/abluecup.

p.303 © iStock.com/JuSun.

p.304 © iStock.com/Dimitrios Stefanidis.

p.309 © iStock.com/wragg.

p.311 © iStock.com/gheatza.

p.312 © iStock.com/Massonstock.

p.317 Used with permission: George Sanger and Susan Penn.

p.319 Used with permission: Hiroki Ogawa; Photo Credit: Shinjiro Yamada.

p.321 Used with permission: Troels Folmann.

p.323 Used with permission: Simon Ashby.

p.325 Used with permission: Guy Whitmore.

p.327 Used with permission: Jonathan Mayer.

p.333 Used with permission: Tommy Tallarico.

p.335 Used with permission: Or Kribos.

p.336 © iStock.com/ARTQU.

p.337 Used with permission: Austin Wintory.

p.338 Used with permission: Game Audio Network Guild.

p.340 Used with permission: Indiana University Jacobs School of Music. Photo by Curtis Smith.

p.341 © iStock.com/RaStudio.

INDEX